Morals
&
Stories

Morals
&
Stories

Tobin Siebers

COLUMBIA UNIVERSITY PRESS
NEW YORK

Columbia University Press
New York   Oxford

Copyright © 1992 Columbia University Press
All rights reserved

Library of Congress Cataloging-in-Publication Data

Siebers, Tobin
Morals and stories / Tobin Siebers.
p. cm.
Includes bibliographical references and index.
ISBN 0-231-07846-3
1. Literature and morals. I. Title.
PN49.S552   1992
801′.3—dc20   91-44863
CIP

Book design by Teresa Bonner
Printed in the United States of America
c 10 9 8 7 6 5 4 3 2 1

For Jill Greenblatt Siebers
ētheiē

CONTENTS

vii

Contents

ACKNOWLEDGMENTS

I wish to express my gratitude to the John Simon Guggenheim Memorial Foundation whose generous support gave me the leisure to plan and to write most of this book. The University of Michigan graciously offered to supplement the fellowship and made additional sabbatical time available to me. I thank in particular John Cross, Associate Dean for Faculty Appointments, John D'Arms, Dean of the Graduate School, and Linda Wilson, former Vice President for Research and Development. I have the good fortune to work with two generous chairs, Stuart McDougal, Director of Comparative Literature, and Robert Weisbuch, Chair of English, both of whom have stood firmly behind my teaching and research projects. I am also indebted to Jean-Pierre Dupuy and the Centre de Reserches en Epistémologie Appliqué at the Ecole Polytechnique for allowing me to join their research team and providing me with office support and space during my year in Paris in 1988–89. Among others at CREA,

Acknowledgments

Mette Hjört, Paisley Livingston, and André Orléan helped to clarify my ideas.

Ross Chambers, Karl Kroeber, and Gustavo Pellón read various parts of the manuscript at times when I was in need of reassurance about ideas and style. I certainly could have used more of their help, and they would have gladly given it, but I took pity on them because each suffers from a generosity of spirt that threatens his own time for work and because I get as much help from reading their writings as I do when they comment on mine. I thank Mark Anderson for inviting me to speak on Kant to the German House at Columbia University. Finally, much gratitude is due to Eric Gans, René Girard, and Martin Meisel who have supported my work over the years.

Reading to my children, Claire and Pierce, has encouraged me to understand how stories work, and my wife, Jill, has helped me to find better ways of writing about this work. My largest and most enduring debt is inscribed in my dedication to her. After a long wait, I have finally written something that can carry her name.

The editors of *The Centennial Review* and *Philosophy and Literature* have generously given permission to reprint in revised form chapters 3 and 9.

Morals
&
Stories

MORALS
WITH
STORIES

CHAPTER I

&

A Childhood Memory

WHEN I WAS GROWING UP and learning about the world of work—and thought belongs to the world of work—my father taught me how to use tools. He taught me to use the right tool for the job. There existed an adequation in his mind, and I have found that he was not at all peculiar in this among craftsmen, between the tool and the job. I imagine now that his understanding of tools and their adequacy carried something of a universal import for him, so strong was his conviction in it.

But what my father taught me in principle or theory was not always borne out in practice, when we were in the heat of the moment. Our attachment to the work and to its place was so powerful that we often felt reluctant to fetch the right tool, if we did not have it in hand. Often enough we made do with the tools that were there. The right tool was usually within walking distance. It was in the basement of the house, if we were working in the garage, or, perversely, in the garage, if we were working in the basement. Work was divided at our house between the basement and garage, depending on the season. In the winter we worked in the basement.

3

It was at those moments when my father used the wrong tool that I saw revealed his genius as a craftsman. He made the tool work in his hands in spite of itself and the job. But I have to say that I always wondered and continue to wonder to this day whether he would have finished the job faster, just as efficiently, and just as creatively, if he had turned his enthusiasm for the job to an enthusiasm for fetching the right tool. None of my wondering has made much difference in my own practice. I honor the principle of using the right tool in theory, but I bend the rule in practice, although not with anything resembling the genius of my father.

What if thinking involves a like attachment to the work and its place? Certainly, we are always somewhere when we think, even though the mythology of thought celebrates its ability to take us to other places. "Thought has wings." I believe that is the expression. But I doubt whether the wings of thought often take us to the place where the right tool is for the expressed purpose of fetching the tool. I imagine thought as somehow less committed to the work. It would very likely go for the tool and forget about it by the time it arrived at its destination.

Maybe my father was right to stay put. When he did go to fetch a tool, he sometimes returned without the right tool in his hand, having been distracted in his task in a way that he would never have been distracted when his hands were on the work.

There will be many objections, no doubt, to this idea of a "right tool," especially since I am proposing to talk about the relation between literature and ethics. Moral philosophers are suspicious about the use of the word *right*. Literary critics avoid it too.

What kind of tool am I talking about anyway?

I am tempted to name this tool as a hammer. But, in fact, the hammer has a special status among laborers. It is the tool least likely to be replaced by an experienced hand and the most likely to be replaced by an inexperienced hand. The experienced craftsman will always go in search of a hammer instead of using a board, a shoe, a wrench, or anything else in its place. A child will use anything for a hammer.

How do I know this? I have lived among people who use hammers.

Is it the same case with the hammer in philosophical usage? Is Wittgenstein's hammer or Heidegger's hammer a privileged tool for the same reason, or is it what comes to mind first as the exemplary tool when in fact it is something else?

Why are philosophers always reaching for hammers in the first place?

Are Wittgenstein and Heidegger experienced or inexperienced crafts-

4

men? Do they take up the hammer because it is what they need? Or are they grabbing for anything to use as a hammer?

For Heidegger, the hammer is usually broken anyway. When the hammer breaks in the hand, he explains, its user understands in its absence what the tool is in a way impossible to attain through mere reflection. Perhaps, but if you try to use a board to pound in a nail, and the board breaks, you will still understand what a hammer is, and you had better go get one or call it quits for the day.

I am not being entirely serious. But it is a good idea to joke on the job, and truth, as they say, is often told in jest.

For Wittgenstein, in *On Certainty*, the hammer raises the problem of language: "Isn't the question 'Have these words a meaning?' similar to 'Is that a tool?' asked as one produces, say, a hammer? I say 'Yes, it's a hammer.' But what if the thing that any of us would take for a hammer were somewhere else a missile, for example, or a conductor's baton? Now make the application yourself" (§351).

I have trouble making the application myself. I think that Wittgenstein went to get the hammer, but he forgot that he needed it when he returned to the work. Or he came back with something else. He should have stayed where he was, in that place where a hammer is a hammer, as my father did, instead of running off to wherever a hammer is a missile, for example, or a conductor's baton. It does not matter to Wittgenstein here whether he has a hammer or not. He is pounding nails with anything he can lay his hands on. It is a language game, where the pleasure is in pounding philosophy. If he were working with nails, he would have his hammer or he would have to go get one.

A point that I will be making in what follows is that it matters where we are. My theme and theory privilege place, as craftsmen privilege the hammer, as a way of talking about literature and ethics. We have an attraction to where we are not only because it is the site of work and living but because we make our tools and ideas work there and because we use only those tools that are in the vicinity and that have been used there for a long time. More specifically, I will focus on the idea of character as that "place"—for the Greek *ēthos,* in addition to suggesting "character" and "ethics," originally meant "to be found somewhere"—in which ethical ideas and literary ones gather together to help us work out the best way to live with other people in the places where people live. There literature and ethics join forces in the search for the good life for a human being.

It is important that place be seen to have both a thematic and theoretical dimension. A claim can be theoretically grounded only when it is thematically grounded. To discuss a theory of some practice, idea, or thing in a work of literature or philosophy in which this element is not a theme is a misstep, as is any theoretical claim that an idea or phenomenon is central to a body of literature in general without our having established its presence as a theme throughout that literature. Theory is bad theory when it has no empirical claim to exist within the ideas and themes of a work. I will therefore try to read philosophy and literature in terms of a theme of character and a theory of it, and the first must be there if I am to say anything at all about the second.

It has been said that to thematize is to moralize, and if this is true, I need not worry about being insufficiently theoretical about ethics.[1] The moral, as it were, always follows the story.

This is another way of saying that literature and ethics do have some relationship.

I intend to honor my father's principle of using the right tool, but I cannot forget his practice and his attachment to the work and its place. One tool is the right tool for the job, but the other tool, nearby or in hand, the hand makes it work. The hand makes the tool, and makes it work. Working with my father, I always had the sensation of reinventing the wheel.

CHAPTER 2

❧

Life Stories

WE THINK OF a life story as taking the form of a biography or an autobiography. But all works of literature belong in a sense to the genre of the life story. To be human is to tell stories about ourselves and about other human beings. Sometimes we tell stories to ourselves. More often we tell them to others. But we rarely, if ever, tell stories to ourselves without thinking about other people, and I suspect that the stories that we tell to others have as much to do with ourselves as with anyone else.

To be a successful story, a narrative must tell about human beings (or about characters endowed with human qualities), their actions, and their problems. If any of these elements is missing, the reading or hearing of the story draws upon the interests of those who are reading or listening to provide what is missing. No interest. No story. The great test of a story is its ability to attract people who desire to become the next teller of the tale, so that the experience of the story cannot be separated from its passing from person to person. Stories that seem for all practical purposes to be untellable are still told and retold, if we find something in them that interests us or if we have another reason to tell them. And some stories are retold because only in retelling them can we deal with their apparent untellability.

If it attracts interest, the story finds its proper place as a communication from person to person, and both teller and told cooperate to keep the story alive. At the immediate level, keeping a story alive means questioning how its characters and their actions relate. When faced with a narration of an action, we inevitably ask what kind of person would perform the action. When faced with the description of a character—a characterization or portrait—we wonder what will he or she do? More primary than the typical question posed by the professional critic of literature— "What does it mean?" (a question for artifacts not for people)—is the series of practical questions: "What does she mean?" "What is she doing?" "Who is she?" "Why is she doing this?" These are questions that belong to a life story, and they confirm the link between literature and our everyday experience of human relationships, where such questions carry ethical and political weight. These questions are decisive in everyday life because they issue forth in our actions toward others. They are no less decisive for the understanding of literature, because literature is one way by which we learn how to act and how to be toward others.

The study of literature therefore raises both literary and philosophical questions. It confronts literariness, but the nature of literature cannot be separated from ethics. Any theory that does not wish to abandon literature to the margins of culture needs to ask how storytelling relates to the everyday world of ethics, politics, and practical experience. It needs, in short, to ask how literature contributes to the asking and the answering of the ethical question, "How should I live?"[1]

The vital issue of most stories, I repeat, concerns how characters and their actions are to be related because this problem touches most intimately our own preoccupations with life. First, we wish to know why characters conduct themselves in particular ways because we wonder about similar problems in everyday life. Every meeting with another person involves questions and transactions of this kind. Second, we all conceal the optimistic and sentimental hope that we may somehow change our own life by studying literary characters. We live in secret lives the lives recounted by stories. We retell ourselves the happy stories that we hear in order to live those happy lives as our own, and we retell tragedies to measure our own life's tragedy and to avoid, if we can, further misfortune.

8

Life Stories

What is the relation between character and action? This is a general way of putting a question that we most often ask for the particular circumstances of a story. It is an old question, and it has been posed by literary critics and moral philosophers alike. It is especially pertinent to the understanding of morals and stories because it focuses on the area of concern implicit in the many meanings of character. The word *character* carries so many different associations and summons any number of disciplinary approaches. It refers to "moral disposition," "individual personality," "linguistic sign," and "dramatic persona," and it naturally confronts theories in moral philosophy, human psychology, linguistics, and literary criticism. No single context or disciplinary model seems sufficient to the problem. To what extent, then, does the question of character involve a series of complex relationships among moral ability, individual personality, alphabetical sign, and dramatic personage? And where might we find a place, if at all, to examine this problem? Permit me to tell one story about it.

The Danish explorer Peter Freuchen recounted his life in the frozen North in his book *Arctic Adventure*. Freuchen's account is filled with awesome tales of survival as well as the boredom of everyday life. It also gives practical advice for the arctic explorer, should anyone be tempted by the profession. For example, if you should be inclined, after a day's strenuous march in subzero temperatures, to remove your coat to refresh yourself a bit, do not take more than a few moments to cool yourself down. Freuchen did, and the residue of perspiration in his beautiful fox coat froze, causing the coat to become so brittle that it split open when he tried to slide his arms back into his sleeves. One minute he was trying to cool off. The next he was trying desperately to keep warm.

On another occasion, Freuchen was trapped on an ice pan for five days with two Inuit couples, among them his friend, Akrioq, his wife, Arnanguaq, and their small baby, Navarana. Being trapped on an ice pan is not much of a holiday. As the pieces of ice revolve in the water and collide, they take the form of circles and grow increasingly smaller, until they will no longer support anyone's weight. At this point, one has to jump onto another pan of ice. After leaping from pan to pan for five days, with no more than four hours of sleep, Arnanguaq was growing noticeably upset, for her child was crying incessantly, and both were tired and cold. Suddenly, she turned on Freuchen and accused him of having lice that bite like wolverines. Her husband apparently felt that he had to say something about her behavior to Freuchen:

Akrioq motioned me away from the women and said confidentially that Arnanguaq, after all, was a woman, and "she belongs to those who are angry when adrift on an ice pan if they have small babies." I admitted that one did not encounter the type every day and that if this was her specialty she might as well take advantage of it when she had the opportunity. (446)

Here we have a description of a perfect adequation between character and action. Arnanguaq is, first, a woman and, then, the kind of a woman who gets angry when adrift on an ice pan if she has a small baby. This is how Arnanguaq behaves, so she is the kind of person who behaves this way. The characterization is a minimal narrative, providing the story necessary to connect character and action, although, as I will soon explain, the description is trivial. A practical understanding of a story usually involves this kind of adequation between character and action. This is most obvious in moral philosophy, or in law, especially, where a trial takes place to tell the story of the relation between character and actions.

The Aristotle of the *Poetics* would, perhaps, have had a true appreciation for Akrioq's understanding of character. Aristotle argued that tragedy displays, first and foremost, human actions and that character exists for the sake of action and not vice versa. It appears that in literature we should begin by describing actions and allow ideas of character to flow naturally from these representations. Who is Oedipus? He is a man, and he belongs to those who blind themselves after having discovered that they have killed their father and married their mother. As Freuchen might say, one does not encounter the type every day, and if this is his specialty, he might as well take advantage of it when he has the opportunity.

But the Aristotle of the *Nicomachean Ethics* might well disagree. Here he argues that actions are subservient to character. Actions in accordance with virtue, Aristotle concludes, have a certain character (1105a30). Indeed, Aristotle defines virtue as a state of character concerned with the choice of action (1107a). They tend, he explains of the virtues, to the doing of acts by which they are produced and that are in our power and voluntary (1114b26). When Aristotle wishes to describe a just action, for example, he does not detail instances. Instead, he reasons that actions are just such as the just man would do and who does them as the just man (1105b5). The character of the just man is therefore crucial to an understanding of just actions. But Aristotle does not describe the just man. Indeed, the *Ethics* is remarkably free of moral portraits and examples.

Despite Aristotle's desire to be practical, he offers few descriptions of those good people from whom we are to learn the virtues.

It appears as if we have encountered a kind of vicious circle. Since actions and choices reveal character, according to Aristotle, we may recognize the just man only by his actions and choices. But these choices and actions may be performed only by being such as the just man is. How is anyone interested in building character to learn from such logic?

Part of the problem is that this circle appears more vicious than it is when we discuss the relation between character and action in the abstract. Aristotle is not proposing a syllogism. We make the circle less vicious by recognizing that actions and dispositions of character develop in a social context and under the pressure of a certain story about what "characteristic actions" are.

The Miss Dashwoods in Jane Austen's *Sense and Sensibility* have a problem not unlike our own. The attractive Mr. Willoughby has just made the acquaintance of Marianne and Elinor Dashwood. Marianne fell down a hill, and he carried her to the safety of her cottage. Mr. Willoughby looked very manly in his shooting jacket, but now the Miss Dashwoods want to know whether he would make a good husband. This is, after all, a Jane Austen novel. Mrs. Dashwood inquires about his character to her neighbor Sir John. "And what sort of young man is he?" she asks. "As good a kind of fellow as ever lived, I assure you," replies Sir John. "A very decent shot, and there is not a bolder rider in England." Marianne is reasonably indignant. "And is *that* all you can say for him?" she cries. "But what are his manners on more intimate acquaintance? What his pursuits, his talents and genius?" (32).

Sir John is rather puzzled and has nothing more to add.

Now if the Miss Dashwoods were literary critics, they might well assume that Mr. Willoughby's boldness as a rider does not recommend him highly as a husband. For, as we later see, he rides rather too boldly and too imprudently over Marianne's feelings and those of Colonel Brandon's ward. But the Miss Dashwoods do not have the benefit of Freudian sexual symbolism to decipher Willoughby's horsemanship, nor sufficient information concerning his character to perform, at this point, the extrapolations necessary to understand that these particular actions are characteristic of him. They do not know enough about Willoughby's character to make Sir John's description of his actions exemplary of virtues or vices.

Sir John's characterization of Willoughby may be correct, but it does not have much to recommend it to the Miss Dashwoods. Who is Willoughby? He is a man, and one of those who shoots decently and rides more boldly than others. The description may be adequate for Sir John, who is looking only for a hunting companion, but as a statement concerning character it is trivial. It appears that we are at a disadvantage if we try to understand character solely with actions. Or, rather, we should understand that some actions are more "characteristic" than others, by which I mean that these actions reveal character better than others. Many of us perform the same actions every day: we go to bed; we sleep; we get up; we eat. The fact that we all perform these actions is important because these are the kinds of actions done by human beings. But not all actions are equally useful in coming to an understanding of character.

How do we begin to describe the relation between character and these so-called characteristic actions? Are these actions such as they are because they reveal character? Or is character merely a convenient way of trying to describe those people who perform these actions?

Is the idea of a "characteristic action" a cheat because it motivates the connection between character and action by throwing, as it were, the ball of action into the court of character?

We have encountered the same vicious circle, and there are two ways to see it as less vicious than it appears in the abstract. But they both lead to the same place. First, the relation between character and characteristic actions develops in a social context, in which the benefits and disadvantages of certain actions will be relative to that society as well as to human society in general and, consequently, marked by society as notable. The people who perform these actions will be equally notable, and it will always be advantageous for living in that society to know when one has encountered such and such a person.

Moreover, people observe each other, and individuals who are less successful than others tend to imitate the actions of those who seem to be doing better. This form of imitation has several effects. On the one hand, it gives way to a series of beliefs, languages, and conventions concerning how to act and to be, and these patterns are often internalized so strongly by people that any diversion from them becomes psychologically painful. On the other hand, conforming to the actions of those around us not only produces conventional ways of describing our activities and dispositions but fulfills a psychological need to be part of a group. Social and family life proceeds much more smoothly when members share the same language and beliefs, and we obviously work very hard to educate others, especially our children, about the conventions governing life in society. It is in everyone's interest to have a notion of character in order to make interaction, communication, and cooperation easier.[2]

Second, people live with other people and not with actions. In some sense, of course, we must live with other people's actions as well as with our own. But people attract our attention, and we wish to know something about how they are. Character is a way of describing how people are in an efficient way but not because of the concept of character in and of itself. Character is efficient because it describes those dispositions, desires, and emotions that are most important for living a life among other human beings in the places where they live.

Akrioq's characterization of his wife as a woman and one of those who gets angry when adrift on an ice pan if she has a small baby describes personality on the basis of what we might call an uncharacterizable action. It may be important among the people of the polar North not to become upset when trapped on an ice pan, but it is still so less important than other things that the characterization appears as a joke. It presents a strong adequation between character and action, but it is trivial because it cannot be made to work. It does not have sufficient currency in everyday life. Similarly, Sir John's characterization of Willoughby does not work. One could imagine that it could work better in special circumstances. If England were at war and Willoughby were a soldier expected to shoot and to ride in combat, Sir John's description could well be seen as a useful characterization. But even in this case the characterization would be relatively trivial, suitable only for the activities of shooting and riding. We would have to wait, for example, to see whether Willoughby could be convinced to ride and to shoot in war.

In both cases, the way to soften the viciousness of the circle leads to the fact that people have to live with people and that any rapport between their characters and actions will be subject to that interest. Indeed, at the heart of ethics resides the overriding human desire to live in community with other people, and no ethical concept exists for long that does not ultimately work to satisfy this interest. Action of itself is therefore not sufficient. It must be performed by someone, and this means that the problem of action leads directly to the question of human character. I am justified, then, in referring to a "characteristic action," for actions that are not characterizable will not interest us for long.

Notice, however, that people will go to great lengths to characterize actions. If we could envisage a drama or a film (it would probably have to be a film, since it would be too difficult to present actions without agents in "live action") in which inanimate objects acted upon each other or in which shapes, colors, and forms were presented to us, the strength of our interest in the presentation would depend directly on the extent to which we could imagine those objects as characters in a story (or, in an extreme case, on the extent to which we were rebelling against the fact that we expect characters and a story). If no such characterization or story were supported by the presentation, it would have no interest, and it would not sustain our attention.

We may now say something about the idea of character in general and why it does not often appear to rely solely on action.[3] Virtues and vices are dispositions of character, properly defined, because they participate in the social transactions among people who require a way of anticipating and describing the way that people are. They are explanatory comforts, in a sense, that allow people the ease of relaxing expectations and anxieties (or raising them) in everyday situations, and they permit the high degree of communication among people about people necessary to human cooperation.[4] The idea of character is used as a medium of communication in order to advise others what they will find when they deal with other people. Virtues and vices are what Bernard Williams describes in *Ethics and the Limits of Philosophy* as "thick concepts," if we understand that their apparent thickness is a condition of their being a gathering of many ideas about disposition that are expedient to communicate in the social world rather than a condition of some particular essence connected with the state of existence described by them (140–45, 200). For any concept may thicken, as it gains importance for the social world.

Several objections may be raised against this description of character. First, it may be argued that the language of character can be no different from any other language. We may think that we use the word *good* differently in such sentences as, "He is a good person," or "He is a good chess player." We may believe the goodness of the good person to be a more absolute, a thicker goodness than that of the chess player, but we have merely succumbed to metaphysics, or at least to nonsense, as Wittgenstein pointed out in his "Lecture on Ethics."

It is not clear how human beings can succumb to metaphysics. As for nonsense, this remains to be seen.

The difference between these two goodnesses, however, is real enough, and in the most obvious ways. The problem is that this difference cannot be inferred by looking at words and sentences in isolation from their surroundings. Thickness does not rely on individual concepts but on a larger story. When Akrioq described his wife as a woman and one of those who gets angry when adrift on an ice pan if she has a small baby, he was describing a "vice" analogous to that described in the sentence, "She is a bad chess player." Her flaw is too trivial to be considered a vice, and Akrioq in fact offers his characterization to excuse his wife (in his own sexist way) and not to accuse her. The characterization appears as a joke, which is to say that it has the quality of a momentary entertainment that appears to have little to do with the context from which it sprang. But if Akrioq had used the language of character and its catalogue of virtues and vices, it would have demanded a different kind of response. The language of the virtues and vices in general may be applied to many situations. It permits a great deal of generalization about people that is useful, if properly employed, and dangerous, if not. Most specifically, it engages people in the act of telling a story about how human beings will react to different events, and it causes people to focus on their immediate situation. If Akrioq had said to Freuchen, "Arnanguaq is a bad woman," the explorer's reaction would probably have been different. The value of that phrase is different in terms of communication, and Freuchen would have had to consider what it said about Arnanguaq. He would have had to ask himself about what Ross Chambers in *Story and Situation* calls the "point" of the story. Why is this characterization being given now? Whose interests does it serve? What does it hope to accomplish? Is it reasonable, given the situation, to lend credence to Akrioq's characterization of Arnanguaq? If not, what kind of character is he? If so, what may I expect of Arnanguaq? Should I think about countermeasures? Should I leap to another ice pan?

The characterizations produced by the language of virtue and vice are stories that demand additional acts of storytelling. It is as if these characterizations contained the kernel of a plot that needs to be related in story to the immediate surroundings of the persons confronted by it.

The linguistic objection to character is finally not viable because its adherents wish to submit character to a linguistic analysis, but one cannot get to character on the basis of an examination of words and sentences. Character relies on a larger story, and its pressure on individual formations, descriptions, and sentences can only be inferred, not completely discovered by analysis, especially by linguistic analysis. We understand character only by telling and retelling stories. I will return to this argument in chapter three because it has special pertinence to work currently being done in literary criticism on ethics.

Another objection may dispute the idea of character for ethical reasons.

"Character" will always be an explanation, it will be argued, and explanation is supposedly never free from the particular interest of the one who explains. Using descriptions of character therefore exercises power over other people; and in most cases, it will be an unjust use of power. (Notice here, however, that those who object on these grounds do possess a theory of character. They believe that human character is essentially wolflike: unjust and bloodthirsty.)

This argument contains a real, if impractical, objection. As far as character can be seen to be an abstraction, explanation, or theory, it involves us in the dangers of such thought in a manner unrivaled by any other context. Theory always risks a process of derivation that may leave its original object behind. We distrust theories and abstract ideas because they are often unfaithful to life as we live it. Yet few of us could get through the day without taking the ominous leap of faith involved in abstract ideas, conventions, and theories. But when character is the object of abstraction, this leap of faith may become a fall. The idealizations and stereotypes created by theories of character risk doing violence to people, for ideals of character may be used to deprive individuals of their rights as human beings. All the great prejudices—racism, sexism, nationalism, and classism—depend on specific theories of character to maintain themselves at the expense of their victims. Perhaps the little prejudices of everyday life harm people on an even larger scale: how many times in a week do we reject or recommend people at a moment's notice, after having decided that they are this or that type of person?

To ask what character is, then, requires ethical care and moral character, if the perils of theory are to be avoided. The student of character confronts the problem of ethics in an unprecedented way because the study of character not only belongs, as Aristotle knew, to the science of ethics but requires the utmost sensitivity to ethical matters.

The real question, however, to be posed to those who object to character on ethical grounds is the following. Given their idea of human character, would it make any difference to eliminate the tendency to characterize people in various ways? In short, is this tendency the cause of the general evil that they see? If the world is as they see it, teeming with wolfish and power-hungry people, the elimination of characterization would not matter significantly. If the world is not as they see it, the elimination of characterization would cause a great deal of hardship.

In point of fact, there is no question of eliminating this tendency anyway. The argument against it arises from a philosophical position that has lost its hold on the world.

A final objection may be that character is either fiction or nonsense. I grant the first point but not if "fiction" is to be seen as a derogatory term. We should already be beginning to understand that character is both a literary and ethical concept, and I will have much more to say about this connection in what follows. *Morals and Stories* is meant to circumscribe the area of concern shared by literature and ethics, and as its argument grows more clear, it will, I hope, address to what extent the belief that both ethics and literature have no value for practical life because they are forms of storytelling is not worth supporting.

That ethical notions such as character are nonsense is a stronger objection because it has so often been made. But the idea of nonsense is not as coherent as it may seem, and it is not clear that the objection that something is nonsense makes any sense itself. It usually means that we have not looked far enough for an answer. The objection became especially popular with the rise of linguisticism, and it may well be that the term *nonsense* makes sense only in an isolated linguistic context. For as soon as we examine the context in which various "nonsensical" remarks are made, we will understand in all probability that they have some role to play. Nonsense usually has its point too.

Indeed, the point of the argument that ethical concepts are nonsense has most often of late turned on an ethical desire to thwart the apparent authority of these concepts. Calling ethical concepts nonsense or calling for nonsense in response to ethics possesses a transgressive force that makes sense only as a reaction to ethics. It belongs to the characteristically modern distrust of institutions, systems, and authoritative bodies. Our current sense is that authority is implicated in power and violence, and we feel as a result that ethical concepts are inherently immoral. But, of course, no one can launch this critique of ethics without planting his or her feet firmly in the tradition of ethics. Moreover, this critique of ethics grows out of the ethical tradition in the first place. Those who end by putting their feet back in the tradition to critique the tradition discover that they never took their feet out to begin with. It is a case of wishing to lift oneself by the bootstraps and discovering that the boots have no straps.

Character is, above all, a social idea, and it cannot be eliminated without a great deal of difficulty and many extreme changes in the ways that people live and think. The awkwardness and genius of the concept of character remains that it is a descriptive and prescriptive form that cannot be readily described or prescribed. Its stability is not easily demonstrated either by those who fear stability or by those who wish to approach it through the medium of linguistic analysis. Moreover, most discourse about character ends by being the same kind of storytelling that gave rise to character in the first place. Its indescribability excites the temptation to evaluate it, and once we begin to evaluate it, we tend to use the very concepts that we purport to be evaluating.

Perhaps this tendency accounts for Aristotle's reluctance to describe character in the *Nicomachean Ethics*. Aristotle, as I hinted above, does not provide a characterization of the virtuous man. There is nothing in the *Ethics* comparable to a moral portrait. We glimpse the great-souled man in its pages but once, when Aristotle describes his gait. (Does Willoughby's riding have something, after all, to do with his character?) But the great-souled man is too much on the march, and before we can catch a closer look, he walks deliberately out of sight.

The absence of this portrait presents no grave flaw in Aristotle's account. Rather, it derives from his idea of the Greek polis or city-state. Only if we believed that a book on ethics should take upon itself the task of establishing a vision of character apart from human society, as some say Kant did, would we be tempted to criticize Aristotle on this point. He does not himself believe it possible, for he tells us explicitly that ethics belongs to politics. The reason, then, that Aristotle does not describe the virtuous man is that he defines society as that domain in which we gain the experience necessary to compose this character for ourselves. In short, he need not provide a moral portrait because culture is that place where this work is done, which is to say that culture is an ethical culture. Indeed, to attempt such a characterization in a book would seem to be an act of theory removed from the practices gained by living in the places where people live. This was Plato's mistake according to Aristotle. Plato succumbed to the idea of the idea, and to the belief that he could provide a theory of good character apart from the experience of both storytelling and living in the world.

There is no question of such a theory succeeding in its intentions because no theory really gets off the ground. All theories have practices, although not every practice has a theory. But theories are successful in a more important way. If culture is that place where the work of characterization is done, then theory is as much a part of this work as any other activity. We count on theory as much as on anything else to compose our ideals of how human beings should act and be. Aristotle's reluctance to describe the virtuous man should not, therefore, be taken as a dogmatic refusal of theory. He affirms, of course, the contemplative life at the conclusion of the *Ethics*, and he gives us many moral portraits in the *Rhetoric* (although these chapters are seldom read anymore), thereby initiating the tradition of characterization in the West. That he included characterizations in his *Rhetoric* reveals his faith in our ethical culture and his desire to participate in it as well as his idea of what rhetoric is supposed to be. Rhetoric, Aristotle explains, is an offshoot of ethical studies, which, in turn, spring from political science (Rh 1356a25–30). The *Rhetoric*, then, is written in the same place as the *Ethics*.

Today, laboring as we do under the idea of language, we often reverse Aristotle's proposition and reduce both politics and ethics to rhetoric. This means, of course, that we still believe in an ethical culture, since this "beautiful" rhetoric remains a symbol of morality. But the absoluteness of the application of the idea of rhetoric means that we have fewer places to express ourselves. Rhetoric has its more proper place in human society, where its applications contribute to the ways that people talk to and think about each other. Its stake in persuasion makes it an instrument for moving people to actions and opinions, both wrongly and rightly, and as this way of talking, it joins the power of storytelling to that of ethics.

CHAPTER 3

∾

The Case Against
Linguistic Ethics

THE DISPLACEMENT OF character by language has immediate and often unfortunate consequences for both moral and literary thinking. When relieved of the problem of character, moral philosophers usually turn their attention to the meaning of meaning, or what people really intend when they use moral language, and despair of talking about moral or political conduct. G. E. Moore's *Principia Ethica* focused moral philosophy on its own language at the beginning of this century, arguing that some of its failures result from the inability to phrase questions properly. A. J. Ayer later disputed any relation between the moralist and the moral philosopher, reducing the task of ethics to the analysis of statements: the objective of the moral philosopher is to show "how ethical statements are related to, and how they differ from, statements of other types, and what are the criteria which are appropriate to them" ("Editorial Foreword" 7). Finally, C. L. Stevenson's *Language and Ethics* consummated the trend in linguistic ethics by claiming that the primary function of moral language is to persuade other people of our own opinions. For Stevenson, "It is good" is a disguised version of "I like it." Thus Anglo-American philosophy recovered the perspective of Nietzsche, who believed that ethical statements allow the weak to bend other people to their wills through the cunning of language. An entire movement in moral philosophy could be characterized in such terms and, only lately—through the efforts of Stanley Cavell, Alasdair MacIntyre, Martha Nussbaum, and Bernard Williams, among others—has philosophy moved again beyond the preoccupation with the meaning of meaning to the problem of how ethics relates to activities in practical life such as marriage, storytelling, political contestation, and states of character and emotion.[1]

Literary critics today, however, continue to deny the importance of character for the reading of literature, preferring to stress the power of language, the arbitrariness of the sign, and the ambiguities of interpretation. We have in effect abandoned the hope of describing character at any level, be it ethical, psychological, or literary. Language, as the interpretive category of modernity, frames the response to every problem. Any attempt to find a coherent and sensible way of talking about the self fails, we complain, because it ends by inventing the self rather than finding it. Character is then said to be an abstract and artificial construct created out of language and used to give unity and order to human personality. Where we once looked for character we now find language. The coherence of the self, it seems, is nothing but an illusion of language.

What better proof of this illusion than the fact that characters in books are capable of exciting our love, anger, and fear? From the dawn of time, the history of literature has been the story of one long Pygmalion complex, except that not all characters in stories are beautiful statues. They are more like scarecrows, composed of bits and pieces of language, but if the slightest breeze appears to animate them, we fly into emotion nevertheless, like addled birds, flapping about in fear or lovingly clutching.

Notice that language represents a vehicle for a skeptical attitude toward the nature of the self and the grounds of character, but the skeptics do not ask whether one needs grounds for doubt.

"The world," it has been said, "cannot hover in the heavens of its own accord."

"Atlas holds it aloft," is the response.

"And how does Atlas stay in the air?"

"He sits on the back of an elephant."

"And where does the elephant stand?"

"He stands on the back of a turtle."

"And where does the turtle stand?"

"I'm afraid, from there, it's turtles all the way down."

By such stories the world stays in the heavens, and language acquires the power of turtles.

The insistence on the theoretical and linguistic dimension of character appears to be inevitable, especially in this skeptical world of ours, although it may not be equally inevitable that we respond to it in such foreseeable ways. The skepticism of modern theory is necessary because we have come to learn that doubt forms an integral component of moral consciousness. But skepticism can never be more than one component among others, by which I mean that it cannot stand alone and in itself as a form of morality. Skepticism needs a ground as much as anything else, and the temptation of absolute skepticism, although a strong one, is ultimately a fantasy of belief, especially in its drive toward completeness, which is, after all, the great hallmark of all ethical dreams.

Although the modern view of language does have enormous tactical value in exposing the dangers of theories and abstractions, it ultimately fails, and for three general reasons. First, the skeptical attack on character depends on an ideal of character. The theorist of language suspects the coherence of character and associates it with an ethical crisis in which authority based on ideology creates a regime of oppression. Phrases such as "the power of language" or "the politics of literature" often focus our attention on the deceitful nature of authority. Authorities usually cement their power through a language of value embodied in words such as "personality," "virtue," "vice," and "moral character." The current theory of language among literary critics exposes the will to power and fictive nature of such linguistic constructs. But by offering this critique, the theorist of language makes an ethical argument against character that implies another theory of good character. The act of doubting moral authority and language is a moral virtue to be desired and cultivated. This ideal of moral character even has a name. We call it Language. Today we speak of language more and more as if it were a personality. This is not merely a form of shorthand convenient to the academic writing of philosophy, linguistics, and literary criticism. The moral personification of language carries the residue of character displaced by those same ideas of language.

Notice, however, that this model of character is vastly inferior to the one that it replaces. If modern thought has any contribution to make to ethics, it lies in the remarkable consensus that we hold concerning the treatment of our fellow human beings. We are disgusted by the torture of human beings and concerned about the abject conditions in which many people are forced to live. Modern theories of the decentered or linguistic subject negate these important ethical feelings. They deny the feeling that a human being is eminently worthy of being helped and treated with justice. They consider ideas of human dignity and value to be linguistic fictions unworthy of serious philosophical reflection. But these ideas, which are apparently so unphilosophical, are responsible for the great advances in moral sensibility identifiable with modern life.

Second, this theory of language fails because it leaves no place for language itself. How, for example, does one define language within a field of exploration that is wholly linguistic? Since language does not apparently ground itself in reality, theorists today describe language as a play of languages or discourses. They talk of language affecting language, of discourses struggling with other discourses, but such descriptions do not provide a real definition of language. Indeed, such descriptions only capture metaphorically the same types of struggles and battles that were found in nonlinguistic descriptions of character. (They apply, more precisely, the model of liberal individualism to that abstract entity called language.) In short, metaphors of language applied to character are more metaphoric and more abstract, more suspect finally, than the figures of speech traditionally used to discuss personality and ethics. Ironically, if we probe current ideas of language with any kind of rigor, we will discover that the generation of literary critics who has invested more in the problem of language than any other has yet to arrive at anything resembling a theory of language. The poststructuralists do not have a theory of language, and time is running out for the movement.

Third, literary criticism that denies the importance of character loses touch with the experience of storytelling itself. It therefore loses touch with those people who care about literature. The huge gap on the present scene between theories of literature and the everyday practice of reading is a direct result of abandoning all interest in character. People read for character, and a theory that rejects character can have nothing in common with this kind of reading, nor is this sort of theory bound to be intelligible to many people. It does not retell stories with sufficient care to interest most people, and the stories that it does tell, for it does tell stories, conceal, almost willfully, every connection with our daily life. We learn little from them save how to practice the theory itself.

In a related development, skeptical thinkers confronted by the supposed groundlessness of ethical ideas have tended to succumb to another predictable temptation. They denounce ethics in favor of politics. I note from the outset that the choice of political analysis is not in itself flawed. In principle, the political analysis of literature and philosophy represents one of those areas most needed on the current scene, and I have no desire to raise objections to its development and practice. No reason exists to make a strong distinction between ethics and politics because practical and political wisdom are intimately related. But, habitually, the embrace of politics by literary critics has had the most feeble results. The opening gesture of many political theorists of literature is to establish an artificial (and moralistic) distinction between ethics and politics based on the belief that politics is more concrete and historical than ethics, and therefore less prone to mystification and airy theorizing. Simply put, for them, politics is a good mode of interpretation, and ethics is a bad one.

Consider, briefly, Fredric Jameson's influential *The Political Unconscious*. Jameson makes two of his objectives remarkably clear. First, political analysis must obey the opening imperative of his book, "Always historicize!" Jameson identifies neither the source nor the authority of this universal statement. It levitates, suspended in midair, through the sheer power of moral command. Second, and dubiously, Jameson argues that his method differs from others because it is political, whereas the "predominant code" of literary theory today must be called an "*ethical* criticism" (59). One of Jameson's stated goals is to present an alternative to the temptation of ethics because ethics, in his view, lives by exclusion and by inventing certain types of evil or otherness. Moreover, ethics appeals for its authority to such outdated and reified notions as the "self" or the "ego," and every enlightened modern thinker, Jameson believes, knows that such notions need to be eliminated (60). By nature, he infers, ethics conceals the genuine stakes in social conflicts, allowing inequities and cruelty to exist, whereas politics, again by nature, appears able to sidestep such difficulties with ease to expose the reality of history.

But Jameson fails to offer anything remotely resembling a historical analysis, and he, in fact, bases many of his readings on the most formalistic devices of structuralist linguistics (such as A. J. Greimas's semiotic rectangle). More significant, his division between ethics and politics does not stand up to analysis, for his avowed orientation is, of course, Marxist, and the force of Marx today is more ethical than political. Marxism as a political theory is dead. It has nothing either in its current political applications or in its economic achievements to recommend it. Marxism today lives largely as a skeptical theory of culture, and like many such theories, its orientation is decidedly moralistic. Marxism is no longer directed toward history or even practical matters. It focuses on culture in the abstract, and its readings derive much of their power from a strictly critical orientation. The remarkable force of Marxism, for I do not deny its power, resides in its critiques of class consciousness, alienation, and exploitation. In short, its present viability derives from its vision of ethical individualism and its ability to criticize both the patterns of domination in society and the alienating effects of industrial technology. But Marxism has nothing practical, nothing really political, to offer as a concrete alternative. Perhaps this is why Marxists have run for cover to the area of literary theory. Literary study suffers from a long history of political somnambulism, and in contrast to most literary critics, Marxists look like bona fide political activists.

The call for a "politics of literature" has not yet demonstrated its value (although I remain optimistic), and one looks in vain, outside the province of feminist criticism, for anything having the political instincts of a book such as Hannah Arendt's *Eichmann in Jerusalem*, where the examination of political language carries immediate and potent consequences for an understanding of how social and political forces drew a generation of people into a whirlwind of hatred, prejudice, and genocide. Similar occasions await political commentary, but few dare to step forward. In fact, many literary critics who embrace political analysis seem to be so drunk on generalities that they no longer know how to speak about political realities, and they too easily separate ideas from people's character and past actions, a weakness that becomes overwhelmingly clear in their blind admiration of thinkers who could not follow their own convictions or who embraced the political philosophies of evil regimes, Paul de Man and Martin Heidegger being among the most recent examples. The attempts to defend such men against their own unfortunate actions and applications require great feats of interpretation and excuse-making, and they reveal to what extent a genuine commitment to politics has too little meaning for us today.

Quite expectedly, some literary critics have argued that we need a new idea of ethics based on the structure of language. Julia Kristeva and J. Hillis Miller, to give the most obvious examples, have both praised the ethical orientation of language in itself. According to them, the ethics of language is released in the act of interpretation or of reading, and it is therefore worthwhile examining the method behind their interpretations, for it will give us a better idea concerning what linguistic ethics consists of and what its failings are.

The Case Against Linguistic Ethics

The early work of Julia Kristeva is preoccupied with ethics and politics, and the titles of her writings enthusiastically bring together social and poetic ideas, as is the fact, for example, with *The Revolution in Poetic Language*. In her later work, however, she has turned away from political analysis properly defined to psychoanalysis, although this turn is not without its ethical consequences. Kristeva's most sustained statement on ethics may be found in *Polylogue*. She devotes a long section of the book to "the ethics of linguistics," and it climaxes with a specific description of the ethical qualities of Russian futurist poetry. These ethical qualities spring essentially from the nature of language itself. According to Kristeva, poetic language captures another mode of expression that consists of a practice of sustained contradiction. Poetic language sketches out the limits of the self and of the scientific rules given by judgment. To arrive at a linguistic ethics, then, critics must come to an understanding of language as an "articulation of a heterogeneous process." The heterogeneity of language apparently releases marginal, negative, and destructive forces, and these forces subvert repressive political regimes.

When Kristeva turns to the poetry of Khlebnikov and Mayakovsky, and Roman Jakobson's analysis of them, we see what her theoretical claims do methodologically. Kristeva describes murder, death, and unchanging society as the impossibility of understanding poetic language. According to her, poetic language is composed of pure sounds, rhythms, and signs that are detached from reality and anterior to any reference to an object or an emotion. Societies murder their poets precisely because they wish to stress rhythm and the purity of words, for these practices cannot but threaten and transform the rigid organization of political systems. The time of the poem, according to Kristeva, is a future anterior, which will never take place, and as such it subverts place and present meanings—those linguistic practices used by the authorities to exercise control.

Enter, of course, the Russian futurists. In Mayakovsky, the revolution of poetic language takes the form of his battle with the sun and his use of suicidal images. In Khlebnikov, it takes the form of glossolalia. In both, the "I" of the poem is radically linguistic, unstable, and antisocial, and the ethics of linguistics consists in determining how this "I" struggles against repressive social languages and regimes.

Note well, however, that the revolutionary language of Russian futurism in Kristeva's view does not attack a repression particular to the Russian society of the time but a general repression associated with all societies. There is something unpolitical in this gesture, and it gives rise to a kind of theoretical thinking that fails at every turn to come back down to earth. It is a Romanticism that composes a moral position from a general skepticism about the possibility of a just society. Despite its apparent political orientation, then, it has little to say about specific societies and no political practice to recommend. Rather, Kristeva's goal is purely theoretical. For her, the heterogeneity of the linguistic self inherently composes an ethics. Only by recognizing the linguistic nature of the self and its instability, then, may we come to an understanding, Kristeva argues, of what ethical character really consists. But Kristeva's description of this form of selfhood, although it deals largely in generalities such as the "self" and "society," still leaves her in possession of an ideal of character, however heterogeneous or poetic it may be. The rub is that the self has no choice about its heterogeneous conditions any more than society does about its repressive hierarchies. Everything depends on the oppositions found in linguistic structure, including, especially, the possible forms of the ethico-political.

J. Hillis Miller has established himself as a major spokesman for the ethics of reading by returning to the topic with dogged determination. Like Kristeva, Miller relies on language itself, more precisely on its supposed contradictory nature, to define the ethics of reading. According to Miller, readers confront a "linguistic imperative" when they read any text, and it commands that they give themselves over as a duty to the coercive power of language. Language by its nature is ambiguous, and it is impossible to impose a single, precise meaning within it. Reading becomes, à la Paul de Man, the impossibility of reading, Miller concludes in his essay "The Critic as Host," "if by 'readable' one means open to a single, definitive, univocal interpretation." The text gives the law, but the law does not give itself, and Miller confesses, as a result, that "Nihilism is an inalienable alien presence within Occidental metaphysics, both in poems and in the criticism of poems" (447).

In practice, Miller's nihilism produces what he calls a lateral dance, in which the critic follows words through their contradictions and waltzes from text to text. "The Critic as Host" provides the cleanest example of the method and its limitations. Miller analyzes the meanings of a number of words used by an opponent in the debate over pluralism: "parasite," "host," and "guest." He compares them to Freud's analysis of *unheimlich* and *heimlich* in his essay "The Uncanny," claiming that each word embraces two contradictory meanings. These words destroy the possibility of a single meaning, for whenever we use them, we supposedly encounter a linguistic trap that undoes our intentions and meanings. Our choice is to fight against language and to lose, or to give in to it and to embrace the linguistic imperative. If we give in, we come to understand a new value, "the value of recognizing the great complexity and equivocal richness of apparently obvious and univocal language" (443).

"The Critic as Host" shares its method with Miller's more specific statements on the ethics of reading, although he does not couch the essay in ethical argument per se. In the prizing of complexity, richness, and equivocalness, we recognize the great ethic of liberal individualism and its skepticism toward any claims to obligation or purely social responsibility. But in *The Ethics of Reading*, Miller's most complete sketch of his linguistic ethics, we witness how this doubting of obligation becomes an obligation. This is best demonstrated by remarking that Miller repeats and distorts the ethical theories of Kant, as is immediately evident in his substitution of the term "linguistic imperative" for Kant's "categorical imperative."[2] Miller claims that the reader, when reading, experiences an ineluctable duty that arises in the form of a transcendental command to affirm the undecidability or radical ambiguity of language: "In any ethical moment there is an imperative, some 'I must' or *Ich kann nicht anders*. I *must* do this. I cannot do otherwise. If the response is not one of necessity, grounded in some 'must,' if the response is a freedom to do what one likes, for example to make a literary text mean what one likes, then it is not ethical, as when we say, 'That isn't ethical'" (4). Remember that the freedom to make a text meaningful, according to Miller, is limited by the fact that language is undecidable and therefore an inappropriate tool for making meaning, and not by the ethical belief, as E. D. Hirsch has argued, that readers should not impose their private and eccentric meanings on a work.

Apparently, some part of this linguistic imperative requires Miller to break into German as well. Miller *must* feel German when he reads. But *"Ich kann nicht anders"* is not, of course, the German of either Miller or Kant, despite its similarity to the categorical imperative. It is Martin Luther's response at the Diet of Worms. When threatened by the Council, Luther refused to recant, asserting that his conscience was captive to the Word of God and not to popes or councils. Miller's allusion to Luther does not mean in any sense that he shares Luther's view of scripture. Miller most often works to deny scriptural claims for textuality as mere metaphysics. Rather, Miller's use of Luther plays a double game. He appears to stand where Luther stands (*"Hier stehe Ich. Ich kann nich anders. Gott helfe mir. Amen."*), but he cannot stand Luther's meaning. Miller's metaphor is devoid of everything that makes Luther's statement metaphorical. Miller is a Lutheran who is skeptical of Lutheranism.

When Miller turns to Kant, we discover a similar operation. Miller elaborates a Kantianism that is not Kantian. This is obvious, first of all, in Miller's mingling of Kant and Freud. Miller sprinkles the chapter on Kant with Freudianisms, and the effect is that the Kantian good will begins to look rather like the Freudian unconscious. For instance, repeating his method in "The Critic as Host," Miller interprets Kant's use of *versprechen*, "to promise," in the light of Freud's idea of the "slip of the tongue." Consequently, when Kant claims that promises must be kept, according to Miller, he actually loses the ability to promise, a linguistic necessity that Miller defines as "lying promises." The idea of a lying promise reveals an "intrinsic feature of language," Miller explains, and the "sad linguistic necessity" that we are destined never to keep promises, whatever our intentions, because the structure of language itself prevents it. "Lying becomes a universal principle," Miller claims, and this principle is the only form of universality understandable in Kantian terms (39).

Second, Miller focuses on the footnote in the *Foundations of the Metaphysics of Morals* (the second note in the "First Section") in which Kant describes the "respect" that people feel for the law. Miller claims that we will be able to have at least a preliminary grasp of Kant's theory of ethics as well as of what is most problematical about that theory, if we can read the footnote accurately in the context of its surrounding paragraphs. But this accurate reading ends by being a close examination of one word, "respect" (*Achtung* in Kant's German).

Miller's analysis of Kant's footnote exposes the limitations of deconstruction and the contradictions of its claims. He gives close attention to the word "respect," while arguing simultaneously that there is no theory of ethics without storytelling. This last argument has rich possibilities. But we are left, sadly, to make the application for ourselves because Miller ignores Kant's stories about the categorical imperative to focus on those particular words that allow him to engage in a lateral dance. The word "respect" permits Miller to destroy Kant's argument for respect. Kant, apparently, bases his theory of ethics on a word that does not enhance his theory but subverts it. "Respect," according to Miller, represents a knife-edge that Kant must walk, and to either side lies an abyss. On one side is the abysmal thought that respect is a "mere reflex action of desire or fear";

on the other side is the abysmal thought that respect "creates or projects its objects" (19). In the end, Kant falls into the abyss because he has tried to name something that has no name. He succumbs, then, to the metaphoric and undecidable nature of language.

Miller's maverick Kantianism plays with all the familiar Kantian themes: freedom, autonomy, duty, and universality. But the result is rather different from Kant's. On the one hand, Miller attacks Kant's ignorance of history, pretending to speak in the name of historical analysis. On the other hand, Miller emphasizes only particular texts and claims that we can do nothing but close readings. Miller, in fact, rarely has recourse to historical analysis, and in each of his close readings, we hear the clear, transcendental voice of duty, requiring us not to tell the story of our best self but to interpret a poem or story as undecidable. The result is a monotonous view of literature and a fantastic and unworldly view of human life. Lying and promising bring us the same truth; both get us nowhere. In fact, the linguistic imperative exists nowhere, outside history, and neither social nor historical forces impinge upon it. Here is Miller's claim for it: "This ethical 'I must' cannot, I propose to show, be accounted for by the social and historical forces that impinge upon it. In fact the ethical moment contests these forces or is subversive of them" (8). In its transcendental quality, supposedly, resides the force of ethics, for Miller claims that its existence (if that is the word here) subverts history and society. But he never makes it clear how an ethic of nowhere can subvert an ethic of some place.

But all is not pessimism, Miller reminds us, recalling Paul de Man's theory of radically undecidable language. "I would even dare to promise," he writes, "that the millenium [sic] would come if all men and women became good readers in de Man's sense" (58).

There is really only one sad linguistic necessity in all of this, and it is the sad necessity that linguistic ethics is not adequate to the task of understanding either ethics or literature. The current generation of literary critics seems to have been struck with a case of selective amnesia; they have simply forgotten what ethical and literary arguments sound like, as Stanley Cavell would say, and consequently, their arguments have lost the dense texture and human touch found in that precious talk in which human dilemmas, choices, emotions, and triumphs are described. They seem to have accepted the idea expressed by Jonathan Culler that literary criticism "advances by becoming increasingly formalistic, just as linguistics does" (5). One hears in such ideas the hopefulness of the early years of structuralism, when literary critics first discovered linguistics and claimed it as the solution to the problem of validity in interpretation. After all, literature is language, and a science of language should allow students of letters to take possession of a science of literature. But the present tendency to focus on one word or only on those words that are puns produces a limited interpretive method. It ascribes to language as a whole the features that Freud gave to a few "primal words," and it then uses one or two words as the basis of an entire reading, assuming that because they can be shown to be ambiguous, it proves that the whole work collapses.[3] It presents no evidence for this claim except for a general theory of language, which has never been proved and which, moreover, asserts that it is impossible to demonstrate its truth because of the nature of language itself.

Even if one or two words are undecidable, it does not mean that the work is so flawed. The Venus de Milo has lost its arms, but no one whom I know of has as yet claimed that it is a statue of a woman without arms.

Structural linguistics has not lived up to its promise. One recalls, for example, the early excitement generated by Roman Jakobson's and Lévi-Strauss's analysis of Baudelaire's *Les Chats*. They purported to find in a purely linguistic analysis of the sonnet the connection between linguistics and anthropology. The result was dry reading indeed: discussions of word placement, rhyme schemes, labials, and feminine and masculine endings. In the end, they could not sustain the analysis at the linguistic level, and they turned to Baudelaire's personal understanding of words, as revealed in his other writings. For many years, this essay was mandatory reading in courses on literary theory and for graduate students. Today it has disappeared from the canon, remaining only in memory as a curiosity of an early and enthusiastic era. As Michael Riffaterre later summed up the method in his little essay "Describing Poetic Structures," "No grammatical analysis of a poem can give us more than the grammar of the poem" (213).

The Yale School of Artificial Intelligence has arrived at similar conclusions in its analysis of how stories work. I am not making a joke at the expense of the now defunct Yale School of deconstruction but referring to the work done at Yale in computer simulations of stories. Roger Schank and Robert Abelson and others have arrived at a series of simple classifications, such as scripts, plans, goals, and life themes, for analyzing how people understand stories. Their book, *Scripts, Plans, Goals, and Under-*

standing, begins with the useful assumption that "the appropriate ingredients for extracting the meaning of a sentence . . . are often nowhere to be found within the sentence" (9), but they then try to discuss how different contexts may be classified. They argue that people have "scripts" informing them which actions are appropriate in particular situations, and that they follow these stylized and stereotyped sequences. Individuals also use "plans" in order to organize various scripts, and their "goals," in turn, organize plans. Finally, we have a use of "life themes" that gives us, among other things, an idea of how the roles occupied by people relate to their behavior. If, to use one of the book's examples, I say that "Larry the lawyer picked up the garbage from all the cans on the street," we find this sentence to be unintelligible, if we try to explain it on the basis of Larry's profession (133). We need more information to decide whether this is a community service performed in times of need, or a punishment for drug-trafficking, for instance, handed down by a community-minded judge.

Speakers, unless they are trying to trick their listeners, understand that their audience knows which actions are being named. Speaker and listener have a common point in mind, or a context, and we need a practical way of thinking about this point in order to begin to discuss how interpretation works. Schank and Abelson give the example of the simple sentence: "The policeman held up his hand and stopped the car" (9). We could interpret this sentence to mean that the policeman possesses the magical power to stop automobiles with the simple movement of his hand, or that he is really Superman, disguised as Clark Kent, the policeman, and that he stopped the car with his superhuman strength. These interpretations are coherent, but we have no reason to make them, unless a specific "script" calls for them. More reasonable, of course, is the idea that the driver of the car, understanding traffic laws, saw the policeman's signal and stepped on the brake, bringing the car to a halt. The point remains that this sentence presents little difficulty for understanding, despite the fact that it does not provide within itself all of the information needed to read it. It summons for most of us a familiar script that provides the necessary context for understanding it.

People often leave out the connections between sentences in a story, but this does not guarantee that their meanings will be unintelligible because we infer the implicit connections in most narratives. It is necessary to look for meaning not only in sentences but at the level of the whole story and, beyond, at the points where the story relates to its contexts and the history of those contexts. It is not at all easy to trace how inference uncovers the causal and other relations between elements in a story; it is easier to perform linguistic analyses of sentences or to dance from word to word in order to construct the grand and skeptical narrative that meaning cannot exist, thereby making a closer and more difficult examination of the foundational level of narrative, its politics, ethics, and rationalities a moot point instead of the point.

The work of Schank and Abelson presents its own difficulties, and I am not at all claiming that it solves the problems of literary and ethical interpretation. It does have the virtue, however, of orienting interpretation away from individual words and sentences toward a recognition of that place where language is used. It richly demonstrates the fact that both literary and ethical notions of character rely on a dense social context that is responsible for their applications and that is influenced in turn by those applications. Language does not in and of itself create either the places where people live or those people who ask how and where they should live. Both people and the places where they live have their part in the story of language. This story is difficult to tell, but it is, in my view, the only story worth telling.

The heresy of paraphrase is correct, then, although it does not recognize that interpretations of literature are ethical in nature. The heresy of paraphrase explains that every interpretation of a work is a paraphrase that violates its object, and that the only way to prevent such violence is to recite the work verbatim, without commentary. We cannot, it is true, interpret a story without paraphrasing or moralizing it, thereby adding to or subtracting from its economy. But neither can we understand a story without engaging in such paraphrasing or moralizing because most statements require us to summon various contexts, conventions, and norms. This thematization, if we can use the term, is a moralization insofar as it connects the story to the places where people live. Literature is ethical in its need of interpretation, which means that the value of literature resides in its ability to summon the idea of human life. The heresy of paraphrase misses the point when it opposes interpretation in the name of saving literature from "violation."

We need an idea of this practical domain of literature, and not simply a theory of literature. We may ask, for example, what literature is, but our descriptions will be inadequate because the real practical force of literature resides not in itself but in interpretation, in its relation to the human world, and this knowledge cannot easily be abstracted by a theory, though continue to theorize we must. The knowledge given by literature, like that of ethics, must be read and experienced repeatedly to advance toward maturity. It must be told, heard, and retold, creating around itself the same kind of gathering described within it.

CHAPTER 4

༂

The Moral
of the Story

THE VALUE OF STORYTELLING for building character appears to be an assumption widely accepted by both the history of moral philosophy and the history of thought about literature. To understand justice as a virtue, for example, is not merely to understand how it may be embodied in a character but to see what place it holds in a certain kind of story and to desire to occupy that place and to tell that story. We give our children their moral education by telling them stories, hoping that they will wish to recollect and retell them; and when we argue with each other over ethical problems, we make our points with stories of various kinds.

The purest form of argument of this type is argumentation by proverb, in which a speaker invokes parables, maxims, sayings, or Biblical quotations as part of his or her case. Today, however, we are increasingly distrustful of proverbial wisdom, and so it has fallen out of use to some degree. Or, perhaps, the modern love of citation satisfies the urge for proverbs. To the extent that both forms of communication desire to summon a community of people who share the same beliefs, language, and ideas, citation in scholarly argument works like argumentation by proverb, except for the fact that its quotations do not usually carry the universal import given to proverbs.

But proverbs and fables still present a striking analogy for the relationship between moral philosophy and literature. "A proverb," as Walter Benjamin defines it in "The Storyteller," "is a ruin which stands on the site of an old story and in which a moral twines about a happening like ivy around a wall" (108). Proverbs and sayings are the ruins of stories with a moral, or fables, and they attain their power to be applied by having survived, though in piecemeal condition, both their reality and its story, while still managing to preserve some part of each. Some moral philosophers have lately described the doctrine of character in a similar light. Alasdair MacIntyre explains at the beginning of *After Virtue* that we must conceive of the situation in ethics today from a postnuclear war perspective. It is as if an enormous catastrophe has struck our civilization, separating us from our understanding of the past, and the virtues are like little proverbs whose stories have been partially lost in the din of time. So strong is MacIntyre's belief in this analogy that he advises us to form new types of communities within which moral life can be preserved until our current dark age passes.

But the ruins that proverbs are continue to tell a story and a moral. The moral, Benjamin reminds us, penetrates the story as ivy does the wall. Does the ivy break down the wall or hold it together? Can we separate the ivy and the wall without destroying both of them?

Like the story and its moral, literature and philosophy seem to be made of different substances. Moral philosophy is traditionally concerned with general understanding, whereas literature appears closer to particular events and characters. The story with a moral, or fable, brings together these two incongruent desires, combining both the general and the particular; but, like the chicken and the egg, it is not easy to say which comes first or which one has first importance in life. Do chickens lay eggs to make more chickens? Or are chickens merely, as the saying goes, the way that an egg has of making another egg?

There are, of course, two obvious ways to describe the adequation between the story and its moral. On the one hand, we may conceive of fables as the illustration of a universal principle. Gotthold Lessing called a fable an application of a universally valued maxim to a particular event. If we reduce a general moral statement to a particular case, pretending that it really happened but presenting the case in a manner that easily recalls the general moral assertion, then the result will be a fable. On the other hand, we may give the strongest focus to the story, remarking that it encourages many abstract statements, none of which is wholly adequate to the story. But whatever way that we choose to describe stories and their morals, we end by recognizing some kind of desire for moral generalizations, and it seems clear at least that stories help us either to acquire or to verify them, if not both. It is a matter, then, of trying to talk about how this movement between particular and general works, if it is possible, and about its stake in such familiar activities as exemplification and characterization as well as in such traditional oppositions as practice and theory, and literature and philosophy.

The modern writer of advice stories, Sadeq Hedayat, tells a fable called "Story with a Moral."[1] Its title is too perfect to resist:

There was an ordinary man named Mashdi Zolfaqar. He had an ordinary wife called Setare Khanom.

As soon as Zolfaqar came through the door, Gowhar Soltan, his mother, ran up to him and began to pick at him about Setare Khanom, saying:

"Gutless! You should be very proud of yourself. You know that your wife has many lovers. In my day, when a stranger knocked at the door, the young woman of the house would put pebbles under her tongue to sound old. Even today they still preach this from the pulpit, but who listens? Earlier today, for a handful of ice, Setare went half way down the street with nothing on but her slip. This morning she was gathering up the bedclothes on the roof. I came up and caught her talking of heaven and earth with Ali the tinker who was in the street below. Good Lord, she looks like a corpse out of the grave. I could kick myself for not marrying you off to Ostad Mashallah's daughter. She was like a bouquet of flowers. A thousand skills flew from each of her fingers. I have been killing myself to teach her how to make dough. Do you think I can? She spoiled a whole bag of flour. It went sour and I had to throw it away. I prepared the dough again and divided it into loaves. No matter what I say, she answers, 'I came to pretty up, not to patch up.'"

When the mother's complaints reached this point, Zolfaqar was boiling with rage. Frantically he ran into the room. As usual, he took the whip off the peg and lashed into the helpless Setare. He hit her harder than ever. The serpent-like black leather of the whip coiled around her body, leaving L-shaped marks on her arm. Setare shrouded herself in her prayer shawl and moaned while no one came to help her.

Half an hour later, the door opened. Biting her lip, Gowhar Soltan came between them. With a cunning look she caught Zolfaqar by the hand and said:

"God won't approve of this. You act as if you caught a Jew! Why are you hitting her like that? Get up Setare, get up, love. I have kindled the fire. Go get the basin of dough and let's start baking."

Setare took the dough from under the basket. When she was near the oven, she saw her mother-in-law bending over the fire, blowing on it. As fate would have it, she stepped into the water bucket and fell with the dough basin on top of Gowhar Soltan. The mother-in-law was thrust up to her waist deep into the oven. Half an hour later, when Setare recovered from her fake swoon, half of Gowhar Soltan's body was done to a crisp.

The moral of the story is never to leave a bride and her mother-in-law alone near the oven.

Hedayat is a modern writer, and his "Story with a Moral" turns to surreal silliness at the end, for his moral is too specific, too uncharacteristic, or too unexemplary to be of any great moral value. Nor does the story readily avail itself of the kind of allegorization and generalization normally associated with fables. Particular virtues and vices do not spring forth from it to present themselves for serious comparison with our life. But Hedayat's use of the fable form for comedy does show us something of the modern distrust of morals. Rather than succumbing to general moralizing or explanation, he chooses to describe. But, then, why attach a moral to the story? Perhaps Hedayat is mocking an impulse that we all feel when we hear stories.

The experience of reading Aesop's fables would seem to bear out the existence of such impulses. When we read an Aesop's fable, we make several different types of calculations, depending on the relation between the story and ourselves, and the story and its moral. First, we must make the calculation that leads us into Aesop's animal kingdom. But, in fact, this calculation is made either very easily by human beings or it has been made for us by the experience of a thousand and one childhood hours of being surrounded by stuffed animals and of hearing stories about animal adventures. Second, we make the calculation to verify or to acquire the moral of the story. This calculation is, however, more complicated than the first. Reading a fable as an adult, for that is all I can speak of at present, I may experience the moral as either just, redundant, or inadequate, or sometimes it makes me think of another fable better suited to its application. But in general I find it extremely difficult to express an adequation between most stories and their morals.

The Moral of the Story

It may be that I am too theoretically inclined to appreciate the practical relation between stories and their morals. It is easy to drive a wedge between a story and its moral by imposing aesthetic, critical, or ethical theories on them. First, we are inclined today to ignore morals "in general," which is to say that we have a moralistic tendency to reject morals just because they are morals. Second, it often seems that the story conveys a moral of its own apart from the one affixed to it, and we consequently take pleasure in rejecting the moral that officially closes the story. Finally, other fables seem to outfox their moral by giving away advice before the end, and this seems to indicate that morals cannot keep up with stories. The fact remains, however, that fables are stories with a moral, and the fact that this fact exists must be faced.

Consider several fables, then, beginning with Aesop's "The Fox and the Goat."

A fox had the misfortune to fall into a well from which, try as he might, he could not escape. Just as he was beginning to be worried a goat came along intent on quenching his thirst.

"Why, friend fox, what are you doing down there?" he cried.

"Do you mean to say that you haven't heard about the great drought, friend goat?" the fox said. "Just as soon as I heard I jumped down here where the water is plentiful. I would advise you to come down, too. It is the best water I have ever tasted. I have drunk so much I can scarcely move."

When the goat heard this he leaped into the well without any further ado. The fox immediately jumped to the goat's back and using his long horns was able to scramble out of the well to safety. Then he called down to the unhappy goat the following advice: "The next time, friend goat, be sure to look before you leap!"

Moral: It is not safe to trust the advice of a man in difficulties.

"Look before you leap" has outfoxed the formal moral of the fable. It has crystallized into a proverb that carries its own general applicability. It is not, perhaps, more just than the moral, "It is not safe to trust the advice of a man in difficulties." Indeed, it appears to be more general because it does not carry the specifications of the moral. It is difficult to say whether the moral or the saying is more storylike. The saying is clearly more metaphorical, but the moral has the apparently storylike feature of being more particular. In any case, one can see how the moral could not survive in face of the more memorable saying. The same may be said about the moral for "The Fox and the Grapes." We tend to remember the saying,

"Sour grapes," and not the moral, "Any fool can despise what he cannot get."

"The Farmer and the Nightingale" presents an opposite example of how fables may sometimes contain generalizations that nevertheless fail to replace their morals.

A farmer, after a hard day's work, chanced to hear the beautiful song of the nightingale. So pleased was he by the songbird that he decided to set a trap for it. The next night, he captured the nightingale.

"Now, my beauty," said he, "you shall hang in a cage and sing for me every night."

"But nightingales never sing in a cage," replied the bird, "and if you imprison me I shall sicken and die and you shall never hear my song again."

"Then I'll put you in a pie and eat you," said the farmer.

"Please do not kill me," begged the nightingale. "If you set me free, I promise to give you three great truths more valuable than my poor body."

The farmer eagerly released the bird, and he flew up into a bush. "Hold on," said the farmer, "what are the three great truths you promised me?"

The nightingale trilled a few happy notes and said: "Never believe a captive's promise. Keep what you have. And never sorrow over what is lost forever." Then the songbird flew away.

Moral: A bird in the hand is worth two in the bush.

The moral of the story is just, and it has survived the bird's three great truths, despite the fact that they are such truths. Each one deserves to attain the grandeur of proverbial wisdom. What is particularly striking about "The Farmer and the Nightingale" is its rather obsessive desire to give advice, as if the work of the fable was itself overcome by its need to be useful. It tries, as do many fables, to find a shortcut from the story to the application, but it fails, in this instance, because we have not retained the advice that the nightingale is so desperate to give and that the farmer is so eager to receive. Perhaps, such is the case for the simple reason that this fable does contain a human being, and its human audience tends to identify more with the farmer's loss of the beautiful nightingale than with the advice given to prevent and to comfort such loss.

Other fables end with morals that seem ill-fitted to them. In the case of "The Wolf in Sheep's Clothing," Aesop tells a rather complex story to which the moral does not readily stick.

A wolf had been lurking near a flock of sheep for several days. But so vigilant had been the shepherd in guarding his animals that the wolf was becoming desperate.

Then one day the wolf found a sheepskin that had been thrown away. Quickly he slipped it on over his own hide and made his way among the flock of grazing sheep. Even the shepherd was deceived by the ruse, and when night came the wolf in disguise was shut up with the sheep in the fold.

But that evening the shepherd, wanting something for his supper, went down to the fold, and reaching in, seized the first animal he came to. Mistaking the wolf for a sheep the shepherd killed him on the spot.

Moral: Appearances often are deceiving.

It may be that the title of this fable, which has itself become a proverb, interferes with the sense of the moral. But I think that something else is at work as well. The fable is more of a morality tale than some others because it enacts a scene of poetic justice against the wolf. The wolf's hypocrisy destroys the animal. The moral may be right, but it strikes one as trivial and inadequate compared to the wisdom of the story. The story refuses to exemplify the moral, tempting the reader to add a more suitable one.

Finally, it is important to stress that the attachment between the story and its moral is itself fragile. The various ways in which stories and morals work together, which I have been surveying rather casually here, sometimes do not stand up well, and given the tendency of fables to give advice, it is to be expected that we would find one that has precisely this moral.

A boy was given a piece of cake by his grandmother. Not knowing how to carry it, he held it so tightly in his hands that he was left only with crumbs by the time he got home. His mother told him that in such cases he should, for example, protect the cake under his cap. The next time, he got a pad of butter, and the boy blindly obeyed his mother, without noticing the difference in his prize, and returned home with his hair sticky and yellow. His mother repeated the lesson, explaining that in such cases he should put the butter in some leaves and dip it in the river from time to time. During his next visit, the boy was given a puppy. He wrapped it in leaves, smothering it, and then held it under water until the poor beast died. This time his mother threw up her hands and said to the sheepish lad, "There are some little cakes fresh from the oven in the pantry. Crush them with your feet!" The boy did it on the spot.

The fable does not, understandably, end in a moral, since it seems to explain that morals do not work. Here is a fable tailor-made to modern consciousness, although its skepticism attaches too much value, perhaps, to the boy's inability to learn in the short run what he will in all probability learn in the long run, if his mother persists in the dedication to education that the story all too eagerly grants her. It verifies our modern suspicion that morals are for the foolish, and it provides a nice little allegory justifying our most critical and skeptical tendencies. It is the kind of fable that a modern moral philosopher, disappointed in philosophy, might tell. But when one tells the fable, has one stopped being a moral philosopher and become a storyteller? Or has one begun to relate only a different story about moral philosophy?

Fables bring out, perhaps more than any other genre of story, our desire to outmoralize the moral. We cannot accept the generalizing impulse of fables, but we cannot help generalizing about them nevertheless—which is to say that we like to formulate our own morals. We no longer find pleasure in listening to the morals of fables. We prefer to hear ourselves talk. Aesop originally composed his fables for kings. But today we have few kings and fewer still who would have the patience to listen to an Aesop's fable. The audience for Aesop in our day is generally assumed to be composed of children, perhaps the only human beings left on the planet who love stories enough to beg for them and to spend time with them. Am I being too naive, too nostalgic, or too childlike, when I assume that children have some understanding of the practical adequation between stories and morals? If only they would deign to tell us what it is. But children are not interested in that kind of telling. Instead, they ask us to tell them the story one more time, and when we refuse, as we often do, they retell it themselves.

If I were to succumb to the very urge to generalize that I have been trying to detail with these fables, I might try to map out the relation between story and moral or between literature and moral philosophy according to a general scheme of classification. No doubt, for example, we could find many cases where the tendencies that I have been describing appear in philosophical texts that use literary examples. In some cases, the stories will outfox the moral theory. In others, the theory will have more purchase as a story than the stories on which it relies. Finally, we will find some cases where the literary examples appear to be mere ornaments for philosophical writing.

While this classification might be useful, it could not be sufficient to serve as a theory of how examples relate to theories or of how literature relates to moral philosophy. For in every case, our awareness of the relation between story and moral, as it accords to some idea of classification, will be far less interesting than when we begin to read between the two and to obey the urge to tell their story. A classificational or theoretical approach to stories with a moral does not do them justice because stories do their work when we live with them, and if we are too eager to test them before we have made their proper acquaintance, they refuse to work for us, and rightly so. Stories work best when we dwell with them and on them. Ethical ideas work best under the same conditions. The experience of literature, which counts precisely as experience for this reason, consists of finding the story and the moral doing their best work together.

Moreover, how can we limit the problem of classification to cases in which the story is attached to the moral in as obvious a way as we find in fables? We would have to single out larger and more difficult domains, and look at how, for example, some famous general phrases advance or follow their stories.

"It is a truth universally acknowledged, that a single man in possession of a good fortune, must be in want of a wife." Does the first line of *Pride and Prejudice* provide the moral of the story that the story then tries to tell? If we placed the line at the conclusion of the novel as an application, what would its resonance be?

In addition, the titles of Jane Austen's novels, *Pride and Prejudice*, *Sense and Sensibility*, or *Persuasion*, seem to be morals in themselves, telling the reader that the story should be read in a way to make it adequate to a demand for moral allegory.

Which character represents Pride? Which one represents Sense?

"Every art and every inquiry, and similarly every action and pursuit, is thought to aim at some good; and for this reason the good has rightly been declared to be that at which all things aim." Aristotle's maxim opens the *Ethics*, but had it closed it, what meaning would it have to carry? Or is its tautology an invitation to immerse ourselves in the circle of sense, the polis, in which every aim finds its good?

"All happy families are alike but an unhappy family is unhappy after its own fashion." Tolstoy's first sentence sums up in general what *Anna Karenina* works out in particular, and it aspires, as Tolstoy does himself, to describe the good life as a single life for all people. But with what compass, with what grace, or by what act of faith, do we find the path leading from this saying through the grandiose and cluttered world of Tolstoy's novel?

"Act only according to that maxim by which you can at the same time will that it should become a universal law." What kind of story does Kant need to tell to make the categorical imperative carry the force of the moral?

Whenever we view a story as an example of a moral, we will confront the paradox inherent in the leap from story to moral, or from example to theory. In *Whose Justice? Which Rationality?* Alasdair MacIntyre describes this paradox with two truisms, both of which seem to be valid but which cannot be valid because they contradict each other. He argues that no theory or concept can be elucidated apart from its examples. But he also reasons that each theory is, among other things, a story of how examples are to be described, and how we describe an example will therefore depend on which theory we embrace.

Bernard Williams presents the paradox of the story and its moral from the wider perspective of the relation between literature and moral philosophy, but the paradox is no less vicious. "Can the reality of complex moral situations," he asks in *Morality*, "be represented by means other than those of imaginative literature?" (xi). The dilemma cuts two ways. On the one hand, how much of what is genuinely important to people can be rendered in universal theories? On the other hand, are stories valuable for ethics, if no moral is attached? To make examples work for moral philosophy, Williams concludes in *Ethics and the Limits of Philosophy*, we need to put in more detail. But if one puts in the detail, the example may begin to dissolve, losing its value for moral philosophy. To emphasize the story as a story, giving all weight to its detail and none to generalization, cuts it loose as an example from ethical theory.

Like proverbial wisdom, the relation between a story and its moral does not develop overnight. Our leaping and jumping back and forth from example to idea, or from story to moral, or from literature to ethical theory misses the point. Like the awe with which we watch the trapeze artist, the awe of the leap from story to moral depends on the distance covered by the leap and the great height at which the artist accomplishes the trick. It also requires practice, and it takes time to master its techniques. The trapeze artist makes the trip with the greatest of ease, but we may not be as adept, and in the final analysis, it is not showmanship or acrobatics that we are seeking but an understanding of the ground between the two points in question. We do better, then, to pace it off than to climb to the trapeze, and this means living and working with the story and its moral.

The better the story, the more work it does, but stories demand that we do work as well. They present us with a task, and to accomplish it, we must pass time together. All stories have moral lessons to give us, just as morals tell a story, but to uncover the practical relation between stories and morals demands patience, and it is never without its contradictions, questions, and paradoxes.

Examples do determine theories just as theories give us examples of themselves. But such truisms do not capture the fact that a fit must sometimes exist between an example and a theory or between a story and a moral. The fit is never precise, but it works well enough for us not to notice, and that is what counts. I find myself wanting to use the example of storytelling to picture how this fit works. The fit depends on a story for its rightness, and without the right story, people have no idea of which examples belong to which ideas, and vice versa.

Nelson Goodman's idea of the sample, as he elaborates it in *Of Mind and Other Matters*, provides a clear case, although he does not stress the narrative elements important to making samples work. He remarks that samples, such as the swatch of cloth at a tailor shop, represent their objects in a particular and limited way (59–60, 89). We do not believe in a pure adequation between the sample and its object but focus on a few special characteristics of the sample.

We are approaching another fable, "The Tailor and the Businessman."

A businessman heard of the great handiwork and precision of a certain tailor, and he decided to have him make him a new suit. He went to the tailor's shop, and the tailor showed him his work. Never had the businessman seen such beautiful suits, and he eagerly agreed to the tailor's price. The tailor took the businessman into a back room in which he kept thousands of rolls of fabric and swatches of cloth.

"Here is the material I use to make my suits," said the tailor proudly. "Which material would you like to have?"

The businessman's eye caught a particularly attractive material. He picked up one swatch from among the others and gave it to the tailor. "This is my choice."

"This is something of an unusual request for current fashion," remarked the tailor, "but the customer is always right."

A month later the businessman returned to the shop to pick up his new suit. But when the tailor brought it out, the businessman found to his dismay that the tailor had made his suit by sewing together a thousand swatches of the material.

"What kind of suit is this?" demanded the unhappy customer. "I ordered a suit not a quilt."

"But this is the fabric that you picked out," the tailor explained. "Did you expect I would use another?"

Moral: A sample is not its object.

When we use examples, we do not expect that all of their characteristics will be active in the work of representation. But if an example has too many characteristics, too many details, that is, it may present a problem for exemplification, because it grows more difficult to connect the example with the idea, or the story with the moral. This difficulty exposes the fact that there is another story of some kind involved in the affair. It is the story that tells of the exemplariness of the example. It tells which characteristics are needed in the example.

Examples work much as character does in this respect. When we try to determine a person's character, we watch for characteristic actions, as determined by both our society and human society in general, and after our acquaintance has grown sufficiently, we begin to have a sense of the person's characteristic traits. We call these his or her character. Character is cut from a larger length of cloth, but there are plenty of samples available to tell us how to do it. I am reminded here of the way that the Greeks thought about fate. *Moira* or fate is the length of cloth that makes up a person's life, and of course, the cut is not finished until that life comes to its end.

In the case of examples, we also rely on a larger story whose pressure weighs on our sense as to whether an example and theory fit together, and when we use examples, we tell this story as well as the story of the example. Such stories compose the ethical culture in which we live, and like the proverbs described by Benjamin, they are twined with ivy. In every case—that of character, example, and proverb—we will not in all probability be able to tell their suitability by looking at them in isolation. The elements that determine their fitness are not within them or under our eyes. We cannot easily tell, for example, how the saying, "Look before you leap," compares in various respects to the moral, "It is not safe to trust the advice of a man in difficulties." It is therefore nearly impossible to explain precisely why the one survives in common parlance and the other does not. But we may hazard to guess that the first has been picked up by people, perhaps through a story such as "The Fox and the Goat," and that they have applied it to many situations, so that its applicability, usage, and meaning are composed and communicated by its being passed from person to person. The fable of "The Fox and the Goat" is no longer needed to give the saying its legs; it stands in the place made by its daily use.

Little work has been done, until recently, to characterize to what extent stories and morals share various features. The best work has appeared in moral philosophy within the last decade, and it is distinguished by both its attentiveness to storytelling and the stories that it tells.[2] Alasdair MacIntyre is perhaps the most visible proponent of this new view in ethics. *After Virtue*, as I suggested above, relies on an idea of virtue akin to that of the proverb, for it sketches the descent of virtue within a general narrative setting. Character, for MacIntyre, is both ethical and literary, and to stress it is to adopt a view of the narrative character of human life. MacIntyre's argument is useful because he conceives of the looseness of human representations, their bagginess, without despairing of their value. Character, for him, is not merely a social role or linguistic construct arbitrarily attached to a person. It is imposed through the way in which others regard and use characters to understand and to evaluate themselves. "A *character*," in MacIntyre's definition, "is an object of regard by the members of culture generally or by some significant segment of them" (29). Furthermore, individuals inherit a particular place within social settings and relationships. To know oneself as such a social person is not merely to occupy a static or fixed position but to find oneself placed at a certain point on a journey with set goals. To move through life is to make progress, or to fail to make progress, toward a given end. "The unity of a human life," concludes MacIntyre, "is the unity of a narrative quest" (219).

To conceive of the unity of human life as a narrative quest is not, as might be suspected, a romantic notion in MacIntyre. It is not Don Quixotism. It is MacIntyre's way of describing the necessity of examining moral issues at the level of cultural conversations and not in terms of minute phrases, words, or singular meanings. It is a recognition of the existence of an ethical culture, in which questions such as "What does it mean?" are better phrased as ones such as "Who is he?" and "What is he doing?" The novels of Jane Austen make this point for MacIntyre. Austen represents, for him, one of the last great imaginative voices of the tradition of thought concerned with the theory and practice of virtue. Everything tends to be particular within her world. She writes about individuals living with others, being changed and challenged by them, and trying to find a place within their life, however humble it may seem when compared to the grandiose action—the wars, rivalries, and adulteries—usually pictured in novels. In Austen's novels, we see the progress, or the failure to progress, of people in a vivid and particular way.

In addition to its view of character, *After Virtue* provides a theory of the cultural settings in which dispositions of character find their place. The virtues are embedded in and formed by what MacIntyre calls "practices." Most often, MacIntyre illustrates the idea with the example of games. Throwing a football is not a practice, but the game of football is. Bricklaying is not a practice, but architecture is. Chess, politics, science, and the arts also represent practices. Practices tend, for MacIntyre, to be any coherent and complex form of human cooperative activity. They are socially established and possess goods that are specific to them and that may be realized by achieving the standards of excellence that define them. In short, practices are activities that have precise rules and standards of excellence, and they tend to be engaged in for themselves. One begins to see how the virtues might arise from engaging in such practices, since they would demand specific habits to be perfected and seem to exclude any interest in the activity that is not internal to its particular excellence.

After Virtue reveals a strong awareness of the cultural practices and settings that ground human actions and character, but MacIntyre does not in fact describe them in other than a schematic and highly theoretical fashion. One problem, of course, is that MacIntyre does not talk about those people who do not have the luxury to engage in activities for themselves, and the various activities that he does not deem to call practices are often, precisely, the types of activities in which people in the work-a-day world engage: bricklaying versus architecture, etc. But most of these activities do have specific rules and standards of excellence, and if MacIntyre were to devote some time to bricklaying, for example, he would soon discover them, or find himself out of a job. In short, MacIntyre ignores the habits, specific knowledges, and doings associated with forms of work and play in the everyday world; and the idea of practice remains largely a theoretical entity. For if practices were as important to the formation of virtue as MacIntyre supposes, he would not have so much trouble finding examples of them. Nor would he need to have recourse so often to the example of games.

The theory of practice is nevertheless valuable because it stresses the types of activities necessary to the formation of character, that is, activities that are viewed as good in themselves, that submit themselves to the formation of habits, that exist according to some idea or standard of ordered conduct, and that may be passed on by experience and imitation. The idea of practice has everything, then, that MacIntyre needs to describe a successful notion of virtue, but this does not mean that such practices exist. Nor does it exclude the possibility that virtuous activity possesses these properties in and of itself. MacIntyre needlessly obscures the notion of practice when he removes it from the practice of something. He cannot establish the idea of practice as a context for the virtues, if he removes it from context. It is preferable to speak of the practice of virtue in itself rather than trying to bring to virtue a theory of practice formulated in the abstract.

MacIntyre's sequel, *Whose Justice? Which Rationality?*, continues to stress the place of storytelling in human life, but it gives far greater detail than the earlier book, and it has a stronger historical flavor. Here MacIntyre emphasizes the idea of tradition as a means of describing how the clash of cultures and intellectual domains creates and resolves moral conflict, and we are meant to understand that practices are embedded in traditions just as the virtues are embedded in practices. Traditions, according to MacIntyre, are always having their history written and rewritten by their members, and these histories take a narrative form. "A tradition is," in his definition, "an argument extended through time in which certain fundamental agreements are defined and redefined in terms of two kinds of conflict: those with critics and enemies external to the tradition who reflect all or at least key parts of those fundamental agreements, and those internal, interpretative debates through which the meaning and rationale of the fundamental agreements come to be expressed and by whose progress a tradition is constituted" (12). This means that MacIntyre's idea of ethics still has an overtly theoretical dimension, for intellectuals and academics take a large role in telling the stories of these agreements and disagreements, and their accounts filter down to society at large to influence the nature of rational inquiry, although he also points out that philosophical theories give expression to concepts and theories already embodied in practices and types of community (390).

The point, however, is not that individual intellectuals constitute the tradition. For, in MacIntyre's eyes, individuals reason as members of a particular type of political society and not just as individuals. Members of a tradition actively write its history both from within and with an eye on competing traditions. It is in some respects a matter of the resources used to describe and to settle conflicts. Tradition is an overriding pressure insofar as it appears to its members as the limit of their community, and when this community is threatened from without or within, the forces of tradition exert pressure over time on its members to reshape their account of the tradition to face the threat, either by absorbing, reworking, or repulsing its definitive elements. In the end, it appears, two traditions will always merge when faced with each other over a long period of time, and MacIntyre consequently argues that conflicting ideas of justice and practical rationality not only can be resolved but that they simply will be. For him, then, it is largely a matter of keeping alive the tradition in which he believes so that it may survive. One suspects in fact that the historical detail and breadth of *Whose Justice? Which Rationality?* are put in place for this very purpose.

I have not retold MacIntyre's story here. I doubt, in fact, whether it could be retold without turning the discussion over to him entirely. His argument is both too particular and baggy to bear a paraphrase. It is somewhat ironic that someone like J. Hillis Miller, who insists on the importance of history and close reading, reduces the Kantian tradition to the words "I must," while MacIntyre, who insists on the importance of philosophical theory, produces a book on tradition that is too thick, literally, to be retold. What I have repeated, somewhat schematically, is MacIntyre's stress on the narrative dimension of tradition, justice, practical rationality, and character. Without debasing the idea of fiction or storytelling, he places it at the foundation of society and history. It lies there not to subvert human efforts but to represent our best attempts to live the life of a human being in the places where human beings live.[3]

No doubt, the modern distrust of theory has in part led moral philosophers to turn to literature for a nontrivial description of human life. They see in the complex scenes of literature a means of representing human choices, actions, and patterns of behavior. But moral philosophers rely on literature for more than the "metaphor of life." They have moved storytelling to the base of social life because they recognize in it a specific human tendency found in many aspects of our existence. In "Life and the Narrator's Art," for example, David Carr points out that our idea of life takes the form of a story. People see themselves quite naturally as the heroes of their own life's novel, he explains, and not because, like Flaubert's Emma Bovary, they have read too much bad fiction. The idea of human character is a reflective device that permits people not only to organize their immediate and long-term goals but to cooperate and to communicate with each other. If life appears at times to imitate art, it is not because life is an artificial concept, a bag of tricks, but because it depends on our narrative impulses. Art owes its existence to the narrative impulses found in life, and it survives only because it so successfully imitates them. The present emphasis on character in moral philosophy recognizes the importance of this idea of a life story, and it brings literature and ethics together for the express purpose of examining the nature of human life. In fact, it represents an embrace of human life that would not have been possible two decades ago when the linguistic climate of philosophy, literary criticism, and anthropology effectively outlawed the idea of the human.

Consequently, many moral philosophers are now more skeptical about ethical theory than they are about ethics per se. They have returned to a concern for practical life and tend to shun theory in and of itself. It is no longer considered an absurd idea, as Bernard Williams argues in *Ethics and the Limits of Philosophy*, to see the world from a human point of view. Rather, it is absurd to think that human beings should not be concerned with human beings. This is not to say that we should identify the point of view of the universe with the human point of view. It means, according to Williams, that our arguments have to be grounded in a human perspective, and Williams's work devotes itself to this grounding. Ethical theory fails when it attempts to derive its positions from no one's point of view. We cannot get beyond humanity, despite what Nietzsche preached. There is no reason to want to be citizens of nowhere.

Bernard Williams does not use literature as an anchor in the way that Alasdair MacIntyre does, but he does rely on the idea of character to tell his story of moral philosophy, and this story is worthy of notice. He divides ethical development into two types. The first he calls "ethics," and it emphasizes character and dispositions toward virtue. Ethics is not, in Williams's mind, either theoretical or systematic. It flows from human nature and culture, and settles in various concepts, practices, and histories, through which people come to believe in those various dispositions of character, or virtues, that lead them to choose or to reject actions because they are of a certain ethically relevant kind. Williams argues that the formation of ethical dispositions is a natural process in human beings, and these dispositions, as Aristotle believed, belong to the content of the self. This means that it is not easy to describe ethics because its explanation does not lie in a statable rule. Nor do people summon an internal law when they are faced with ethical decisions. Rather, ethics is ongoing. Ethical value lies in the continual production and reproduction of ethical dispositions. In short, as Otto Neurath put it, we repair the ship while we are at sea.

The second type of ethical development is closer to moral philosophy itself. Williams calls it "morality," and it represents the desire for generalizations, sharp boundaries, and rule-governing behavior. It places its stock in authority and what Williams sometimes calls the "midair position." Williams contends that people cannot call a time-out when faced with a moral difficulty, so that they can leap to a universal position; they must continue to live while they come up with a solution. Morality tends, in Williams's description, to make obligations and laws the key to living a life, but by taking this position, it asks people to leap beyond life.

Consequently, *Ethics and the Limits of Philosophy* is skeptical about the enterprise of philosophical morality but not about the value of ethics. It is difficult, however, to describe this value precisely. For Williams refuses to give a definition of ethics, thereby deliberately frustrating the demands of morality. Rather, he tends to associate ethics with such loose ideas as "intuition," "experience," "importance," "luck," and "custom." In the emphasis on custom in particular, Williams appears to share ideas with Alasdair MacIntyre, for both men wish to see ethics in terms of practices that cannot be abstracted from their cultural environment. Williams explains, for example, that we may be able to show how a given practice hangs together with other practices in a way that makes social and psychological sense. But we may not be able to find anything that will meet a demand for justification made by someone standing outside those practices. We may not be able, in any real sense, to justify it even to ourselves. Practices are so directly related to our experience that the reasons they provide will simply count as stronger than any reason that might be advanced for them (114). Similarly, when Williams turns to dispositions of character, he stresses that the excellence of a life depends on "having" certain beliefs. A person who believes in thick concepts, for example, will have a better chance to have the life that he or she believes in than people who have no such beliefs. In short, Williams, like MacIntyre, believes that people must have a "life," and having a life means having a story in mind that one can believe in.[4]

Part of Williams's story asks that we refuse to see in morality a story that people can believe in. Modern philosophy would not be modern if it did not hesitate over moral generalities and principles. Yet people do believe in laws and rules, and often enough they govern their behavior

54

according to them. Williams's sketch of ethical development fails to account for the continued existence of what he calls morality. For him, the story is sufficient, and we need not add the moral. But we add the moral nevertheless. It is part of the story that people want to tell. Perhaps what Williams calls morality does cause much damage in the world by frustrating people and making their life more rigid. Perhaps it would be better if we could do away with it. But morality does exist, and it is not entirely unbeneficial. It also gives moral philosophy a reason to exist. Ethical theory watches over "morality" and "ethics," as Williams defines them, and morality and ethics work together in constant interaction. Indeed, one reason that Williams produces such a pure and innocent idea of ethics is that he refers everything contradictory and problematic to morality. Morality and its problems (rules, boundaries, obligations) cannot be settled by dismissing them as merely a "powerful misconception of life." For this gesture is itself dependent on the "midair position" that Williams associates with morality.

Does it make sense to say that the desire for the moral, the desire to go beyond both the human and the story, is equally a human aspiration? If we hold any belief at all in bettering ourselves, we must experience what might be called the temptation of sainthood. The desire to be a saint is all-too-human. It is an ethical attitude, but it is an aesthetic or literary attitude as well. Saints desire to make their lives conform to a perfect story. Their asceticism is finally an aestheticism, and their torment, of course, lies in enduring the distance between this story and their own life, between the moral and the story.

In her beautiful essay on Isak Dinesen, Hannah Arendt tries to capture what she calls Dinesen's "philosophy of storytelling," and this philosophy weighs heavily on any thoughts that we may have about dividing morals and stories. Dinesen, of course, considered herself to be a "mere story-teller," but stories, in her view, carry the enormous burden of revealing the meaning of what otherwise, as Arendt puts it, would remain "an unbearable sequence of sheer happenings" (104). The path between stories and life appears to cut both ways. Storytelling reveals meaning, for Dinesen, without committing the mistake of defining it, and it brings about reconciliation with things as they really are. We may even trust storytelling to give us the last word that we expect from the "day of judgment." But we must also be aware that things fall apart and that the slightest misunderstanding may ruin everything. "If it is true," Arendt muses about Dinesen's philosophy, "that no one has a life worth thinking about whose life story cannot be told, does it not then follow that life could be, even ought to be, lived as a story, that what one has to do in life is to make the story come true?" (105). We all face at one time or another the temptation of wishing to make a story come true, of wanting to interfere with life to make it fit a moral, rather than waiting with patience for the story to emerge on its own.

These two forms of thinking, if they may indeed be called two forms, have been artificially divided and relegated to the separate worlds of philosophy and literature. Literature must tell the story. Philosophy must tell the moral. And while it may be true, in the way that a truism can be true, that we may tell stories about life but that we cannot make life into a story, it does not follow that literature is destined to succeed where moral philosophy is doomed to fail, or that storytellers will never add the moral, or that moral philosophers will never recount the story. In any case, if we do not manage to make life into a story, we shall surely not fail for lack of trying.

My daughter's favorite story at the moment, for children favor stories for moments, is a modern rendition of Charles Perrault's "Les Souhaits ridicules" called "The Three Wishes."

One day, after many hours of work in the forest, a woodcutter expressed his disappointment with his life. "Why is it," he asked, "that I must work so hard and never have what I want?"

A fairy overheard the woodcutter and feeling sorry for him, she granted him three wishes that he might find happiness. But she also warned him that he would have only three wishes and that he must consider them carefully.

The woodcutter rushed home to tell his wife of their good fortune, and they decided to have supper while considering what to wish for. The wife brought her husband's soup to the table. "Soup again," he sighed. "I wish I had a nice fat sausage for a change."

In the blink of an eye, a nice fat sausage appeared before him. "Now see what you've done," scolded his wife. "You've wasted one of our three wishes." She complained and complained and would not give up her disappointment. She made such a fuss that her husband grew angry.

"I wish this sausage were stuck to the end of your nose," he cried. In an instant the sausage flew up to his wife's nose and stuck there. They pulled and pulled on the sausage but to no avail. No matter how hard they tried they could not get the sausage off her nose.

"At least we still have one last wish," the woodcutter said, trying to console his wife.

"What are you saying?" she answered him. "I can't go about with a sausage on the end of my nose." The woodcutter could only agree. "I wish the sausage were gone," he said.

In the end the woodcutter and his wife did not even have the sausage to eat for their supper.

The woodcutter finds himself in a moral situation. (In fact, it is a Kantian situation with a vengeance, where there is no issue whether "ought" implies "can.") The fairy gives him the power to extend his will, to make choices, and to act beyond his present circumstances. He may now will his life to be whatever he wishes it to be. It is within his power to be happy. But his will is so attached to his life as it is that he can will only according to it. He wishes merely to have a nice fat sausage; and in the end, the three wishes are sufficient in number only to restore to the woodcutter and his wife the very life whose existence they threatened to take from them in the first place.

Who knows what the moral of the story is?

My daughter's version, being a modern one, does not, of course, include a moral, and it requires us to make the application ourselves.[5]

My own sense is that the story tells about how stories and the theory of morals fit together to tell a story. The woodcutter may wish to make his life conform to his will, to make his life fit a theory or a moral, or to use the power of gods or fairies, but he ends by telling us the same old story about himself. And yet he arrives at this story of his life by trying to change his life.

Who are we to say that this path, however ridiculous or otherworldly, is not part of his life?

There is a wisdom to be bought from both the story of the story and the story of the moral. The wisdom of the story may be the wisdom of old age, but it comes only to those who, when young, learned the wisdom of the moral from those as wise as they themselves were to become.

also in Homer that we should see the place of literature for the first time? The *Iliad* is the "first" work of literature, and in it as well we find literature in its first place as both a form of comfort and of moral education. The heroes of Homer's epic tell stories to each other to please, of course, but they tell their stories more often to teach each other how to act and to live. And school children then and now repeat their tales.

What is the place of ethics in Homer's *Iliad*? Its ethics is not, most fundamentally, about either the rationality or irrationality of Greek religion.[1] Whether Zeus is just or not, for example, is an interesting but secondary question for Homer's poem. The question asks merely whether the gods of Greek religion possess the moral capacity of human beings, and it can be answered, if it can be answered, only by bringing the gods down from Mount Olympus to the plains of Troy—which is to say by doing to the Greek gods what Homer has already done: to anthropomorphize them. Confine a telling of Homer's story to Mount Olympus, and it loses both its interest and value for most people. For Troy is, after all, where the action is. Ethics in Homer is the story of how those people who find themselves at Troy try to live there among one another. More specifically, ethics in Homer tells how people come to live somewhere. Homer recounts how what we call ethics springs from some place, just as Homer's poem provides the ground from which moral philosophy in the West emerges.

The coincidence is not accidental. If ethics is a knowledge concerned with the place of human beings, and if this knowledge is seen for the first time in Homer, then we cannot but return to this place when we try to arrive at an understanding of ethics. But Homer does not give us easy answers. He does not tell us much about ethics as such. He tells a story that requires an interpretation, and it is true that this interpretation has always been ethical, but do we need to assume that the story is itself ethical?

I cannot pretend to tell all that there is to tell about either the place of ethics or the place of literature in Homer. All I can do is to try to pace off the ground. It is familiar ground but not so familiar that we do not forget it. It begins with a word, but it is not a matter of telling the story of this word. It is, rather, a matter of telling the story in which this word figures. This story is that of the *Iliad* itself, beginning with the wrath of Achilleus, moving through the amity between the brothers, Agamemnon and Menelaos and Hektor and Paris, and concluding with the deaths of Patroklos and Hektor and the return of Hektor's body to his father, Priam.

CHAPTER 5

❧

The Place of
Ethics in Homer

WHEN WE RETURN TO A PLACE, we often see it for the first time. It is an oddity of language that the phrase, "to see for the first time," almost always implies that we are not in fact seeing for the first time but perceiving anew what we have seen before. There is nothing paradoxical in this familiar idea. People understand that they must see something many times, sometimes, to see it for the first time.

This is, above all, true of being somewhere. We live in a place for a time before we come to understand the lay of the land, and then we never forget it.

This fact is also true of stories. We must be told a story and tell it ourselves many times before we begin to see it for the first time.

Stories and places have at the very least this feature in common.

We have not, I think, seen enough of Homer's *Iliad*. Or so it would appear from the fact that philosophers continue to return to it in their attempts to write a history of moral philosophy in the West. It is in Homer that we see the place of ethics for the first time. Is it an accident of history, and of the history of moral philosophy in particular, that it is

The Place of Ethics in Homer

The word that I have in mind is *ēthos*. It is a strange oversight that most accounts of ethics in Homer do not have much to say about it. For most writers of the fifth century B.C., *ēthos* means "character." In earlier writers, however, and Homer is among them, the word signifies "the place where animals are usually found." *Ēthos* is a word about a "place," a "haunt," or a "habitat" that becomes habitual and eventually characteristic of its inhabitants.[2] The word brings together a collection of ideas, demonstrating rather dramatically the ties among moral character, literature, personality, language, and place. It also suggests, as I have been arguing, that literature and moral philosophy cannot exist without one another.

The word appears in the *Iliad* twice in its plural form (*ēthea*) and three times as an adjective (*ētheios*). The first refers simply to the "haunts" of animals. The second means "one who is found in a certain place" and thus "dear." But both words refer to a place of belonging, an arena or range in which the animal or person lives. Homer's first use of the word occurs in a simile designed to describe the individual character of Paris, and he later reapplies the same simile to the character of Hektor. The simile is identical in both cases, but it will be necessary to examine each use in its turn because they contribute to each other's story. Indeed, part of my interest is to trace how the word begins in association with the Trojans and passes to an association with the Greeks and with Achilleus in particular. Homer's last use of the word, in its adjectival form, occurs in one of Achilleus's speeches. When the ghost of Patroklos appears in Book 23, Achilleus addresses his dead friend as *ētheios* or "dear one." I hope that I am not exaggerating when I claim that the *Iliad* is in part the story of how Achilleus comes to say this word to the shade of his departed friend.

Homer uses the simile first in a passage following the famous and sad encounter among Hektor, Andromache, and their son on the wall of Troy. Previously, Hektor had scolded Paris for delaying his entry into the fighting, and Paris promised to arm himself and to meet his brother on the wall before he gained the field of battle. Here Paris hurries into battle not so much because he wants to fight but because he does not wish to disappoint his brother:

> But Paris in turn did not linger long in his high house,
> but when he had put on his glorious armour with bronze elaborate
> he ran in the confidence of his quick feet through the city.
> As when some stalled horse who has been corn-fed at the manger
> breaking free of his rope gallops over the plain in thunder

to his accustomed bathing place in a sweet-running river
and in the pride of his strength holds high his head, and the mane floats
over his shoulders; sure of his glorious strength, the quick knees
carry him to the loved places [ēthea] and the pasture [nomos] of horses;
so from uttermost Pergamos came Paris, the son of
    Priam, shining in all his armour of war as the sun shines,
laughing aloud, and his quick feet carried him; suddenly thereafter
he came on brilliant Hektor, his brother, where he yet lingered
before turning away from the place where he had talked to his lady.
It was Alexandros the godlike who first spoke to him:
"Brother [ētheios], I fear that I have held back your haste, by being
slow on the way, not coming in time, as you commanded me."
    Then tall Hektor of the shining helm spoke to him in answer:
"Strange man! There is no way that one, giving judgment in fairness,
could dishonour your work in battle, since you are a strong man.
But of your own accord you hang back, unwilling. And my heart
is grieved in its thought, when I hear shameful things spoken about you
by the Trojans, who undergo hard fighting for your sake."   (6.503–25)

Homer likens the character of Paris to a spirited horse that cannot be subdued by attempts at domestication. The glory, freedom, and beauty of the horse parallel those of Paris as well. But the principal idea of the simile remains the depth of habituation effected on character by place. It appears that you can lead a horse to water, but you cannot make him drink. The horse, held in a stall and well-fed on corn, rejects all efforts at domestication because it has already been habituated to another place. This power of habituation is too strong, and the animal returns as soon as it can to the place that has formed its character. The relation between character and place is wholly coherent.

An irony arises, however, in the fact that the horse is far more enthusiastic about its destination than Paris would appear to be. By his own accord, Paris hangs back from battle. His enthusiasm is not for his ultimate destination, the pasture of Troy where men fall in mortal combat, but for the reunion with his brother.

But surely he is not seeing Hektor for the first time? Nor has it been long since the brothers were in the same place.

Paris is hurrying to be where he has already been. He hastens to a place of belonging in a world that will not soon, for him, have such a place.

Homer establishes the importance of this place of belonging for Paris's character through the use of the simile, and Paris interprets the simile after a fashion by passing the idea of belonging to Hektor. Paris, Homer tells us, speaks first to Hektor, calling him "*ētheios*" or "one who is found in a certain place." Paris and Hektor have had a life together in the same place. Paris may slight himself, calling himself slow to obey, but Hektor will correct and praise him, just as he has scolded him. And Paris will hurry to battle, if it means that he may stop on the way at the wall to see Hektor. It is because Paris has always found Hektor and continues to find him in a certain place that Richmond Lattimore rightly takes the liberty of translating *ētheios* as "brother."

It is not without reason, then, that Homer applies the simile for a second time to the character of Hektor. Family resemblance assures that the characters of the brothers have certain features in common. Here the god Apollo has just spoken to Hektor, assuring him of success in battle. Unfortunately for Hektor, Apollo is a liar. Confident and eager for glory, Hektor leads his men against the Greeks:

As when some stalled horse who has been corn-fed at the manger
breaking free of his rope gallops over the plain in thunder
to his accustomed bathing place in a sweet-running river
and in the pride of his strength holds high his head and the mane floats
over his shoulders; sure of his glorious strength, the quick knees
carry him to the loved places [*ēthea*] and the pasture [*nomos*] of horses;
so Hektor moving rapidly his feet and knees went
onward, stirring the horsemen when he heard the god's voice speak.

(15.263–70)

The simile is not, at first glance, especially appropriate to the situation if we consider that Hektor charges into battle, while the horse gallops to its favorite pasture. Homer would seem to be commenting on Hektor's natural inclination toward battle, as if the battlefield were his home. Or Homer may have wished simply to convey Hektor's fatal enthusiasm. Both of these interpretations, however, miss the point because they choose the displacement of irony over the beloved place that Homer wishes to describe. The principal idea of the simile has already been established by its application to Paris, and it remains the same. It reveals the place of habituation in Hektor's character.

It is neither an accident of composition nor an example of the repetitive and oral nature of the poem that the simile is used twice to describe Trojan warriors, for they are fighting to save their city from invaders.

Hektor enters the fray with the enthusiasm of a horse returning to its beloved places because he is seeking to return his beloved place to the tranquility of its former times. It is not that the battlefield is his home. Rather, his home has become a battlefield, and he intends to drive the Greeks away from it.

The relation between place and moral character is also evident in the evolution from the plural form *ēthea* or "beloved places" to the singular form *ēthos* or "character." Character is more abstract in some sense than place, but students of character continue to insist on the importance of place for building character. Aristotle, for example, explained that only mature people can successfully study moral philosophy because only they possess those good habits acquired over time and through experience with life among other people. Indeed, it is difficult to discuss ethics in Aristotle without considering politics, here defined in the sense of the life led in that place called the city.

Incidentally, Homer's simile contains a second word that undergoes a similar process of evolution. When Homer describes the "pasture of horses," he uses the word *nomos* for pasture. *Nomos* later comes to mean "law." Indeed, the plural *nomoi* is the standard word for "laws" in classical Greece. Quite often the idea of human character occurs in association with the idea of law. Cities have a certain character (*ēthos tēs poleōs*) owing to their constitutions, and people living in those cities for a long time have a certain character as well. Both Plato and Aristotle take up the notion of *ēthos tēs poleōs* at crucial moments in their philosophy. Plato devotes considerable attention to it in Book 8 of the *Republic*, and Aristotle revises Plato's use of the idea in his *Politics*, most notably in Books 6 and 8.

It appears that even legal abstractions have an attachment to place. Certainly, this sense haunts those legal theories that stress particularity in their application and herald particularity as the best indicator of good legal practice. Aristotle again offers an example. He said that a good law, a good rule, should resemble the measuring rule used by the architect. The rule is made of flexible material so that the architect may bend it to the shape of the arch being measured.

Aristotle is more theoretical than Homer in his ethical formulations, but he keeps Homer's usage in mind. In part, Aristotle was able to trace the evolution from habit to ethical understanding so effectively only because Homer told the story of the ties between place and habit. This means that Homer's preoccupation with the relation of place and character is not merely a general theme of his poetry. This relation of place and

STORIES

WITH

MORALS

character is captured within the form of relation that is his storytelling, and it makes up a Homeric ethic that informs an entire tradition. It is not only that the Homeric poems "narrate what happens to men and women," as Alasdair MacIntyre points out in *After Virtue*, but that in their narrative form they "capture a form that was already present in the lives which they relate" (124).

If we are to capture Homer's ethics with any kind of effectiveness, we should understand that everything stands or falls on the many devices of this "relation."

Homer's story informs both the ethics of his poems and the ethics of the tradition. Indeed, his ethics cannot be separated from his storytelling. Both the story and the ethics go together to form the relation between the life narrated and the narrative dimension of the life. That the Trojans are defending their beloved places against the Greeks gives them a natural advantage in the conflict, and this fact is as much a part of Homer's story as of his ethics. The Trojans know the lay of the land, and they fight among those who belong among them. The Greeks live ad hoc. In fact, the major obstacle to the taking of Troy remains the inability of the Greeks to find themselves at home among one another. Significantly, the quarreling among the Greeks is not duplicated among the Trojans. Their city is in harmony despite the battle surrounding it. The Greeks may have occupied the plain of Troy in great numbers, but their numbers do not make up a city comparable to Troy, in which the hierarchy remains intact and unthreatened by disputes. Or if the Greeks do make up a city, it remains a city without character. To put it in other words, the Greeks must face the family of Priam to take Troy, but they do not themselves make up a family. The so-called humanity of the Trojans, especially of Hektor, is largely an effect of this difference. Hektor's death arouses our sympathy because it is so terrifying, but it is terrifying largely because his family witnesses it and Achilleus pursues Hektor to the kill along the same paths in which he played as a boy. Our sense of Hektor's love of family also grows from the fact that he remains close to home. No Greek warrior has the opportunity to show his affection for his wife or son. They are estranged from him, and we must wait for the *Odyssey* to see a Greek find his beloved ones in their certain place.[3]

The notable exceptions to this rule are Agamemnon and Menelaos and Achilleus and Patroklos. Agamemnon and Achilleus have no great love for each other, but they both bring their families to Troy in the persons of Menelaos and Patroklos. Agamemnon, of course, goes to war on behalf of his brother Menelaos, and Achilleus returns to battle only because his friend Patroklos has been killed. When Homer does use the word *ēthos* to describe the Greeks, then, it is proper that he reserves it for these two pairs.

Agamemnon and Menelaos are shown to be of one mind in this passage from Book 10. Achilleus has just refused Agamemnon's apology and gifts, and the lord of the Greeks lies awake, his wits shaken within him. Uncannily, the same trembling seizes Menelaos, who rouses himself to find his brother Agamemnon beside his ship, putting his splendid armor about his shoulders:

"Why this arming, my brother [*ētheios*]? Is it some one of your companions
you are stirring to go and spy on the Trojans? Yet I fear sadly
there will not be any man to undertake this endeavour,
going against enemy fighters to spy on them, alone, through
the immortal night. Such a man will have to be very bold-hearted."
Then in turn powerful Agamemnon answered him:
"You and I, illustrious, o Menelaos, have need now
of crafty counsel, if any man is to defend and rescue
the Argives and their ships, since the heart of Zeus is turned from us."

(10.37–45)

Agamemnon claims to be "the best of the Achaians," and this claim brings him into a terrible conflict, but he has no such difficulties with his brother. Indeed, if we consider that most brothers in literature exist in deadly hatred, the *Iliad* is a grand exception. For fraternal rivalry does not figure significantly within it. These brothers experience the same trembling and worries, and they put their heads together when things fall apart. This loyalty has, of course, advantages as well as disadvantages. The Greeks are at Troy because of it.

The love between Achilleus and Patroklos is of a similar kind. But it is troubled by a difference. Achilleus is a different sort of man from Menelaos. He does not need to call on his friend or on anyone else. The easiest way to classify this difference is to recall that Achilleus was born of the immortal Thetis. Within the context of the *Iliad*, it means something different for Achilleus to say "*ētheios*" to a human being than it does, for example, when Paris says it to Hektor, or Menelaos to Agamemnon. Indeed, Achilleus keeps his confidences most often with his goddess mother, and not with Patroklos. He thinks of his mortal father, Peleus, only with a certain pain. Achilleus's place of belonging is not entirely of this world, and this difference is the source of his greatness and of his great tragedy.

If I delay discussion of the passage in which Achilleus finally says "brother" (*ētheios*) to his friend, it is only because Homer delays it as well. There is a reason for this delay. Achilleus is a young man. He must live longer before he can speak this word. Things must happen to him. Things must fall apart. The story of the *Iliad* must be told. For the *Iliad* tells what happens to Achilleus as a result of his inability to find people dear to him in their certain place.

When Odysseus meets Achilleus in Hades, the fallen hero laments that he would rather be a slave among the living than the king of all the dead. In short, Achilleus seems to be saying that this is his only choice. Hell, as Dante understood, is where you get what you deserve, when you no longer want what you deserve. Achilleus has succeeded in becoming king over all the dead, including, at last, Agamemnon, but now he wants to be the opposite of a king. For Achilleus, it seems, one is the king or a slave. There is no middle ground.

This scene from the *Odyssey* captures Achilleus's sense of the world in the early parts of the *Iliad*. In the beginning, he does not understand, as Odysseus puts it, that "Surely not all of us Achaians can be as kings here" (2.203). But the scene does not take into account what Achilleus learns afterward. Achilleus is lamentable in the *Odyssey* not because he was lamentable in the *Iliad* but because the *Odyssey* can support only one heroic figure, and it must be Odysseus. Obviously, Achilleus never loses his great pride in the *Iliad*, but he does abandon his wrath and his ambition to be the king of all the Achaians.

In Book 1, however, Achilleus has no such understanding. He wants to be the king or nothing. His quarrel with Agamemnon arises as a result of an insult, to be sure, but the dispute cannot be separated from Achilleus's sense of his own difference and his ambition for kingly power. This is not to claim that Achilleus is at fault in the dispute with Agamemnon but to recognize an opposition evident from the first lines of the poem. The division of conflict between brilliant Achilleus and Atreus's son, the lord of men, puts pains thousandfold upon the Achaians. In other words, Achilleus's opposition to Agamemnon is functionally equivalent to an opposition to the Achaians. Thetis makes it clear in her plea to Zeus that only the destruction of many Greeks will prove the worth of her son. She does not ask Zeus to strike down Agamemnon alone.

Book 1 plays out Achilleus's alienation and displacement in many ways, but the most obvious signs are found in the language of the quarrel itself and in the nature of Achilleus's wrath. Achilleus's wrath or *mēnis* is not a human anger. The word refers specifically to a wrath felt by gods, usually toward human beings. It suggests a sacred and vengeful anger, and according to C. Watkins's philology, Achilleus is the only mortal in the poem to be associated with it. When the members of the embassy try to persuade Achilleus to abandon his anger, Aias makes it clear that Achilleus's anger is a form of forgetting his friends and his place among them: "He is hard, and does not remember that friends' affection/ wherein we honoured him by the ships, far beyond all others" (9.630–31). Aias bids Achilleus to respect his own house and to see that all the Greeks are under one roof, but Achilleus cannot beat down his anger, even though he must admit that Aias speaks justly.

In Book 16, when Patroklos asks to reenter the battle, he again represents the hardness of Achilleus's anger but in words that drive home precisely what it means for his relation to other people:

"May no such anger take me as this that you cherish!
Cursed courage. What other man born hereafter shall be advantaged
unless you beat aside from the Argives this shameful destruction?
Pitiless: the rider Peleus was never your father
nor Thetis was your mother, but it was the grey sea that bore you
and the towering rocks, so sheer the heart in you is turned from us."

(16.30–5)

Achilleus's anger is neither human nor divine. It has neither Peleus nor Thetis as its parent. It is purely inanimate. It is incapable of being moved. Its hold on Achilleus alienates him from his Greek company and eventually vents itself on the Trojans. He is desperately and utterly alone.

The politics of the dispute between Achilleus and Agamemnon leads to the same conclusion. Whether Agamemnon is right to take Achilleus's prize is a question that I will not enter into. It is clear, however, that Agamemnon, as king, has the right to distribute gifts (see, for example, 1.209 and 9.330–33). He is at the center of his society, if only for that reason. The Greeks bring their booty to him, and he distributes it according to his idea of merit. He distributes, therefore, tokens of excellence to his men, and their worth is won or lost within this hierarchy.

Achilleus dares to step outside this system. His own sense of his excellence far exceeds what he receives in consideration. No matter what gifts he receives, he must feel to some extent that they are too little. No amount of gifts can satisfy him precisely because his idea of his own value bankrupts the economy of the social system that determines value. He is therefore incapable of being moved by the offering of gifts, and he views Agamemnon's preoccupation with gift-giving as mere greed.

To gain recognition as "the best of the Achaians," then, Achilleus must face Agamemnon, whose great kingship makes the epithet his own. Achilleus becomes the "man who speaks up against" Agamemnon, who challenges him before all others (1.230). At first, he challenges Agamemnon gently, as G. S. Kirk points out in *The Iliad: A Commentary*, but as anger overcomes him, the lines of force become apparent, and they expose Achilleus's resentment of the king's unique position. A quick examination of the speeches shows that Achilleus usually tries to separate Agamemnon from his people. He also speaks uniquely to Agamemnon on most occasions. Agamemnon, to the contrary, usually speaks to the assembly as a whole. Even when he requires that the people find him another prize to replace Chryseis, he employs the plural imperative: "Find me then some prize that shall be my own, lest I only/ among the Argives go without, since that were unfitting" (1.118). It is usually clear that Agamemnon is trying to show himself the lord of his people, whereas Achilleus becomes too soon concerned with the fact of his difference and alienation from the others. Indeed, it is particularly striking that Athene stays Achilleus's hand by telling him that she represents Hera, who loves both Agamemnon and him "equally" (1.209). Achilleus desires such talk and more.

Heroic society, according to Alasdair MacIntyre, lacks what many modern moral philosophers have taken to be a defining characteristic of human selfhood. Members of heroic society, he argues in *After Virtue*, cannot detach themselves "from a particular standpoint or point of view, to step backwards, as it were, and view and judge that standpoint or point of view from the outside" (126). The man who tries to "withdraw himself" from his given position in heroic society, MacIntyre claims, would be trying to make himself disappear. MacIntyre seems to be forgetting here that Achilleus does precisely this. Achilleus withdraws from his society but not to make himself disappear. He withdraws to make himself appear in the eyes of the Greeks as that person most valuable to them. But Achilleus's withdrawal has other effects. He understands that his withdrawal means that many Greeks will die, but he does not recognize that his friend

Patroklos is one of them. Once Achilleus withdraws from his place, he cannot expect to find those who are dear to him to remain in their certain places.

It is Nestor who reminds both Achilleus and Agamemnon that their greatness lies in their respective places in society. He tells Agamemnon to be the great man he is, and not to take Achilleus's personal antagonism personally. But Agamemnon does not give up his anger (1.318–20). Nestor also advises Achilleus not to match his strength with Agamemnon, "since never equal with the rest is the portion of honour/ of the sceptred king to whom Zeus gives magnificence" (1.278–79). Agamemnon is greater, Nestor states, because he is lord over more than Achilleus rules. But Achilleus does not give up his anger, and he withdraws from the very domain in which his sense of excellence is determined.

Achilleus remains outside the conflict. He detaches himself from his own society to celebrate himself and to make others celebrate him. The others feel the need for him, as they die, but they do not celebrate him. They are too busy, and he is idle. Homer gives us the impression at many points that Achilleus spends most of his time surveying the battle from afar. He has become the unmoved spectator of the domain in which he should be acting. When he does finally enter the battle, it is through the person of Patroklos. First, Achilleus takes the battlefield by proxy, as Patroklos dons his friend's mighty armor. When Hektor kills Patroklos and strips him of this armor, a part of Achilleus dies too. Achilleus experiences his own mortality in the death of his friend. To this point, Achilleus has managed not to think about death. He makes his confidences to Thetis, an immortal, and does not think about his mortal father, Peleus. Now with the body of Patroklos in his arms, Achilleus is stirred into action once again. He enters the field himself to pursue Hektor, who is now dressed in Achilleus's armor. The new Achilleus pursues the old Achilleus, as it were, and when Hektor falls so, too, does Achilleus, for it is fated that his death will follow quickly upon the death of his enemy.

We should not exaggerate the psychological content of the scene in which Achilleus pursues Hektor in his own likeness. It does not have to mean that Achilleus wishes to kill himself to placate his guilt over Patroklos's death, or that he kills his old self to achieve a greater self-awareness. These interpretations moralize the scene according to various ethical and psychological models. The interpretations are true enough because they capture Achilleus's feelings of grief, but they make the mistake of emphasizing anew his egotism and alienation. No doubt, Achilleus remains an egotist, but he takes the field of battle to avenge the death of Patroklos and to save the Greeks from his killer. In other words, he enters the conflict for the most likely reasons, as conceived by his society. He is not celebrating himself when he sets to work this time. He is thinking only of Patroklos and of Hektor. But as the passing of armor shows, he cannot think about them without thinking in some way about himself because thinking about them is an entirely different way of conceiving himself. This is the most important psychological and moral element of the scene.

Books 23 and 24 describe Achilleus in the act of thinking about himself in this different way. They make an end of the *Iliad* as well as of Achilleus's withdrawal from others. In Book 23, he buries Patroklos, and the Greeks collectively honor the dead hero with funeral games. In Book 24, Achilleus returns the body of Hektor to Priam and turns his thoughts to his own human origins. But Achilleus does not accomplish the burial of his friend before Patroklos appears to him in a dream and instructs him on the necessary. It is in this scene that Homer finally allows Achilleus to address Patroklos as "*ētheios*" or "dear" to him:

> "You sleep, Achilleus; you have forgotten me; but you were not
> careless of me when I lived, but only in death. Bury me
> as quickly as may be, let me pass through the gates of Hades.
> The souls, the images of dead men, hold me at a distance,
> and will not let me cross the river and mingle among them,
> but I wander as I am by Hades' house of the wide gates. . . .
> And you, Achilleus like the gods, have your own destiny;
> to be killed under the wall of the prospering Trojans. There is one
> more thing I will say, and ask of you, if you will obey me:
> do not have my bones laid apart from yours, Achilleus,
> but with them, just as we grew up together in your house,
> when Menoitios brought me there from Opous, when I was little,
> and into your house, by reason of a baneful manslaying,
> on that day when I killed the son of Amphidamas. I was
> a child only, nor intended it, but was angered over a dice game.
> There the rider Peleus took me into his own house,
> and brought me carefully up, and named me to be your henchman.
> Therefore, let one single vessel, the golden two-handled
> urn the lady your mother gave you, hold both our ashes."
> Then in answer to him spoke swift-footed Achilleus:

"How is it, o hallowed head of my brother [*ētheios*], you have come
   back to me
here, and tell me all these several things? Yet surely
I am accomplishing all, and I shall do as you tell me.
But stand closer to me, and let us, if only for a little,
embrace, and take full satisfaction from the dirge of sorrow."
So he spoke, and with his own arms reached for him, but could not
take him, but the spirit went underground, like vapour. . . .

                                  (23.69–100)

Patroklos stands apart from other men, and although they be mere
images as he is, he still wishes to join them. He wants what Achilleus has
not wanted. He wants, in death, what has caused him to die. Patroklos
has faced the possibility of being ostracized from other people early in
life, and he has found that he wants no part of it. For Patroklos, too, has
had his problems with anger, and this anger threatened to cut him off
from others. He was but a child when he murdered the son of Amphida-
mas over a dice game. Achilleus has been equally childlike in his anger,
and, perhaps, the dispute over Briseis has resembled too much a dice
game, as Aias implies at one point.[4] But Achilleus is the "child" of a
goddess, and his wrath divine has cost many more lives than the temper
of Patroklos.

The shade of Patroklos tells Achilleus the story of their life together.
He tells of his own life, but he cannot tell of that life without telling also
of Achilleus's life. For they have lived together under the same roof. They
are brothers by virtue of this fact, just as Paris and Hektor or Menelaos
and Agamemnon are brothers by virtue of nature. Achilleus's answer to
Patroklos's story of their childhood retells the same story, although it has
the proverbial effect of being expressed in one word. He calls his friend
"*ētheios*," remembering that he belongs with him by virtue of their having
grown up together in the same place. Achilleus has accepted the gifts of
Agamemnon in Book 19 and he has, of course, reentered the war, but he
accepts the gifts with hesitation, and it is easy enough to argue that he
has personal reasons for wanting to kill Hektor. When Achilleus addresses
Patroklos as "*ētheios*," however, he truly ends his withdrawal from other
human beings, and he accomplishes it by telling himself in a dream the
story of their growing up in a mortal household under the care of a mortal
father.

Similarly, in Book 24, the supplication of Priam has the effect of making Achilleus reconsider his human origins. When Priam makes the plea for his son's body, he forces Achilleus to turn his anger toward Hektor to thoughts of Priam and of his own father. Priam asks Achilleus to remember his father, and to turn to a kind of thinking that he has not frequently had in the epic:

"Honour then the god, Achilleus, and take pity upon me
remembering your father, yet I am still more pitiful;
I have gone through what no other mortal on earth has gone through;
I put my lips to the hands of the man who has killed my children."
    So he spoke, and stirred in the other a passion of grieving
for his own father. He took the old man's hand and pushed him
gently away, and the two remembered, as Priam sat huddled
at the feet of Achilleus and wept close for manslaughtering Hektor
and Achilleus wept now for his own father, now again
for Patroklos. The sound of their mourning moved the house.

(24.503–12)

Father and son mourn together over a dying father and a dead son. Each mourns in turn for himself. For Achilleus will soon join Hektor, and Hektor's death means the death of Troy and with it, Priam. Thetis does not remain too far from Achilleus's thoughts. He gives Priam something to eat, as she instructs, but it is striking that Achilleus's last scene is dedicated to his father, when the epic has turned so frequently on his relationship to his mother.[5] The scene is not necessarily patriarchal as a result. The idea of mortality overrides any patriarchal effect because Homer's story necessarily links Achilleus's death with the mortality of his father. Since Achilleus must die as a man, it is also necessary that he should have lived as one, and it is therefore appropriate that the last books of the *Iliad* show Achilleus to be reflecting on the story of this life.

Homer's poem maps the relation of place to character, and we may see in it for the first time a story that links ethics to place and character to the social world. Despite the presence of the gods in the *Iliad*, Homer is describing a very human world, and the *ēthos* of his characters fits the place of their humanity. Homer's language has its place as does the language of his characters. For better or worse, it is not Olympus but the pasture surrounding Troy. Homer tells the story of this place, and his story is ethical. It is not a transcendental ethics but a human ethics of the practical kind stressed by Aristotle. Most important, Homer's moral philosophy is literary. No matter how hard we try, we cannot separate his ethics from his storytelling.

CHAPTER 6

∾

Plato's Tragedy

AS AN INSTANCE OF LITERARY ETHICS, the *Iliad* opens the tradition of Western literature. If we doubt the idea that Homer's poetry and ethics share the same place, we should recall that Plato interprets Homer in this fashion. But Plato does not approve. For Plato, beloved places are few, storytellers present a threat to political order, and ethics takes an ideal form; and to preserve its ideal form, he wants to control the ethical force of storytelling. In Books 2 and 3 of the *Republic*, he attacks the idea of ethics found in epic and tragic poetry, and in more than one case repeats in a negative light the Homeric association between ethics and place. Socrates's summary of the first stages of building good character makes the connection explicitly:

> It is not only to the poets therefore that we must issue orders requiring them to portray good character in their poems or not to write at all; we must issue similar orders to all artists and craftsmen, and prevent them portraying bad character.... We shall thus prevent our guardians being brought up among representations of what is evil, and so day by

day and little by little, by grazing widely as it were in an unhealthy pasture, insensibly doing themselves a cumulative psychological damage that is very serious. (401b–c)

For Plato, literature is an unhealthy pasture, and if we bring up our children there, they will develop bad habits and bad character. If we ask what good literature is for Plato, we are forced to ask how he defines good character. If we ask what good character is, we are led to ask how he defines good literature. Plato's attempt to describe character invariably forces him to be literary. In this respect at the very least, Plato and every moral philosopher after him remain Homeric.

Usually the relation between artistic mimesis and Plato's model of ethical criticism is obscured by the theory of ideas, or the argument over *sophia* and *technē*. Plato presses his view that artistic mimesis is an obstacle to justice, education, and self-mastery because it distorts the master ideas upon which such virtues are based. If we were to become overly involved in the specifics of this argument, we would focus on the apparently secondary and degraded qualities of crafts and art in comparison to the absolute primacy of the forms. But the fascination with Plato's theory of ideas already obeys the impulse that defines Platonism: it is the desire to turn ourselves away from things human toward transcendence, and unless we resist this impulse, at least at first, we will never be able to judge Plato's importance. We cannot understand Plato if we begin by accepting the premises that we wish to understand.

Book 2 on education sketches out Plato's notion of literary criticism. He reads Homer and Greek tragedy closely, and he decides that they are simply not realistic. Plato's greatest problem, and it is more ethical than literary, concerns the character of the gods. His specific test case is Homer. Homer and others misrepresent the gods, Plato has Socrates insist, by showing them contradicting themselves, arguing, and losing themselves to their emotions. Plato understands that Homer's gods, despite appearances, live in an all-too-human world, and Plato disapproves of so much preoccupation with things human. If the gods are to be our models for perfection, poets had better perfect the idea of the gods, Plato implies, and he turns to a careful reading of Homer in which he rejects any characteristic attributed to the gods that might be considered a human weakness. Too often, according to Plato, poets misrepresent the gods and heroes, like a portrait painter whose portraits bear no resemblance to the originals (377e), and he contests the examples that storytellers give to their audiences. If people followed the examples of the gods given in most stories, Socrates points out, they would be able to justify the most horrible crimes, parricide, for instance. Moreover, Homer's stories about wars and plots among the gods present them as quarrelsome and deceitful, contaminating young citizens with the wrong ideas about how to live with each other. Plato distrusts in particular Homer's idea that the gods change shapes or disguise themselves to deceive people, and he disputes that they ever tell lies. The gods possess absolute self-mastery in Plato's view, and to represent them in any other way forgets the profound truth that the "gods and the things of the gods are entirely perfect" (381b). Indeed, for Plato, the gods and the good are one and the same, and he insists that good poetry tell no story in contradiction with the principle that "God is the cause, not of all things, but only of good" (380c).

Little by little, Plato purifies the image of the Greek gods, and by the end of his reading of Homer, he has managed to eliminate any show of emotion or contradiction that might lead us to describe the Greek gods as anthropomorphic. In short, he perfects the divine by rejecting the human.

When Plato turns specifically to heroic character, he proceeds in the same fashion. He uses the model of perfection and self-mastery already established for the Greek gods to perfect human nature. In effect, Plato retells the early books of the *Iliad*, but now we are supposed to accept Achilleus's quest to prove his divine superiority. Homer showed that Achilleus has no place of belonging in this world because he renounces his humanity to satisfy his desire to become a god, but Plato appears to find this aim worthy of imitation. He scolds Homer for giving an extreme picture of Achilleus's grieving over Patroklos, thereby excluding those very scenes in which the hero finds his humanity, and Plato refuses to accept Priam's mourning over Hektor. It is entirely inappropriate in Plato's eyes to pour dust on one's head or to grovel in dung, if one is a hero (388b). Nor should one be overcome with laughter, if one lives on Mount Olympus: the spectacle of the gods bursting into laughter over Hephaistos's antics in Book 1 of the *Iliad* enrages Plato (389). Rather, all excessive behavior—anger, laughter, and lamentation—ought to be rejected. Plato prefers that literature provide only examples of self-mastery. In his theory of ideas, he seeks to represent perfection alone, and he takes the same attitude toward storytelling. He praises Odysseus for his ability to call his heart to order and to master his unruly emotions. But examples of the failure to achieve self-control have little value for Plato.

For the same reason, Plato opposes the recitation of Homer's poetry.

Oral performance affects adversely the building of good character because it injects the immorality of poetry directly into the populace. The rhapsode utters the words of gods, heroes, and villains, toying with them, as it were, and he does not attempt to disabuse anyone of the idea that the words are his own (393a–d). His manner of speech brings fictional characters to life, whether moral or immoral, and he sets off a chain reaction of aping, copying, and imitation. People in the audience begin to retell the story and to recite the speeches of the characters. They take on other characters. They forget their own.

Storytelling, in Plato's view, transforms people's personalities by exciting them to act as if they possessed another character. How can anyone exert self-control over oneself, Plato seems to ask, when one is pretending to be someone else? Although he does not find impersonation as offensive in the case of good models, it produces dangerous results in the case of evil ones. "I think," Socrates explains, "that the decent man, when he comes in the course of a narrative to a speech or action by a man of good character will be willing to impersonate him and feel no shame at this kind of representation. . . . But if he comes across an unworthy character, he will be ashamed to copy seriously a man worse than himself, except for his short periods of good behaviour, and will not consent to do so" (396d). Literature leads to impersonation, and impersonation is not a matter of indifference in Plato's view of good character. It is therefore imperative that unsuitable models of character be excised from poetry and that literature in general be examined and approved according to moral and political standards.

What kind of literature remains?

This is not my question. Socrates asks the question as he pauses to summarize the images of the gods and heroes that belong in good literature. His answer is startling, at least for the literary critic. "What is left," he replies, "would seem to be literature dealing with men" (392).

Socrates, it appears, has left the best for last. The issue of a human literature will culminate his discussion.

But, in fact, we are disappointed. "But we cannot deal with that topic at present," Socrates concludes. "Why not?" his interlocutor responds with puzzlement. "Because I am afraid," continues Socrates, "that we shall find that poets and story-tellers are in error in matters of the greatest human importance" (392b).

Plato does not allow a discussion of human literature to take place. We might presume the reason to be that literature inadequately describes the human. From Plato's point of view, more and more, the idea of a human literature is an oxymoron. Such thinking succumbs to Platonism, however, and misses the real difficulty with Plato's argument. The reason that Plato rejects human literature is not because storytelling cannot represent the human but because it represents the human too well.

When a story is told, heard, and retold, it creates an aesthetic community, a republic of citizens, that competes with other political bodies. This aesthetic community not only brings characters to life and offers them as guides for people's conduct. It serves as a community as such, which is to say that the aesthetics of storytelling is always political and ethical. Literature fulfills two of the greatest human desires. It gives people the pleasure of human company, and it places human beings at the center of the world stage. Plato's genius was to have understood that storytelling is a forceful political and ethical action. But, not surprisingly, the discovery catches him between a rock and a hard place. He wants both to expel storytelling from his republic and to be its only storyteller. Literature and philosophy are in an open contest to create character, and Plato wants to eliminate the competition. He therefore expels the poets from his republic.

Literature, then, has a social dimension in Plato's view. Or, rather, it enacts an idea of society, and this society interferes with his desire to build another republic. The kind of mixed and open society that the experience of Homer's poetry represents is a great threat to Plato's political agenda because it competes with his desire to transform human conduct and to create the ultimate philosophic type. No where does this fact emerge more clearly than in Book 6. Plato has been writing a philosopher's philosophy, not a literary one, throughout the *Republic*. His apparent purpose is to educate the philosopher king, a character who can be a philosopher and still be of this world. But, in fact, Plato must confess that "there's no existing form of society good enough for the philosophic nature, with the result that it gets warped and altered, like a foreign seed sown in alien soil under whose influence it commonly degenerates into the local growth. In exactly the same way the philosophic type loses its true powers, and falls into habits alien to it" (497b).

Plato has recourse once more to the Homeric ethic of a place, or of a pasture, in which character grows, and it has two effects. First, it reveals how alien the world of ordinary people is to the aristocratic philosophic type. Second, the image contains a veiled attack against the democratic and open society of Athens. The city of Athens represents the consummate image of a world of open ideas and free citizens, but it is alien to the philosophic type because it allows citizens to mix and to contaminate each other's characters with alien habits. In sum, it has the same effect as reciting Homer's poetry. The evolution from habitat to habits to character is inevitable and, in Plato's mind, deadly for the philosophic type. For its pressure corrupts the philosopher's attempts to transcend the ordinary world and its common people. Elsewhere, Plato concludes simply that "philosophy is impossible among the common people" (494). Unless philosophers wish to degenerate into local growth, they must guard themselves against contamination by common citizens. They must seek out a place apart from the unhealthy pastures of this world, and this means, ultimately, that they must avoid both Homer and democratic Athens.

But Plato is greatly confused, even in terms of his own argument. The problem is not that the philosopher's nature finds the earth or ordinary society to be alien. The problem is that Plato cannot get his philosopher off the ground. He wants his philosophy to soar toward an unearthly ideal, but his philosopher's feet are stuck in the mud. It is Plato's argument, not human nature, that is alien to this soil, for he has chosen to develop a theory of ethics that denies all relation to the human society. According to Plato, the world perverts the virtuous human being. Either the philosopher is human, and society inhuman, or society is too human for the divine agenda of the philosopher. I want to suggest that Plato believes the latter. Society, as Plato describes it, is found wanting because it is human. Plato begins by expelling human literature, but he ends by rejecting human ethics and politics.

Is it an accident that Plato rejects storytelling and the human world simultaneously? I think not. He understands that an intimate tie exists between stories and human society, and that this relation must be destroyed, if he is to build his republic. This Platonic gesture captures, and comes to stand for, the belief in the age-old struggle between philosophy and literature. But Plato's gesture allows us finally to characterize the secret logic holding between philosophical theories of ethics and the literary work. Plato uses or writes stories to define moral law and then expels storytelling as unethical. Indeed, a certain history of moral philosophy always returns to the idea that storytelling is a source of immorality. Plato's work best demonstrates this baffling logic. Here is a philosopher who returns again and again to literature to formulate his theory of ethics, but this very theory rejects storytelling as the greatest threat to ethics.

A clear example of Plato's contradictory method would be "The Allegory of the Cave," but here I will retell a powerful and often ignored story found at the heart of the *Republic*. In Book 8, Socrates turns his attention to a description of imperfect societies. His reason for dwelling on so much imperfection is ultimately to recommend that existing forms of government be replaced by the monarchy of the philosopher king, although this agenda remains an unspoken one. These societies consist of every form of government—with the exception of the monarchy—then known to humanity. Plato tries to demonstrate how each form of government develops out of another, but he does not design this evolutionary pattern on the basis of governmental principles or constitutions. Nor does he present forms of government according to an idea of institutionalization. Rather, he designs the history of government according to a family genealogy and represents each type of government as a "character of society" or *ēthos tēs poleōs*. Each type of government possesses a corresponding type of individual character (*ēthos*), and they share the same flaws (544, 544e). For two books, Socrates narrates a family romance in which the personality traits of these individuals bring about a further decline in the characters of their sons and of their cities.

Books 8 and 9 are, I want to claim, some of the most literary in the *Republic*. We know that the young Plato tried to write tragedy, and in these books, he accomplishes his desire, following the predetermined form of tragedy and its preoccupation with family genealogy and decline. Socrates even begins his narrative by invoking the Muses: "Shall we invoke the Muses, like Homer, and ask them to tell us 'how the quarrel first began'? Let us imagine that they are talking to us in a rather dramatic, high-flown fashion, pretending to be very much in earnest, though they are really only teasing us as if we were children" (545e).

Like the tragic dramatists before him, then, Plato intends to expose what Socrates calls the "pedigree of strife" (547). The story is an antipolitical fable, a political tragedy, and its purpose is to tell how inconsistent and irregular characters are born when the pure mettles of character—called men of gold, silver, and bronze—blend together in bad society. The point is, apparently, that no human society has managed to find by itself a good form of government because it does not possess true knowledge. Society, therefore, has need of Plato's philosopher king. Socrates's tragic fable exposes the weaknesses of each character in the family romance of political forms, and the effect of the story is to denigrate every kind of government, save that of the philosopher king, in order to pave the way for his reign.

The main characters of the tragedy are the timarchic, oligarchic, democratic, and tyrannical personalities. Each gives way in turn to another. The timarchic character has been imperfectly educated, and he loses sight of his natural superiority to those living with him (548d–550c). He is ambitious to hold office, but he regards his military achievements and soldierly qualities as his best qualifications and not the ability to speak or to judge. He conforms to some extent to the *ēthos tēs poleōs* or "character of the society" (549a). But he is perhaps greedier than others. His particular flaws spring from the improper influence of his parents. Socrates recounts how the timarchic boy was raised by an unambitious father and a resentful mother. The boy's father is a good man, but he avoids office and thinks it too much trouble to fight for what he deserves. The mother complains to her son that his father is not a leader and that she is "slighted by other women because of it." She despises the fact that her husband does not wish to make money, and she tells her son that his father is not a real man. The servants in the household repeat the same story to the boy, and he soon comes to believe that those who "mind their own business are publicly called silly." Thus, the son is pulled in two directions. He listens to his father's advice, nourishing the growth of his rational nature, but he also witnesses the ambition of others. He sets a middle course between the two, and he grows into an arrogant and ambitious man.

Eventually, the timarchic man has a son (553–555b). He admires his father and follows in his footsteps, until the boy sees him destroyed by a political disaster. The father's sufferings frighten the boy, and he decides never to lose his property and position. He drifts toward oligarchy, which fires his ambition for social standing and money. He throws off his courage and exchanges his ambition for avarice. Profit-seeking dethrones all other desires in his mind, and he amasses a fortune, while "reason and ambition squat in servitude at its feet." He becomes, in Socrates's words, a "squalid character," who is "always on the make." He sometimes appears to be honest, but his honesty merely derives from the constraint that he exercises over his evil impulses for fear of their effect on his business concerns. He possess "no moral conviction, no taming of desire by reason, but only the compulsion of fear." He is nothing but a grasping moneymaker.

The son of the oligarchic man is the democratic character. He is raised in an atmosphere of brutal economy and greed. He possesses a natural acquisitiveness taken from his father's house, but he soon gets a taste of what Socrates calls "wasteful" desires. He sees that the masses are engulfed in unnecessary pleasures and urges, and he desires to join in the fun. A veritable battle ensues in the boy's mind. Sometimes the democratic element gives way to the oligarchic, and the boy feels in control of himself. At other moments, the democratic element captures "the seat of government," and the boy enjoys his wasteful pleasures. Eventually, however, pretentious fallacies and opinions invade the "vacant citadel of the young man's mind," and the democratic character gives himself over entirely to pleasure. The democratic character, Socrates concludes, believes that "all pleasures are equal and should have equal rights."

Indeed, for Plato, the democratic creed is based merely on such equality. Democratic liberty is usually nothing but licentiousness according to Plato, and it is bound, apparently, to go to extremes. In democracies, slaves—male and female—have the same freedoms as their owners, and there is complete equality between the sexes. "The dog comes," Socrates expresses in proverb, "to resemble its mistress" (563c). Horses come to resemble donkeys, and both, their masters, and, I imagine, men of gold mix with men of bronze. Animals are "in the habit of walking about the streets with grand freedom, and bump into people they meet if they don't get out of their way. Everything is full of this spirit of liberty" (563c–d).

"You're telling me!" Adeimantus complains about Athens. "I've often suffered from it on my way out of town" (563d).

One of Socrates's favorite jokes against democracy is that democrats think that they can turn donkeys into horses by merely voting on it. I take it that the covert sense of this joke is that democracy makes common people believe that they are as aristocratic as horses but they remain donkeys nevertheless. Plato's own comic portrayal of democratic Athens as a barnyard gives this joke an even more venomous twist by representing democratic freedom as rule by brainless beasts. Indeed, Plato's entire political tragedy is pointed most directly against the democratic society in which he lived, and this despite the fact that only in Athens could Plato have found the freedom to practice philosophy and to speak out against the majority without fear of reprisal.

In Plato's eyes, democracy is the worst offender against social discipline and regime as well as against the aristocracy of the philosophic type. It permits any kind of literature. It creates an evil mixture of classes and moral types, and only tyranny, apparently, can result from so much freedom and lack of class distinctions. Indeed, the son of the democratic character is the tyrant (571–576b). The tyrannical character is essentially a criminal in Socrates's mind. The democratic father brings up his son in an atmosphere of complete license, although he calls it liberty. The little tyrant's desires buzz around him, and his passions run wild. The precise definition of a tyrannical man, according to Socrates, is "one who, either by birth or habit or both, combines the characteristics of drunkenness, lust, and madness" (573c). When the son's sources of pleasure fail, his desires howl aloud, and he begins to plunder others. He kills his father and mother when they stand in his way. He takes power over others, although he is his own slave.

Incidentally, Socrates makes a point of noting that tragedians make good company for tyrants because they praise them, and that the tyrant can be expected to hire actors and playwrights to sway large audiences over to tyranny or democracy (568b). This is one more reason, in Socrates's mind, to expel the poet from the republic.

I have failed in this brief presentation to convey the sense of detail, the psychological drama, and the political agenda apparent in Plato's tragedy. Ironically, it represents, in its preoccupation with bad character, the kind of storytelling that Plato would have rejected from his republic. In fact, the story seems to contaminate Socrates as he tells it. The tragedy arouses Socrates's self-pity and pessimism, and Glaucon laments that their ideal society will, no doubt, never exist on earth (592b). "Perhaps," Socrates concludes, "it is laid up as a pattern in heaven, where he who wishes can see it and found it in his own heart. But it doesn't matter whether it exists or ever will exist; in it alone, and in no other society, could he take part in public affairs" (592b). The ideal city can exist only in the hearts of philosophers, and their nature is not compatible with this world. We should understand as a result why the best of them will have nothing to do with common ethics and politics.

What kind of ethics remains?

What kind of literature remains?

Plato concludes that his ideal character cannot have a place in the alien soil of earth, and he assures us that the types of political and ethical characters elaborated in his tragedy must not be given a place in the city. Plato's ethics takes the form of stories, but stories have no place in his moral philosophy. Nor does his moral philosophy have a place. Rather, it exists in the abstract, as an ideal, as a perfect form of self-mastery, toward which human beings may aspire imperfectly. The same may be said of literature, especially of Plato's efforts. Plato aspires to write a perfect literature to suit his perfect ethics, but the results do not measure up to his abstract and unworldly ideals, and he can assign no real value to them. In short, when Plato expels literature, he expels ethics.

Lest it be thought that I have exaggerated Plato's opposition to literary ethics, let us consider a final point. It may be argued that Plato expels only harmful literature and that good poetry has its place. But, given what we know of Plato, is it better to achieve good character through the imitation of good models or through self-mastery? Everything that Plato says about education makes it clear that the final end of learning is to free the self from its dependence on opinion in order to attain knowledge and independence. When Socrates asks about the effect of music and literature on the education of the philosopher king, for example, Glaucon recalls that they earlier found little of value in a liberal arts education. "There was nothing in it," he reminds Socrates, "to produce the effect you are seeking." "Your memory's quite correct," Socrates responds, "we shan't find what we want there. But where on earth shall we find it, Glaucon? The more practical forms of skill don't seem very elevating—" (522–522b).

All of Plato resides in these lines. They are ironic to the point of deadly seriousness. For if we consider how desperately Plato wishes to get his philosopher off the ground, we may well begin to sympathize with Socrates's complaint that a practical education will never be sufficiently "elevating."

Where on earth might we find a more elevating education? Nowhere, and certainly not in literature, if self-mastery is the key to beautiful character. For the pursuit of self-mastery and its godlike superiority must eventually turn away from the consideration of any character other than its own. In this case, all literature, whether good or evil, must ultimately lose its value for building character. Even the best models in Plato's eyes enslave the self and obstruct its pursuit of the good.

CHAPTER 7

ॐ

The Allegory of
the Cave-Dwellers

STORYTELLERS, whether poets or philosophers, are always some place when they tell their stories, and stories usually describe places in one manner or another; and yet many stories do not excite in us the desire to see these places. Dante's *Divine Comedy* is an example of a work of literature that stimulates this desire. We desire, spontaneously, when we read Dante, to possess a map of his vision of heaven and hell. Perhaps the quest for the historical Troy springs from a like desire. Homer's poem binds storytelling and place so tightly that we cannot help but want to map the places celebrated by his story.

Plato, however, makes it clear that his beloved places may exist only in the heart of the ideal philosopher. But we try to turn his descriptions into geography all the same. "The Myth of Er," related in Book 10 of the *Republic*, gives a physical description of the universe, in which the rings of the grand spindle of Necessity form the orbits of the planets and the sphere of the fixed stars, and philosophers have not tired of tracing out its boundaries. "The Allegory of the Cave" hardly represents Plato's ideal republic, but it, too, excites our desire to experience its geography. The

89

allegory brings together into a coherent story the theoretical distinctions described in "The Allegory of the Sun" and "The Analogy of the Divided Line," representing the climax of the so-called "philosophical passages of the *Republic*," if it makes any sense to describe a section in what is supposed to be a work of philosophy with such a phrase. "The Allegory of the Cave" is the map of Plato's theory of ideas, and the theory of ideas, although it is heretical to say so, is in part a map of Plato's world.

But "The Allegory of the Cave" maps a place that cannot be mapped for the simple reason that it is not a place. The realm of the ideas, our philosopher insists, lies nowhere.

Plato, however, never abandons his desire to make a map of this non-place. Nor does he relent in his desire to go where he cannot go.

It is a great irony, and not a Socratic one, that the *Republic* numbers among those great works that excite our desire to draw a map. Plato rejects the reality of a place of belonging in favor of the reality of ideas. He therefore rejects Homer. But he cannot think about the ideas without locating them somewhere and desiring to go there. He therefore remains Homeric, and we desire, with Plato, to see the places described by him, just as we desire to see Troy.

This situation is not so peculiar, however, if we remember that the Greeks perfected the art of geography and that the histories of their conquests and explorations produced our earliest mappings of what is now commonly called the classical world. Herodotus's travels produced the first reliable story of the boundaries of this world, and when we read his accounts, we understand how intimately related are the Greek way of life and their love of maps. For the Greeks studied geography with a reason in mind. They needed maps to find their way to their colonies and back. They drew lines to trace out the boundaries of their property and their world, and if they made many maps of this world, it was because the world was quickly becoming their property.

It is not for nothing that Alexander the Great loved maps. His love of maps was like other people's fascination with their own signature.

The Greeks thought that they lived at the center of the world. Indeed, Herodotus places Greece at the heart of the classical world, and he traces all roads back to it. As we move away from the Greek center of the classical world, however, we become entangled increasingly in what V. Y. Mudimbe has called the "geography of monstrosity." This geography cannot be separated from the colonizing motives of the Greeks because those people who live on the fringes of the classical world are inevitably represented by the Greeks as monstrous. As in Plato, the farther we move from the center of reality—the realm of the ideas—the more monstrous and false become our visions of the world. At the very least, Plato shares this prejudice of geography with the classical historians, and in spite of the fact that he appears to reject the reality of geography.

At one of the farthest points from the center of the classical world, within the continent of Africa, exists the country of Ethiopia, and within it, in a marginal position, live the people whom Herodotus calls the cave-dwelling Ethiopians. On the one hand, the cave-dwellers, Pliny tells us, have no language and live on the flesh of snakes. Moreover, they appear to be the natural prey of the other inhabitants of the area because they are pursued for sport. On the other hand, Diodoros of Sicily reveals that the Ethiopians were the first of all human beings and have been called autochthonous. The Ethiopians are of the earth, and as the founders of human culture, they sent out colonists to the Egyptians, who in turn sent out colonists to Greece. The cave-dwellers would appear to be the most autochthonous of the Ethiopians and therefore at the origin of their culture; and yet the classical historians represent them as the most primitive and savage of their race.

Classical geography partakes of the colonization of Ethiopia, and its images of the cave-dwellers demonstrate the Greek fear of foreigners. But in a startling reversal, Plato's "Allegory of the Cave" takes the idea of cave-dwellers and universalizes it. The Greeks discover the cave-dwelling Ethiopians and return home many years later to find that their philosophy calls their own people cave-dwellers as well.

Socrates tells Glaucon a story about a race of human beings imprisoned in a cave. They have been held there since childhood, and their legs and necks are chained so that they can look only straight ahead and cannot turn their heads. Behind them, a fire is burning, and between the fire and the prisoners runs a road, in the front of which a curtain-wall has been built in the form of a screen, such as one finds at puppet shows. Socrates asks Glaucon to imagine that there are men carrying various objects along behind the curtain-wall in order to project the shadows of the objects on the cavern wall for the prisoners to view.

"A foreign picture and a foreign sort of prisoner," Glaucon responds.

"They are like us," Socrates retorts, making the analogy complete (515a; translation modified).

But, perhaps, Plato's cave-dwellers resemble the Ethiopians more than the Greeks.

In the depths of Ethiopia live the cave-dwellers, marginalized by both their neighbors and classical geography. They are supposedly monstrous and unlike any other race of human beings, if, indeed, natural history permits us to call them human beings. Another race of cave-dwellers inhabits Plato's cave. They, we are told, resemble the Greeks, but the identification will not last long. For Plato's purpose is to relate an allegory in which these cave-dwellers are also colonized and educated. Little, if any, attention has been given to the fact that Plato's cave-dwellers are being colonized in the style elaborated within classical historiography.

When we first encounter the cave-dwellers, they are in chains, and Glaucon calls them *"atopos,"* betraying his sense that they are not of a world know to him. The word *atopos* means "placeless," and it reveals Glaucon's inability to locate the cave-dwellers on the classical map. Typically, Plato's translators render Glaucon's phrase with some variation on the word "strange," but in fact the word "foreign" captures the sense of this nonplace on the classical map with greater precision and anxiety because its etymology associates it with both dark chambers and the darkness of places far from home. The mentality of the classical world is as fearful of places found too far outside its boundaries as of those found too far inside them. Whether it be the darkness of Ethiopia or of Hades, the sensation of foreignness is the same, but the cave-dwellers suffer the misfortune of living in a place that combines both extremes of alienation. Glaucon can find no expression to describe them, except, appropriately, to call them "nowheremen," and his stupefaction ends by being something of an ironic comment on Plato's own desire to represent the realm of the ideal forms, his own personal vision of "nowhere."

In fact, the place of the cave-dwellers, if they have one, is only to know their place. Plato's dark chamber is their chamber of horrors. Their keepers bind them in chains. They drive them like beasts out into the light and back into the cave. They shout at them in the dark and flash strange shadows on the walls of their cave.

But who are these keepers? Who are these puppeteers who carry the objects projected by Plato's magic lantern and who speak from beyond the pale to the abject prisoners? Neither Socrates nor Plato ever tells us.

Interestingly, Paul Shorey, the translator of the *Republic* in the Loeb series, dismisses the keepers as mere machinery: "The men are merely a part of the necessary machinery of the image. Their shadows are not cast on the wall" (2:121 n.b). Keepers who do not cast shadows would be fiercely efficient, and they seem oddly at home in both Plato's world of ideal forms and his coercive republic of earthly guardians and their subjects.

Plato cannot tell his story of enlightenment without embarking on the conquest of territory. He wants to live in the realm of the ideas, nowhere, but he cannot describe his theory without giving it a place in the classical world. In the case of his famous allegory, his avoidance of the material world serves merely to conceal the machinery of slavery, colonization, and coercion at work in the cave. Socrates may say that the cave-dwellers are like the Greeks, but they represent everything that the Greeks should not be in terms of Plato's philosophical agenda. They live in darkness and ignorance. They are slaves, not citizens. The keepers who force the cave-dwellers into the light are more the model of the good citizen or philosopher in the Western world. They arrive in a missionary capacity to educate the cave-dwellers. They lead them out of the cave and into the sun. The men of darkness encounter the men of light, but their first meeting is imagined in terms of a conflict over territory.

The education of the cave-dwellers is as much an occasion for mobilization and colonization as the education of Herodotus and the other classical historians. First, the keepers imprison their captives in the cave and subject them to the test of shadows and noise. Then, they compel a prisoner to look at the fire and to move about the cave. Finally, they forcibly drag him up the steep and rugged ascent and throw him out into the sunlight. The hapless prisoner reaches enlightenment through a process of forced migration. His keepers control him through force, and they are more insistent than Socrates's annoying gadfly ever was.

The space of Plato's cave, I am suggesting, has been individualized by its inhabitants just as this place has inhabited them, and we must read their life there according to the structure of classical geography. "The Allegory of the Cave" represents another geography of monstrosity. We are not accustomed, of course, to thinking of Plato's allegory in terms of geography, and for obvious reasons. Place in Plato is difficult to conceptualize because his philosophy eschews so relentlessly the material plane of explanation. For him, the material plane is mere appearance. But Plato does write an allegory about a cave to explain his abstract theory of ideas, and when he condemns poetry, he describes it as an "unhealthy pasture" (401b–c). Plato denounces the material world, but he cannot theorize about the realm of the ideas without having recourse to a vocabulary of objects and places.

We may question, however, how much the change in surroundings affects the situation of the prisoner. The prisoner is a cave-dweller and understands his environment. This much is clear from Socrates's insistence that a prisoner once freed would have difficulty understanding the shadows if he were forced to return to the cave. That the prisoner's native understanding lacks value, however, is merely a prejudice of the classical world view. Plato simply does not put much stock in understanding darkness and shadows. He values ideas and light.

Of course, what the prisoner gains on the outside is an idea. The one advantage that he has over his fellows is the knowledge given from outside the cave. He possesses an idea of the cave, whereas his fellows live merely in the cave. Plato's allegory stresses this fact in its basic geography, for the cave is the realm of material existence, whereas outside the cave lies the realm of the ideas. When the prisoner steps outside the cave, he steps into a realm where the idea of the cave exists. In short, he moves from inside the cave to inside the idea of the cave.

The cave-dwellers may be trapped in the cave, but the idea-dwellers are trapped in the idea of the cave. And just as the keepers imprisoned the cave-dwellers in the cave, they compel the idea-dweller to inhabit the idea of the cave. Similarly, Plato's *Republic* works to give citizens an idea of the city in which to dwell and with which to escape the cities of the material world. The dialogue proposes a pedagogy for acculturating its readers to a classical model of life based on a rigorous and ascetic devotion to the idea. Given these facts, it is difficult to imagine the advantage of being an idea-dweller, especially if we do not rely on Plato's biased geography of high and low, and light and dark.

It is indeed strange, given Plato's disgust with the material world, that ideas exist in a realm, or a place, and that they cannot occupy the same space. Contradictory notions, Plato explains, always arise from mistaking two ideas for one. If it seems that an idea contradicts itself, it is proof that we are mistaking one idea for two ideas. The theory of ideas obeys the law of noncontradiction. But this logic is less strange when we realize to what extent the philosophy of ideas involves the necessity of place. Two places cannot be one place, and someone cannot be in two places at once. The realm of ideas is as much a dimension or territory as any other, so it is not surprising that classical history is first written as a history of war and not of peace, and that the *locus classicus* of Western philosophy should be an allegory about the colonization of a cave.

It is questionable, then, whether denying the place of philosophy, as some branches of Continental philosophy now require, actually clarifies or obscures the political and ethical dimension of the history of ideas. The ideas of presence, place, and city, if they do nothing else, force us to conceive of the immediate context of philosophical arguments, and they may thus serve as a reminder to concentrate on situations rather than ideas. Whether we are reading literature or culture, we are involved in the taking of territory, so it is crucial to focus on the maps that our readings make. Reading always makes a map, just as mapping always charts a reading. Some of these readings may be more benign than others, to be sure, so we need not always feel guilty. But we should always remain on our guard, for the history of reading has often become entangled with the history of conquest.

The *Republic*, of course, tells one more story about people who arise from the depths of the earth (414b–415d). It is the cultural myth used by the rulers to create the class order necessary to rule the republic. The gods, the myth explains, composed human beings in the depths of the earth of different metals: those made of gold are qualified to be rulers; those of silver are to be guardians; and those of bronze or iron are destined to be farmers and workers. It is the duty of the men of gold to harden their hearts against those people composed of bronze and to force them to occupy their allotted place in the republic.

Now, Herodotus tells another story about the Ethiopians, and it also reflects on Plato's fettered prisoners as well as on his men of gold and bronze. It is not about the Ethiopian cave-dwellers but about the king of Ethiopia. Herodotus tells us in the *Histories* that when Cambyses, the king of Persia, decided to conquer the Ethiopians, he sent the Fish-Eaters as spies among them. The Fish-Eaters presented many gifts to the king of Ethiopia and promised him Cambyses's friendship. But the king understood that the men were spies and answered:

> "The king of Persia has not sent you with these presents because he puts a high value upon being my friend. You have come to get information about my kingdom; therefore, you are liars, and that king of yours is a bad man. Had he any respect for what is right, he would not have coveted any other kingdom than his own, nor made slaves of a people who have done him no wrong. So take him this bow, and tell him that the king of Ethiopia has some advice to give him: when the Persians can draw a bow of this size thus easily, then let him raise an army of superior strength and invade the country of the long-lived

Ethiopians. Till then, let him thank the gods for not turning the thoughts of the children of Ethiopia to foreign conquests." (3.21–22)

The king then treated the Fish-Eaters as guests and asked them about the gold chains worn about their bodies, and when they explained that they were jewelry, he laughed, having supposed them to be fetters, and remarked that he had stronger ones in his country. The following tour of the country proved him to be speaking truthfully. After showing the Fish-Eaters many wonders, the king brought them to a prison in which all of the prisoners were bound in gold chains. For among the Ethiopians the rarest and most precious metal was bronze.

CHAPTER 8

~

Kant's Character

"THE MYTH OF ER" brings the *Republic* to a close, and it recounts, in effect, the failure of Plato's theory of ideas. For, first, "The Myth of Er" is a story, and stories have no place in Plato's theory of ideas, and, second, it is a story about how experience and habit exert more control over human action and choice than philosophy. The myth explains that the departed souls of human beings gather together and throw lots to determine their next life on earth. There is no choice of the quality of character because each soul must assume by necessity the character appropriate to its choice of life. The choice is a dice game, but each soul is told that there are enough lives to choose from to assure contentment.

When given the opportunity to choose their next life, however, nearly all of the souls make their choices by force of the habits of their former life. Our old characters are not easily discarded.

Orpheus, angry at women, does not want to be born of one, so he chooses the life of a swan.

Thamyris, the singer, chooses the life of a nightingale.

Aias wishes to live his next life as a lion.

97

Agamemnon, because he hates humanity, decides to take the life of an eagle.

Thersites, Achilleus's ugly imitator in the *Iliad*, puts on the form of an ape.

Only Odysseus, from among all the departed souls, steps beyond his former character and habits to choose the life of an ordinary man. Plato praises his wisdom. But Odysseus's choice is, in fact, profoundly anti-Platonic. The ordinary man is hardly Plato's ideal philosopher.

From Kant's point of view, however, Odysseus made the right choice. Kant wrote his moral philosophy for the ordinary person, for those whom Plato would have called the "local growth," and not for either philosopher kings or philosophers. "That kings should philosophize or philosophers become kings," he wrote in *Perpetual Peace*, "is not to be expected. Nor is it wished, since the possession of power inevitably corrupts the untrammeled judgment of reason" (295). Kant considered his *Foundations of the Metaphysics of Morals* to be a popular work, not a handbook for kings, and he designed it to provide a simple account of his ideas. It changed the history of thought about ethics, but not because it became a popular guide for the common person. It is comical that Kant ever believed that his work was for ordinary reading because it is, in fact, impenetrable for most people. Kant, the author of *The Critique of Judgment*, misjudged his audience. But his intentions were good, and good intentions are everything in Kant.

It is an irony, however, that Kant did eventually succeed in an indirect way in becoming a popular teacher of ethics. His ideas survived him, and they have filtered down to us through the years to become part of our everyday thinking about ethics. When people on the street speak about ethics, they speak Kant's language. And yet most of his main ideas have been rejected by today's moral philosophers, for whom he serves as something of a whipping boy. Kant symbolizes for current philosophy the error of putting too much stock in metaphysical and otherworldly ideas, and his insistence on duty strikes many modern thinkers as narrow and rigid. But Kant's moral philosophy does have a deceptively simple and practical side to it, and that is what I want to stress here along with its literary dimension.[1] My point will be, in fact, that the practical side of Kant's moral philosophy and his use of storytelling rely on each other. Only on a literary or fictional basis is practical morality possible. This is the real significance of Kant.

But I anticipate.

Kant based his ethics on the thinking abilities involved in what he called practical philosophy. The authority on practical philosophy is not the philosopher. It is the thinking person. The practical philosopher is one who makes reason the principle of his or her actions. Reason gives the kind of knowledge that may be known through the pure logic of thought, and its concepts are known by human beings *a priori*, that is, apart from habit and experience, simply because people possess a higher intelligence. According to Kant, reason determines everything that is valuable in humanity. Human beings have character by virtue (the choice of word is not arbitrary) of being rational beings. They possess dignity by virtue of their reason. They know truth by virtue of their rationality. Indeed, human beings are human only by reason of what they understand through the act of thinking.

One of the stories that Bernard Williams tells about moral philosophy in *Ethics and the Limits of Philosophy* addresses the history of thinking. Williams argues that Socrates opens the history of moral philosophy with the simple maxim, "Know yourself." So begins the history of thinking about thinking beings, or reflection. The Greeks needed to reflect on themselves, Williams explains, but they started something that we have lost control of (155–68). Today we have reached the dead end of reflection in matters ethical. Our consciousness, he claims, destroys our ethical concepts and our confidence in their application. Reflection, it seems, always finds one more skeptical argument to use against moral principles. The more we turn to reflection to achieve morality, the more frustrated we become, because we never measure up to the finer creatures of our ethical imagination. Reflection reveals nothing but moral flaws, and as we become more conscious of our moral inadequacies, we grow more and more alienated from ourselves. We may try to bury our heads in the sand and to stop thinking, Williams argues, but it is a hard road back to unconsciousness from consciousness. Indeed, it is Williams's distrust of reflection that leads him to give such strong emphasis to "thick concepts" and beliefs. Beliefs are ideas that have not yet suffered the skepticism of reflection.

Incidentally, Freud tried to make us believe that we are all essentially unconscious of our motivations. Many of us believe that he was right, but we believe in him too consciously. We remain extremely conscious of our unconscious.

Williams does not give Kant a precise role in this history of the decline of moral reflection. For Kant is not one who doubted the necessity of reflection. This virtue belongs to Hegel, who invented the idea of un-happy consciousness, or the sadness that comes from thinking too much. But Kant does have a place in the story by virtue of the fact that he was the philosopher of pure reason. Kant may offend ethics, in Williams's opinion, by giving the greatest importance to our capacity to reflect on ourselves. He may transform "ethics" into "morality," which Williams de-fines as an ethics based on rigid principles, duties, and laws. But Kant had his reasons. He emphasized reason over experience and habit because he shared the distrust of human beliefs and conventions characteristic of the Enlightenment. For the Enlightenment thinkers, unreflective beliefs were the cause of prejudice, superstition, and mental slavery, and a firmer foun-dation in clear thinking was needed. "Enlightenment," Kant wrote in "What is Enlightenment?," "is man's release from his self-incurred tute-lage. Tutelage is man's inability to make use of his understanding without direction from another" (263).

Kant's ethics are called critical because he wanted to remove the study of morality from learning by rote and everything habitual—from every-thing, that is, relying on our experience with other people in culture and not on the ability of each person to achieve a purely logical existence. Morality is not, according to Kant, learned by the observation of our-selves. It is not learned by observing the ways of the world, what is done, and how people behave. Although the German word *Sitten*, Kant ex-plained, like the Latin *mores*, means only manners and customs, morality should have nothing to do with them. Reason is the only ground for ethics. Reflection is its only method. Kant did not believe in the alienation of unhappy consciousness. In a word, he was not Hegel.

But Kant did believe in the alienating effects of experience on virtue and character. He rejected classical ethics explicitly because he did not think that virtue could be defined and valued as a mere aptitude or as a long-standing habit of morally good actions acquired by practice. Experi-ence, he explained, may teach people what will bring them satisfaction, and it may provide them with the means to seek it. But neither happiness nor satisfaction has much to do with pure reason, and ethics, for Kant, consists of the method by which people may live a life according to rea-son. Neither virtue nor character can be learned from experience, Kant concluded, because our experiences are never adequate to the complexity of life and its decisions. Rational principles are therefore necessary, and unless character is based on these principles, Kant thought, it is not sufficiently armed against either new situations or the temptations that change brings about in our all-too-human nature.

Until recently, in fact, character had fallen out of discussion in moral philosophy for precisely the reasons that Kant outlined. Character appeared for many years as a needless and artificial prop used to strengthen and to buttress morality. But, as Bernard Williams and others have argued, the objection to character and the virtues is, in reality, an attack against ethics itself. Ethics aims to examine the nature of human beings, their lives, and the places where they are found. It tries to explain how to live well in the places where people live, and it makes no sense to expel the idea of character from it, unless one is really trying to expel ethics.

Kant surely did not object to ethics. Nor did he abandon the ideas of character and virtue. He wrote a *Doctrine of Virtue*, and his ethical theory is based on the character of a practical philosopher who reflects upon life to change his or her character. The task that Kant set for himself is, simply, to ground the development of character in a method of reasoning. "When you have no character," Albert Camus writes in *The Fall*, "you have to find yourself a method." Kant's theory does not depend on character in the classical sense, since his purpose is to formulate an imperative for morality in the apparent absence of character; but character plays a primary role in his ethics nevertheless because the categorical imperative sketches out, as we will see, a "life story" that tells what consequences flow from particular situations and certain ethical choices.

Kant's world is, above all, a world of temptation, and if we are to avoid temptation, we must discover what is unchanging in the world, and only reason is unchanging. Kant believed in saintliness and human perfection, or at least in the need to attempt perfection, and this goal led him to a partial rejection of life as a means to knowledge. Here lies Kant's great melancholy and the reason why modern ethical thought has justly rejected him. Simply put, Kant was most concerned with actions of which the world has never, perhaps, had an example, with actions whose feasibility may be seriously doubted by those who base everything on experience, and yet with actions inexorably commanded by reason. He insisted that reason commands what ought to be done even though no example of it can be found and even though we have no experience with the problem in hand. He was, in short, the consummate trapeze artist.

But how do human beings perform actions of which the world, perhaps, has never had an example?

Human beings are not angels.

Neither are angels, if we believe the story of Lucifer.

The problem is, precisely, how to hear the voice of reason through the babel of the world. All human beings possess reason, but they are inclined, according to Kant, to seek pleasure and to follow the examples of other people rather than the understanding given by their own reason. How do human beings, who are creatures of the world, close their ears to the inclinations and desires belonging to their world? By what method, or principle, might they learn to listen to their own reason?

To answer this question is the avowed task of Kant's *Foundations of the Metaphysics of Morals*. Already its title reveals Kant's greatest challenge. How does one bring metaphysics, that is, what is beyond the physical world, down to earth? In Kant's vocabulary, the question is how can pure reason be transformed into practical reason? Practical reason is the application of pure reason through the power of willing to the world of human actions, thoughts, and emotions. It defines an ethics grounded on reasons so pure that they would seem to have little to do with the world. The project is sublime, ridiculous, and inconceivable. It is sublime in the ends that it sets for humanity. It is ridiculous because it requires a human life utterly alien to the nature of humanity. It is inconceivable because there is no way, within reason, to imagine how pure reason may be grounded.

Nevertheless, this is Kant's project, and his *Foundations* attempts to establish the grounds of ethics by sketching two descriptions for its readers. Both descriptions are literary, acts of storytelling, or "heuristic fictions," to use the language of *The Critique of Pure Reason*. First, Kant works to present the formula, the principle, by which people may learn to hear the voice of their own reason. He calls it, of course, the supreme principle of morality, or the categorical imperative. In most of its formulations, it requires people seeking moral understanding to act "as if" (*als ob*) they believed in a certain end or outcome in order to try on the life that it will produce. (For example: "Act as if the maxim of your action were by your will to become a universal law of nature.") In every formulation, it requires people to act according to an idea, that is, according to a story or fiction having no empirical grounds in reality. (For example: "Act only according to that maxim by which you can at the same time will that it should become a universal law.") The method of the categorical imperative, in brief, asks us to see our actions and emotions as part of a life story, and this story tells us whether we are behaving ethically.

Second, Kant opens the book with a quest for a type of character. He wants to isolate what he calls the "good will." By the good will, Kant means the character who has achieved excellence in the exercise of its will. Like Aristotle, who names the virtuous man as his target in the *Nicomachean Ethics*, Kant calls upon us to imagine the good will. But unlike Aristotle, who refuses to give us examples of the virtuous man in action, Kant carefully illustrates his philosophical ideas with stories that show us how the good will goes about exercising its will. We are constantly led to imagine our own actions in comparison with those of the good will, but the good will is ultimately nothing other than an "aesthetic device," as Kant honestly admits. The personification of virtue and vice is always an aesthetic device, Kant claims in *The Doctrine of Virtue*, but it has the virtue of pointing the way to a moral sense (60). It belongs to an "aesthetic of morals," from which spring subjective images and symbols of those ideas necessary to a metaphysics of morals (a morals based on reason). Or, as Kant later put it in the famous formula at the heart of *The Critique of Judgment*, "Beauty is the symbol of morality."

Kant's use of literary devices to describe ethics may strike one as contradictory, but it reveals that he shares at least one tendency with his classical ancestors: his ethics is literary. The *Foundations of the Metaphysics of Morals* is, of course, an ethical treatise, but it stands with *The Doctrine of Virtue* as one of Kant's most literary works. He tells story after story about the desires of people and how they go about trying to fulfill them. In contrast, *The Critique of Judgment*, which supposedly gives Kant's theory of art, is almost completely devoid of stories: Kant gives only a few examples of beautiful poetry, and most people would not agree with his selections.

From the first page of the *Foundations*, Kant makes it clear that the "character of the good will" is of the utmost importance. He is as much in pursuit of an aesthetic of morals as the metaphysics of morals. He begins by isolating willing as the essential component of character, and explains that morality depends for its existence on "character." Kant believed that acquiring good character is the only moral purpose worth pursuing because character lays the groundwork for dealing with all moral problems. The good will, Kant explains, is not good because of what it does or accomplishes or because it achieves a proposed goal. It is good only because it wills. It is good in itself. Unlike his classical forebears, Kant does not think that actions or choices reveal character. Character lies in volition as such. Character is virtuous solely on the basis of its intentions. Kant illustrates this point with a startling and fanciful image. Even if it should happen, he insists, by some unfortunate fate or selfish provision of a step-motherly nature, that the good will should be wholly lacking in the power to accomplish its intentions and purpose, and if its greatest efforts should have no results, if there remained only the good will of itself, this good will would still sparkle like a jewel in its own right as a prize having its full worth in itself. For Kant, good intentions are everything. Of the categorical imperative, for instance, Kant writes: "What is essentially good in it consists in the intention, the result being what it may" (38).

The good will is good in its own right. It depends on nothing of this world but only on the strength of its own willing. Kant's good will is cut off completely from the world in which virtue would seem to have its greatest call, and his ideal of virtue therefore seems inexplicable. But the source of this character's goodness explains its virtue. Kant establishes the good will as the supreme mediator between reason and desire. It is through willing that character exercises reason and shuns the inclinations and desires that abase it. Willing listens to the voice of reason, and through reason, it achieves a form of virtue and character that is invulner-able to accidents, misfortunes, and the corruption of other people. The great classical question concerning happiness had always, until Kant, been formulated in terms of the end of human life. Could a person be called happy while he or she was still living? Only upon death could one's lot in life be assessed, the ancients surmised, and some of them doubted even this principle, cautioning that the fate of one's grandchildren could influ-ence happiness. But Kant's idea of happiness, which is the stepchild of reason, relies wholly on the good will. Virtuous people are in possession of themselves, and virtue cannot be taken from them. No matter what befalls them, if they continue to will and will well, they guard their reason and thus their virtue. The good will is the fulcrum of all morality. It allows reason to lift the world. To destroy the subject of morality in one's own person, Kant warns, is to root out the existence of morality itself from the world. Morality exists in the world only because human beings treat themselves and others according to the dictates of reason, that is, as per-sons. It cannot be handed down from above or enforced by the laws of courts, if each person refuses to summon the gift of reason.

It should now be clear how important the idea of character is in Kant's ethics. Its importance far exceeds anything described in classical moral philosophy, although, admittedly, Kant's description of character is highly theoretical, schematic, and fictive, when compared to the classical idea of character modeled on experience and life in the city. To repeat, for Kant, morality depends entirely on good character, not on action, choices, or social effects, and building character is the only moral purpose worth pursuing. It should also be clear, then, that Kant believes that we can successfully transform our character. Character is not something that we are born with and must live with throughout our lives, except insofar as reason is the possession of all rational beings. Nor does character in Kant consist of a collection of attitudes that we hold toward others. It is an attitude held toward oneself. Kant argues that we can build character through self-reflection, self-analysis, and self-correction. All rational beings possess the potential for good character by virtue of their reason, but virtue must be acquired nevertheless, and not by experience but by practicing the strenuous art of thinking and willing. The good will learns its goodness neither through imitation nor through threats but by being put to the proof of combat with the inner enemy. The field of battle for moral practice is the will itself. The combatant is alone: the self struggles against itself.

The city of the ancients is now the human soul, and it has one inhabitant.

(Notice how incompatible Kant's idea of the will is with Freud's notion of the self, in which the unconscious subverts conscious attempts to rise above neurotic and psychopathological impulses. It is difficult in the age of Freud to understand Kant.)

To conclude that one can build character by exercising the will, as it were, is all well and good. But how does one go about it? One cannot spontaneously do everything that one wills to do. Nor does the unpracticed will have a clear view of its own ends. How does one build character?

As the supreme principle of morality, the categorical imperative provides the means of building character expressed in abstract form. It gives the method by which the good will practices willing according to reason. It clarifies the ends of willing for the good will. Kant defines the categorical imperative as follows: "Act only according to that maxim by which you can at the same time will that it should become a universal law" (44). Here Kant understands a "maxim" to be a subjective principle of conduct and a "law" to be an objective and general principle of conduct. Most often, the categorical imperative has been interpreted in terms of the golden rule: "do unto others as you would have them do unto you"; and to a great extent this interpretation makes sense, because Kant insists that ordinary people may well understand the categorical imperative better than philosophers who look too hard for subtleties.

The categorical imperative appears to be a formula of the most abstract kind, and in the case of the philosophical tradition, its application always raises a series of objections that makes Kant's ideas seem even more abstract and otherworldly. Two interpretations in particular lead us away from what is most practical and literary in Kant's formula, and they must be discussed before we may turn to the idea of literary ethics once more. The first interpretation pivots on the idea of law. According to it, Kant tried to discover the principle of morality, but he managed only to reproduce the ethical attitude of his own time: the categorical imperative is nothing but a manifestation of Kant's Prussian sense of duty. The categorical imperative thus fails to capture a universal idea of morality. Moreover, it represents a most obsequious and demeaning attitude toward law, allowing it to assume an oppressive and awesome power over the individual.

I believe that this interpretation misunderstands the meaning of law in Kant's writings. When Kant introduces us to the idea of the law early in the *Foundations*, he describes it in a particular, although exaggerated way. He begins by supposing the existence of a perfectly good will, a holy will, and proceeds to trace out its relation to the law. Kant explains that the perfectly good will gives itself the law, and that it can bend to no external "ought." Kant continues: "The 'ought' is here out of place, for the volition of itself is necessarily in unison with the law" (35). Laws are for Kant mere expressions of the relation between the objective principles of willing in general and the subjective imperfections of the individual human will. Put simply, good laws are the manifestation of the good will, and if we experience difficulty in obeying them, it is an indication of the amount of character building necessary to bring ourselves into conformity with the good will. The point to stress is that the law is not an order external to character. The law is the supreme manifestation of character. In other words, law is the property of good character. When the good will gives itself the law, it affirms itself. The giving of the law to oneself is the supreme expression of self-sufficiency, virtuous character, and freedom.

Kant's concept of duty, which has blackened him in the eyes of so many modern thinkers, involves the same process, but it expresses it from the point of view of the good will. Duty is simply Kant's term for the application of law to the will through the power of willing. The good will, however, does not consider itself to be willing according to a self-given law. The ends of willing appear in a subjective light "as if" they were the duty of the good will. Duty is the "heuristic fiction" that the good will summons when it is willing. It does not think of the law of the land. It obeys its own individual sense of duty. It is important to stress this subjective feeling for two reasons. First, it reveals how literary devices help to orient the good will. Second, it stresses Kant's belief that law originates in the individual will and not in government or institutions. This is not to say that Kant did not reproduce the morality of his age. He did. It is to say that from Kant's point of view the good will always reproduces the good laws of its age, since these laws are in a real sense already the results of the good will's acts of willing.

The second interpretation that clouds Kant's purpose turns on the idea of universalization. It also depends on viewing Kant's ideas from an excessively linguistic perspective. When Kant discusses the relation between character and law, the inescapable but vertiginous conclusion emerges that both law and character are expressions of freedom. The only laws of willing are laws of freedom, and the good character gives himself or herself this law. The vertiginous circularity of the process represents Kant's idea of individual freedom, or autonomy. Kant states that no example of this freedom can be given. He, in fact, calls it a mere idea, that is, a fiction, but it remains a necessary and practical fiction. Indeed, Kant concludes the *Foundations* by exclaiming that freedom is incomprehensible, although he remains confident that we can comprehend its incomprehensibility.

Now, freedom is tied intricately to universalization as Kant describes it. Kant always insists that freedom, not universality, is the end of morality. Freedom is, in short, the principle of morality. When we apply the categorical imperative to a subjective maxim and will that it be a universal law, the end result must be freedom. A game currently exists in Kant studies in which his critics try to discover subjective maxims that can be universalized according to his formula and still have disastrous results. These critics are interested only in the process of universalization, as if they were playing with a Rubic's Cube or an algebraic equation, and not with questions of human responsibility and survival. For them, universalization is a linguistic process, and not a matter of human beings. (Ironically, they most often ascribe this abstract perspective to Kant himself and attack him for it.) But moral questions cannot be posed in a vacuum. They require a context and an understanding of the particular issues involved. Otherwise our answers will be unintelligible and irresponsible.

Alasdair MacIntyre, in *A Short History of Ethics*, attacks Kant for naively believing that universalization is the principle of morality:

For the Kantian test of a true moral precept is that it is one that I can consistently universalize. In fact, however, with sufficient ingenuity almost every precept can be consistently universalized. For all that I need to do is characterize the proposed action in such a way that the maxim will permit me to do what I want while prohibiting others from doing what would nullify the maxim if universalized. Kant asks if I can consistently universalize the maxim that I may break my promises whenever it suits me. Suppose, however, that he had inquired whether I can consistently universalize the maxim "I may break my promises only when . . ." [MacIntyre's ellipses]. The gap is filled by a description devised so that it will apply to my present circumstances but to very few others, and to none such that if someone else obeyed the maxim, it would inconvenience me, let alone show the maxim incapable of consistent universality. It follows that in practice the test of the categorical imperative imposes restrictions only on those insufficiently equipped with ingenuity. (197–98)

MacIntyre understands only too well that Kant did not desire the ingenious to escape the test of morality. Rather, he believes that Kant made a mistake in formulating the categorical imperative. The mistake, however, lies in MacIntyre's reading. MacIntyre makes the mistake because, like the ingenious, he pays too much attention to the tricks that can be played with language and not enough attention to Kant's stories about how the categorical imperative works. In other words, at this early date, MacIntyre has not yet developed an interest in stories. He is more interested in language than in literature. And I must add that when he turns in later books to the study of narrative, he does not reevaluate or change his view of Kant. MacIntyre defines ethics in *After Virtue* as the ability of thought to capture in stories the narrative dimension of human life, and he insists that the fit between ethics and life be measured according to their parallel interest in narrative form. But he does not recognize that Kant formulates the categorical imperative in precisely the same way, and so Kant remains his nemesis.

When Kant formulates the categorical imperative, he tells four stories. They are not characterized, nor need they be, by an immense flair for literature. They have a plot and characters with specific personalities, virtues, and vices, and they need little else to serve their purpose. They are, respectively, tales about a suicide, about a man who breaks his promise to pay back borrowed money, about another who possesses sufficient comfort in life that he is tempted not to develop his talents, and about a man who is well off but decides not to contribute to the welfare of those less fortunate than he. The last story even has dialogue: "What concern of mine is it? Let each one be as happy as heaven wills, or as he can make himself; I will not take anything from him or even envy him; but to his welfare or to his assistance in time of need I have no desire to contribute" (47).

In the case of each story, Kant decides that the maxim of individual conduct cannot be willed to become a universal law by the person in the story. The reason is not that the world would become a terrible place but that the process of willing would destroy itself, and the will that destroys itself ceases to be free. About suicide, Kant explains, "I cannot dispose of man in my own person so as to mutilate, corrupt, or kill him" (54). Kant often refers to the idea of "humanity in one's person," and it is crucial to accent it because it exposes the great degree to which the categorical imperative describes a process of character building. The good character gives the law to himself or herself, but if the will cannot survive this law, the law becomes not an expression of the will but its contradiction, and the will loses its power to converse with its better self. The categorical imperative puts one into communication with the "humanity in one's own person," and it asks whether we are to become like this humanity or liken it to ourselves. If we remake it in our own image, instead of the reverse, we must live in the world of our own making. The humanity in our person loses its voice, or perhaps we no longer have ears to hear it.

MacIntyre argues that a consistent universalization could be invented in which someone wills a law that applies to oneself but not to others. He makes this point because he believes that universality implies the presence of others, but, for Kant, the good will, not a community, is the center of willing. This is why Hegel accused Kant of creating an ethic of the individual. Hegel was right: Kant's ethics begins with the individual and bases everything else on his or her capacity to will. The good will, then, does not will for others. It wills only for itself. There is only one person involved in the formulation of the categorical imperative, and it is the person trying to discover whether his or her conduct will be moral. The categorical imperative designs a personal and fictional sphere of character building, intentionally removed from the influence of society, the experience of others, and previous habits. It is a method in which I tell myself a story about myself in which I meet myself. If the "man in my own person" allows me to survive, if I can live with myself, my maxim can be treated as if it were a universal law. If the "man in my own person" does not allow me to survive, if I cannot live with myself, my maxim is contradictory and self-destructive.

Kant's description of the categorical imperative finds an echo in his thoughts about conscience. In *The Doctrine of Virtue*, he portrays the conceptions of our conscience with a similar image. The moral disposition called conscience has, according to Kant, something peculiar about it. Even though it seems to be about the private affairs of a person with himself or herself, we experience the necessity of obeying our conscience "as if" it were another person's bidding. The man accused by the court of conscience, Kant explains, is one and the same person with the judge of the court. Kant speaks specifically of "a twofold personage, a doubled self who, on the one hand, has to stand in fear and trembling at the bar of the tribunal which is yet entrusted to him, but who, on the other hand, must himself administer the office of the judge which he holds by inborn authority" (104). This same twofold personage emerges in the exercise of the categorical imperative. Self and self converse, and the world has no ears to hear the conversation. It is a story told about oneself to oneself.

Note well, however, that the method of the categorical imperative does not ultimately exclude the idea of a community of rational beings. As a method for willing, the categorical imperative puts the seeker of morality into contact with reason, and it is a given of reason, according to Kant, that all human beings possess reason. If I learn to live with myself according to reason, then, I have learned to live within the community of rational beings, because each individual's reason puts him or her in communication with the "humanity in one's own person," and respecting this humanity leads everyone to similar moral conclusions. When the good will wills according to reason, then, it inhabits what Kant calls a "notional republic," that is, the city of reason.

In other words, when Kant accepts it as given that all human beings possess an equal capacity for reason, he builds before the fact the very community that is to come about as a result of living according to rational principles. That reason is a political or social way of understanding is presupposed by the claim that all rational beings possess it. Similarly, Kant accepts as given that freedom is exercised in willing and that the will accepts freedom as its end. Nowhere does Kant demonstrate or prove these assumptions. He states merely that they arise from pure reason. They are givens, beautiful fictions, and once we accept them, Kant's other assumptions fall into place.

If Kant is to be attacked, it is against these beautiful fictions that we must arm ourselves. The animal whom Kant wishes to transform into an angel turns out from the start to have been a sheep in wolf's clothing. But I for one have no desire to attack Kant's ideals of humanity's freedom or its innate capacity for virtue. They are among our most beautiful ideas, and we should permit them to remain among us if only to give ourselves a moment of repose from the uglier ideas of the world.

Let me, instead, play out Kant's fourth example about the wealthy man who does not desire to harm or to help others. Tolstoy could have written this story. Indeed, he did write it many times. The man thinks to himself: "I will not harm anyone. I will not envy anyone. I will not be evil. But I want to be left alone. Let each man take care of himself. Let heaven take care of the poor." Kant usefully explains that the human race is not endangered by this view. He in fact concludes that if everyone behaved this way, the world would probably be a better place. There is no problem, Kant finds, that such a law could exist. But Kant insists that the wealthy man could not will that such a law exist: "For a will which resolved this would conflict with itself, since instances can often arise in which he would need the love and sympathy of others, and in which he would have robbed himself, by such a law of nature springing from his own will, of all hope of the aid he desires" (47).

Kant asks the wealthy man to tell himself a story about himself in a world populated only by men in his own person. Can the wealthy man wish that he would live in a world where he would not help himself when in need? In such circumstances, for I insist that the story has precise circumstances in which people with wealth and people in trouble exist, the wealthy man could not survive. By willing that the maxim of his action be treated as if it were a universal law, the wealthy man wills that he not exist. He wills not to be willing, and since willing is necessary to change a maxim into a law, no such transformation may take place because the agent of willing has literally disappeared.

We may now understand why MacIntyre misreads Kant. MacIntyre argues that ingenious people may create a categorical imperative worded in such a way that it would apply to others but make an exception of themselves. But no self and other exist in the categorical imperative. All agents in the story are facsimiles of the seeker of moral knowledge. If I will to be the exception to my will, I except myself from willing, and deny my own existence. Universality is not the key to the categorical imperative. The key is freedom and how character wishes to represent itself. Kant's theory of the categorical imperative provides a method of building character in the absence of all social supports. It offers an ideal of character to an age dreadfully suspicious of everything on which character has been traditionally built. But ethical character, like literary character, cannot exist without a life story.

In the final analysis, then, the life stories illuminating the categorical imperative are more important than the principle of morality itself, or, rather, the categorical imperative would make little sense in their absence, because the end of the imperative is to tell the story of the moral. Without Kant's stories, the categorical imperative would resemble a proverb whose meaning has been lost in the din of time. It would be as airy and otherworldly, as worthless, as Kant's many critics have tried to make it. Stories put the categorical imperative into practice. In fact, there is no way of practicing the method of the categorical imperative without telling a story.

MacIntyre's reading of Kant is therefore inspired in a special sense. He understands that the categorical imperative always contains a gap that must be filled by my subjective and particular conditions. The filling of that gap is an act of storytelling, a hypothetical life story, in which I test my desires and intentions in a world in which I will be the immediate object of my own actions. The categorical imperative carries the necessity of asking, then, whether particular actions may take place in the world, and this world is a place in the ethical sense described by Homer. For all of Kant's otherworldliness and saintly aspirations, this one fact is unavoidable, and it gives his ethics a dimension as practical as any conceived of by his classical precursors. Kant's moral philosophy is practical, but it cannot exist without storytelling because the idea of ethical behavior arrives in the creation of a story. The categorical imperative is the supreme principle of morality, but it is also an invitation to literature.

CHAPTER 9

∽

Kant and the Origins
of Totalitarianism

> The moral principle that it is one's duty to speak the truth
> if it were taken singly and unconditionally, would make
> all society impossible. We have the proof of this in the
> very direct consequences which have been drawn from
> this principle by a German philosopher, who goes so far
> as to affirm that to tell a falsehood to a murderer who
> asked us whether our friend, of whom he was in pursuit,
> had not taken refuge in our house, would be a crime.
> —Benjamin Constant on Kant (1797)

In a certain sense, insofar as it wishes to deny, to correct, or to surpass
him, modern moral philosophy remains something of a postscript to
Kant. But we have not yet learned to see that modern responses to Kant
may well be derived from and surpassed by the modernity of Kant's own
ethics. This, at least, will be my argument here. Indeed, it sometimes
seems that the express purpose of modern ethics is to occult Kant's modernity, either by viewing him as a representative of the outmoded and
failed philosophy of the Age of Reason or as the slave of duty, the one
concept that has come to be most suspected by ethical thought in the
twentieth century. Hitler, it seems, exposes how thoroughly unmodern
are Kant's claims for reason and duty. The dream of reason supposedly
produces Hitler's Germany and, after Auschwitz, the concept of duty ac-

quires the clear and shameful distinction of being able to justify any action, no matter how monstrous. Modern ethical thinkers associate Kantian reasoning and duty with a kind of monstrosity as well. My duty is to obey the imperative of reason, Kant says, and not to look to the world of experience. As long as I do my duty, I will not be held responsible for the consequences of my actions. Few attitudes are as repulsive to modern thought.

Alasdair MacIntyre's *A Short History of Ethics* captures the modern critical attitude toward Kant and alludes to the historical origins of our distaste for him:

> Anyone educated into the Kantian notion of duty will, so far, have been educated into easy conformism with authority. . . . [Kant] hated servility and valued independence of mind. Paternalism, so he held, was the grossest form of despotism. But the consequences of his doctrines, in German history at least, suggest that the attempt to find a moral standpoint completely independent of the social order may be a quest for an illusion, a quest that renders one a mere conformist servant of the social order much more than does the morality of those who recognize the impossibility of a code which does not to some extent at least express the wants and needs of men in particular social circumstances.   (198)

The "consequences" represents as well as any word what modern moral philosophers have singled out as being of primary importance in ethics. Both Benjamin Constant and Alasdair MacIntyre agree on this point. The modern world, they explain, brings unexpected consequences from every action, and we moderns no longer believe that simple rules, codes, or imperatives are capable of regulating the disorder and unpredictability of moral life. Strong adherence to such codes makes society impossible. Rather, we have to look to the consequences, and the only method of doing this is to immerse ourselves in the dense texture and fabric of our society, to come to know ourselves as social beings, that we might understand the network of relations in which our actions take place.

However we describe Kant's ethics, whether as individualistic or as subservient to the authority of duty, it seems to fail to meet this description of how things are. First, Kant's almost solipsistic emphasis on the reasoning individual, in which the good will obeys no one but himself or herself, appears to miss the point: in the modern world of consequences, we must attend to political life and its intricate web of relationships. There is no place for a morality independent of the social order. Kant's preference for moral autonomy appears inadequate as a response to the modern situation in particular and to the ethics of situations in general. Second, duty now belongs to our view of "German history," as MacIntyre puts it. We view duty as an opiate, a blindness, a rationalization, capable of condoning tyranny and conformity to violence. It is not a concept of respect for society but its nemesis. Rigid laws, totalizing views of conduct, duty—these are the tools of fascism and the enemies of the modern ethical project.

It is true that Kant grew rigid in his ethical views, especially in *The Critique of Practical Reason*. It is also true—we need not try to conceal it—that he tends to express his ethics in the vocabulary of duty. Duty begins as a "heuristic fiction" that represents how willing is viewed by the one who wills. It does not, at first, represent law at all, unless it be the law that the individual willingly gives to himself or herself. But Kant easily takes up this fiction and speaks from within it, as if there really were a concept of duty deriving from outside the sphere of willing, and this kind of talk is especially disconcerting to modern thinkers, who are all too anxious to face the immediate consequences of actions and to avoid the kind of conformism that made Germany history possible.

MacIntyre's purpose in the passage quoted above is to render judgment on Kant's role in German history. He expresses his moral outrage at Kant's inability to face the consequences of his ideas for the Third Reich. It is MacIntyre's summary statement on Kant's failings as a philosopher, but it comes, interestingly, after he has analyzed a story that Kant tells to Benjamin Constant. Constant is also concerned that Kant fails to face the consequences drawn from his moral principles, but he does not have the benefit of so powerful an illustration of consequences as MacIntyre finds in German history. It is MacIntyre, of course, who gives Kant's story this modern context, not Constant, but I want to suggest that Kant's modernity lies precisely in the fact that MacIntyre can summon this context. Kant's story fits these circumstances because it is already ahead of both MacIntyre and Constant. MacIntyre has history on his side because he can give Kant's story its proper and complete illustration, whereas Constant cannot, but in the final analysis neither MacIntyre nor Constant possesses as modern a view of consequences as Kant displays in his little story about whether it is right to lie to a murderer in pursuit of a friend. I am not indulging in a paradoxical and painful anachronism. Constant cannot comprehend the kinds of consequences that figure in later German history, and his criticism of Kant takes place, accordingly, on the grounds of the simple argument whether one should sacrifice human life to save the truth. MacIntyre does understand the consequences of trying to save a human life in the context of German history, and he attacks Kant, strangely, for not being ahead of his own time, for not knowing as much history as he does. If we believe MacIntyre's criticism, Kant not only fails to see the moral consequences of the concept of duty for Nazi Germany, he contributes to the construction of this concept and shares in its historical shame. But, in fact, the opposite case is true: Kant's story faces these consequences more directly than MacIntyre can ever hope to imagine.

The story of the Constant-Kant debate is interesting in itself in addition to providing the necessary context for understanding what Kant is trying to say and why modern moral philosophers should object to it.

The topic is, of course, truth-telling. Constant argues that Kant's moral principle against lying would make society impossible, if taken unconditionally, and he attacks Kant for having said, apparently, that we have no right to tell a falsehood, even if it means that we must tell a murderer where to find a friend. Kant's response to Constant, "On a Supposed Right to Tell Lies from Benevolent Motives," accepts Constant's little moral narrative as the testing grounds of his ethics, even though it is not at all clear that Kant can most advantageously explain his ideas with this example. But the topic is truth, and it is rather a matter of telling the truth. "I hereby admit," Kant writes, "that I have really said this in some place which I cannot now recollect" (361). In truth, Kant does not know where he has told this story. He has told it some place. But this place is now, unavoidably, "On a Supposed Right to Tell Lies from Benevolent Motives," which becomes at this moment both a discourse on truth-telling and an example of it. It is perhaps ironic that Kant's forgetfulness means that Constant has the privilege of telling the story to Kant as an example of why his ethics fails, and that Kant must retell it to show that it is, in fact, the one story that demonstrates why we may wish to think twice about rejecting his ethics for the modern world. Whether the story is originally Kant's is hard to say. But Kant makes it his story.

How we understand Kant's story, I insist again, will be a modern problem. The story is way ahead of us, which means that Kant is here more modern than his modern critics. More specifically, he is more modern in his use of storytelling. One of the limitations of my previous descriptions of Kant's storytelling was that I represented it as unavoidably flat and predictable. The categorical imperative commands that we tell a story along predictable lines in order, precisely, to predict an outcome. My point was to illustrate Kant's literary ethics and to show to what extent he needed storytelling to enact his supreme principle of morality, but I suspect that some readers found Kant's stories and my praise of them to be rather self-serving and lacking in aesthetic appeal. The simple fact remains that storytelling in Kant exists to tell the story of the moral. Those who want the story of the story will find him disappointing in matters aesthetical. I do not mean to suggest that Kant's story of the murderer in search of his friend will be any less moral. It still exists to tell the moral of the story. But the situation that it evokes is vertiginously complex, nauseatingly so, to anticipate Sartre, and we have not yet come to appreciate how thoroughly modern are its telling, the situation that it summons, and, I dare say, its aesthetics.

The fullness of Kant's account emerges directly from his desire to meet Constant's objections point by point. Such exposition is characteristic of Kant's rigor as a philosopher, but what is most striking here is the fact that his ethical argument is inseparable from his storytelling. Constant names two major objections. The first is immediately intelligible in terms of the story. To tell the truth is a duty, Constant explains, but only toward him or her who has a right to the truth. But no person, he continues, has a right to a truth that injures others. The second objection is more technical. It concerns what might be considered one of Kant's favorite problems. Once we understand that a principle is true, Constant argues, we must not allow its apparent inapplicability to persuade us to abandon it. For such situations usually arise because we are ignorant of the "middle principles" that contain the means of its application, and we must, consequently, attend to these principles. To put it simply, Constant believes that a truth should never be abandoned prematurely, if it seems inapplicable, because political solutions may be found to put it into action. Kant is, of course, the philosopher most concerned with translating pure reason into the practical sphere, and he will agree to a certain extent with Constant's defense of inapplicable principles, but he refuses to espouse purely political solutions.

Kant's response to these two objections contains a subtle elucidation of his philosophy. To Constant's claim that people have a right to truth, he responds that the claim has no meaning. Rather, he explains, each person has a right to his or her own truthfulness. As always, Kant begins with the individual, and when speaking in terms of individuals, it makes no sense to legislate to others before legislating to oneself. We have no right to be told the truth, therefore, only a duty to be truthful ourselves. In his *Foundations of the Metaphysics of Morals*, Kant made it inescapably clear that morality in the world has no hope of surviving, if it is not based on an individual act of willing for oneself. Kant is here true to that principle.

The issue at hand, however, is not whether one has a right to one's own truthfulness but whether one has the right to be *untruthful*. Moreover, if we accept Constant's objections, the question becomes, as Kant phrases it, "whether, in order to prevent a misdeed that threatens him or some one else, he is not actually *bound* to be untruthful in a certain statement to which an *unjust compulsion* forces him" (362; my emphases). Notice two points about Kant's exposition of the problem. First, he stresses detail. The problem concerns a certain statement aimed at preventing a misdeed. Second, and this will be of prime importance later, Kant insists that the situation involves "unjust compulsion." He makes this insistence no less than seven times in his short essay. I raise these two points because Kant is often attacked for ignoring details in favor of principles and because many critics of Kant's argument with Constant ignore the fact that Kant insists that the person in the dilemma has no choice whether to speak. It is not, then, a situation in which a simpleton in love with the truth sees the murderer's question as one more grand opportunity to run off at the mouth with truth. Rather, it resembles certain events in German history.

Constant desires, as Kant sees it, to transform untruthfulness into a duty. He argues that we are bound, obligated, to lie in such cases. But Kant cannot approve of such a perversion of principle, and he provides two distinct arguments against it. One is an ethical argument, but the second is juridical. The first is familiar to all readers of Kant. Truthfulness cannot be avoided, Kant insists, however great the disadvantage to oneself or to any other, because one does wrong to humanity in general by lying. In *The Doctrine of Virtue*, in fact, Kant goes so far as to name lying as the deed most destructive of moral life: "The greatest violation of man's duty to himself merely as a moral being (to humanity in his own person) is the contrary of truthfulness, the *lie*" (92). When I choose to lie, I create a situation in which all declarations lose their value in truth. My decision to lie is subject to Kant's categorical formula, and once inserted into that formula, it enacts a story in which I cannot be expected to tell myself the truth, and if I cannot expect the truth from myself, no one can expect the truth from anyone else, and all contract based on our common humanity must perish. All rights founded on agreement—and there are many—cease to exist.

Second, Kant finds Constant's argument weak in a juridical sense, and his rebuttal is unexpectedly sensitive to the problems of defending one's choices to other people. It is also at this point that Kant's response becomes most literary. It takes on a denseness and fictive quality unsurpassed by other passages in his work. In fact, its aesthetic quality is so obvious and so well-expressed that Sartre could not resist making it the kernel of his own story, "The Wall." If I choose to lie to the murderer, Kant points out, I make myself legally responsible for the consequences, whereas public justice can find no fault with me, no matter what happens, if I tell the truth. If I lie, it may happen that I will find myself accused of being an accessory to murder, even though this situation can only be described as an accident, that is, fraught with the peril that comes with being caught up in unexpected events that cannot be adequately justified in public accountings of my actions.

Kant elaborates the perils of lying by giving the conclusion of his story two very different twists. Suppose, on the one hand, that I tell the truth to the murderer, and he enters the house to kill my friend. It is possible that in the meantime my friend might have left the house unobserved, and the murder will not as a result take place. It may also happen, Kant says, that the murderer, while looking for my friend, might be caught by neighbors, and the deed prevented. But suppose, on the other hand, that I choose to lie and tell the murderer that my friend has gone out. What if, unknown to me, my friend has actually left the house, so that the murderer meets him in the street and kills him? I might with justice, Kant warns, be accused of causing the death. In the public sphere, he concludes, whoever tells a lie, however good his or her intentions may be, must answer for the consequences of it and must pay the penalty for them, however unforeseen they may have been.

I again remind the reader that Kant's subject is not ethics per se but public justice. He is in no way arguing that we should avoid lying to escape public punishment but exposing the practical fact that lying does have specific juridical and social effects that people will inevitably have to face once they embark on the course of lying. In short, Kant possesses a thorough understanding of political consequences, but he rejects them as guides to moral conduct nevertheless, and perhaps for the very reason that he does possess such a good understanding of them. Rather, Kant concludes, for ethical reasons (the only correct and reasonable guide to conduct in his view), that we should embrace truthfulness when we have no choice whether to speak.

Here we should pause to make some observations about Kant's ethical storytelling. First, Kant's account seems quite impossible and farfetched. How in the world, we might ask with exasperation, can we be expected to attend to such consequences as Kant here describes? Am I really to tell the murderer where my friend is in the hope that he has moved to another location or that my neighbors will suddenly appear to save him? Imagine the shame of sacrificing him to the truth. It may be true that public justice will find no fault in my truth, but I will still suffer publicly for seeming to turn my friend over to a murderer. How, in fact, can I be sure of my own motives? I may tell myself that it is my duty to tell the truth, but perhaps I am really exchanging my life for my friend's. But lying is not necessarily the better choice. What happens if I lie, and my lie gives my friend away in spite of my best efforts? Imagine the piercing absurdity of being tried as an accessory to murder, after having tried to save my friend with a lie.

Kant is describing an impossible situation. There can be no winners here, unless, it seems, fate intervenes to save us.

But is not the impossibility of the story exactly the point of Kant's argument? Anything can happen, he seems to say. Things fall apart. Things fall together. The world is not an ordered and predictable place. Who are we to think that we can see everything with a single glance? Kant does not give voice to this kind of hysteria. He never says, as the Existentialists liked to put it, life is absurd. He believes in reason, and reason dictates for him the simple truth that truthfulness is the unconditional command of reason, and not to be limited by any political expediency. The point to understand, finally, is not that Kant refuses to face the consequences of his principles. He shows a clear understanding of the pain involved in such consequences, and he accepts them. These are the only consequences that he is willing to face because he does not believe that any other consequences can be faced. The other consequences occur too late in the game to count as reasons. They mean the end of reason.

I will return to Kant's story and its consequences below, when they may be placed with greater ease in the context of German history. In the meanwhile, let us pass on to Constant's second objection but not before noting, one last time, how truly unfathomable is Kant's story. There is something raw and distasteful about it. It offends our reason. It reminds us of Kafka (or of Sartre, but without the heavy hand of his philosophizing). And yet, this Kafkaesque tale is Kant's defense against the Kafkaesque perception that lying might become a universal principle.

Constant's second objection explains that we must not lose a first principle to impractical ideas but look for the middle principles by the means of which it may be put into practice. He is, of course, posing his principle that we have a duty to lie to save human life against Kant's impractical idea that we have a duty to be truthful, no matter what the social and political consequences. The argument is technical, I repeat, but what is most important is easily stressed. Constant is making an argument for a distinctly political and social view of justice. He rejects, for example, Kant's unconditional duty to truthfulness because it would apparently make society impossible. He claims that we are bound to lie to the murderer because of the danger to society. Middle principles are the bridge between first principles and practice in Constant's explanation, and his example of them expounds a strictly political case. In a small society, he explains, the first principle of equality may be directly applied because each person can contribute to the formation of laws. But in a large society, with many members, a middle principle is needed. Here it is impossible that each person contribute to legislation, and we require, as a middle principle, the idea of a *representative*, through whom legislation by all can be effected. Constant insists that any attempt to apply within a large society the first principle of equality without the mediation of the middle principle, representation, will infallibly bring about the destruction of that society.

The problem, of course, and Kant notes it, is that no middle principle exists in the case of telling the truth to the murderer. That is exactly the problem with some situations. There are not always easy transitions from first principles to their application. Constant rejects Kant's principle because he can find no middle principle, but he abandons at the same time, according to Kant, his own view of principles. A principle recognized as true, Constant insists, must never be abandoned, however obviously danger may seem to be involved in it. But Constant, of course, denies the truth of Kant's argument because of its dangerous consequences for society.

Kant once again rejects Constant's argument. According to Kant, Constant has an excessively bureaucratic view of justice. He wants his middle principles, "the mechanisms of administration of justice," as Kant calls them, more than he wants first principles. Constant wishes to subordinate justice to a political system, so that it may be suitably carried out. But

Kant's ultimate point, and his reproof against Constant, remains that justice must never be accommodated to politics. Rather, the political system must always be accommodated to justice. All practical principles of justice, Kant concludes, must contain strict truths, and middle principles should contain the closer definition of their application to actual cases and never exceptions to truths because exceptions destroy the universality by which alone truths may bear the name of principles.

I have now taken Kant's argument as far as it will go within the context of his debate with Constant. The context is limited, but its limitations arise more from Constant's side of the argument than from Kant's. MacIntyre gives their debate another dimension by invoking German history and of course he has every right to do so, but not because Kant's ideas lead to this unfortunate history but because his story responds to it before the fact. More than anything else, it is the content of Kant's story, not the history of German philosophy, that compels MacIntyre to invoke the history of totalitarianism, and he is not the first to be stirred in this manner. Both Jean-Paul Sartre and Hannah Arendt, before him, find themselves suddenly Kantian, perhaps in spite of themselves, when they read Kant's little story as an experience of totalitarian history.

In 1937, Sartre published his first political fiction. He called the story "The Wall" ("Le Mur"). It describes the Spanish Civil War and the dilemma of a revolutionary, Pablo Ibbieta, who is captured by the fascist government. Ibbieta and two other prisoners, only one of whom is a revolutionary, are sentenced without trial to die at dawn. Sartre spends enormous energy describing the physiognomy of terror experienced by the three as the night wears on. They grow increasingly numb and alienated from their own bodies. They wet their pants without realizing it. They sweat bullets, although they wear only scraps of clothing and the night is bitterly cold. At one point, Ibbieta captures his feelings of alienation from his own body by thinking that he has been somehow attached to an enormous vermin. His consciousness hovers above his verminous body, both detesting it and disavowing that this body, which is to die, has anything to do with his real person.

Ibbieta takes the same attitude toward the other prisoners. They are physically repulsive to him, and Sartre's description of their bodies lingers over their ugliness, detailing bald patches, rings of fat around bellies, the stench of urine, and dead and inexpressive eyes. Ibbieta feels "inhuman," no longer sensing the slightest sympathy for the suffering of his friends.

He has no desire to touch them or even to reach out to them. The men guarding them are equally inhuman. Ibbieta calls them vampires.

The critics view Sartre's work as an experiment in terror, and the story is usually thought to be about dying and the effect that it has on consciousness and moral feelings. The expectation of death is usually blamed for Ibbieta's attitude toward other people. Death has seized him in its jaws, and sheer terror extinguishes the basic sentiments of human sympathy. All of this is surely true. But the story requires additional commentary on why a person should cease to be one. The important fact to stress is that Ibbieta is being put to death. He is in the grips of a certain history, not exactly the history that MacIntyre calls German, but it is close enough. His captors are fascists, and Ibbieta is powerless before them. They recognize none of his rights. They compel him to speak. He is an instrument to be used for their purposes. The Spanish fascists treat Ibbieta as an object, not as a person, and this explains in part why he no longer behaves like a person. But it does not explain why he allows his personhood to be taken from him. It does not explain, more specifically, why he chooses to adopt the unsympathetic and essentially inhuman attitude of the Spanish fascists.

Here is where Kant enters the story. Ibbieta's alienation from his own humanity is expressed by Sartre in two different but powerful ways. The first turns on character description, both Sartre's characterization of Ibbieta and those of Ibbieta himself. The second depends on plot. Ibbieta's alienation is most vividly expressed in the choice that the fascists force him to make. For Ibbieta is the man in Kant's story who is asked by murderers to reveal the hiding place of his friend.

Throughout the night, Ibbieta engages in an internal monologue, in which he analyzes the personalities of his friends and tests his own character. His friends come off worse than he does. They have few virtues as human beings to hear Ibbieta describe them. They are gluttons and cowards. Ibbieta most often refers to them as if they were slabs of meat or old coats crumpled in the corner. They are figures in a still life, *nature morte*. Ibbieta comes very close to thinking about himself in the same way. He makes sympathetic remarks, to his own stupefaction, in which he does not believe. He loses all interest in thinking about the woman whom he apparently loves. He stares at his friends trembling beside him and at his own hand, motionless, unanimated, and lacking all desire to reach out to them.

Ibbieta's lack of feeling, however, is not in my opinion the effect of his being sentenced to death. Characters in Sartre's fiction do not need such excuses to feel alienated. From the first instant that Ibbieta is pushed into the great white room of the hospital where the prisoners are being held, he reveals his essential detachment from others. Already in the first paragraph of the story, long before he is sentenced to death, Ibbieta describes the look and physical qualities of his fellow prisoners, and his language is entirely anatomical. It dissects its objects, and it exposes his lack of feeling for them. Part of the reason that Ibbieta cannot stand up to the fascists is that he cannot hold himself up. He already hates himself. He does not like living with himself. Let me stress this point. Even though Ibbieta does not crack under pressure, even though he does not intentionally give away his friend to the murderers, he does not, I insist, stand up before his torturers. He cracks in a different way, losing himself to the evil of his captors, and the feeling of vertigo that he experiences in the last lines of the story are actually a kind of delayed reaction to this fact. They are his reaction to the consequences of his deed, but they occur too late in the game to matter. They mean that he is lost to himself. But he is, it seems to me, already lost to himself at the beginning of the story. His deed would never have taken place, if he were not incapable of living with himself in the first place.

Ibbieta's fall is most forcefully exposed in Sartre's use of Kant's plot. The guards enter the room and seize Ibbieta's two companions. But they tell Ibbieta to wait there. Then he hears the shots in the courtyard. He wants to scream and to pull out his hair, but he clenches his teeth and buries his hands stiffly in his pockets. After an hour, the guards return and lead him to the interrogation chamber. Two officials sit him down in the smoke-filled and savagely hot room. The little fat one poses the obvious question about Ramon Gris, Ibbieta's best friend and the leader of the rebels. "Where is he?" he asks. Ibbieta says that he does not know. They make the situation crystal clear. "It's your life or his. We will let you live if you tell us where he is" (230).

What happens next is crucial, if we are to understand why Ibbieta acts as he does. He comes to the realization that his captors have no power over him. Thanks to death, the great equalizer, Ibbieta considers that these two ugly officials are going to die, too. "A bit later than me," he thinks, "but not much later" (230). This is his first mistake. The officials do have power over him. They have had him led into the room like a cow, and now they are compelling him to speak. They can kill him on the spot.

This is power, and the fact that they will die someday does not mean that they do not possess power. Second, Ibbieta tries to put himself in their place. He cannot do it, of course. He finds them both shocking and ridiculous. They are vampires and clowns. They are madmen. The irony here is that Ibbieta does not believe himself capable of putting himself in their place. But he is already in their place. He hates them. They are not human. They wear silly ties and have ferocious and beastly gestures. Sartre never gives us the point of view of the officials. But I do not think it outlandish to imagine that they feel the same way about Ibbieta. We are in a room thick with mutual hatred, with no exit, as Sartre anticipates the suffocating inhumanity and coldness exposed in his future work.

The officials give Ibbieta a quarter of an hour to reflect and send him out of the room. He does reflect. He asks himself whether he should tell them where Ramon Gris is hiding. Ibbieta decides straightaway that he will not give his friend away. He would rather die. But he asks himself why he makes this choice. He does not decide to help Gris because of friendship. He no longer feels friendship for him. He no longer cares for his lover, Concha. Human love is lost to him. Nor does he believe that Gris's life is worth more than his own. "They are going to stick a man against a wall and fire on him until he croaks," he reasons. "Whether it's me or Gris or someone else, it's all the same" (231). Ibbieta admits that Gris is more valuable to the cause of Spain, but he no longer gives a damn about Spain. "Why save Gris's skin?" he asks himself. His only explanation is that he must be stubborn. He has no reason. Suddenly Ibbieta becomes giddy. Life appears to be a joke.

The guards come for him again. He laughs at a rat in the hallway and engages a guard in conversation about it. He also advises him to shave off his moustache. Facing the officials once more, he regards them as curiosities, as "insects of a very rare species" (232). They ask the same question, but Ibbieta does not sacrifice his life by refusing to answer, even though he has chosen to die rather than give away his friend. Instead, he decides to play a practical joke. He lies to them. He knows that Gris is at his cousin's house, but he tells them that he is hiding in the cemetery. "It was to play a practical joke on them," he tells himself. "I wanted to see them get up, buckle their gun belts, and shout out orders busily" (232). They do his bidding, jumping to their feet and rousing themselves to the kill.

It is tempting to say about Ibbieta that practical joking replaces practical reasoning. In Kant, practical reasoning enlists a person's thoughts about an immediate situation, and asks whether one can live with oneself in it. Ibbieta tries to think about himself, but he feels brutal and malicious. Instead, he cannot help imagining the comedy produced by his lie: "I imagined them turning over gravestones, opening one by one the doors of the crypts. I represented the situation to myself as if I were someone else: this prisoner refusing to play the hero, the serious soldiers with their moustaches, and the men in uniform running among the tombs; it was an irresistible comedy" (232). It is important to notice that Ibbieta cannot find himself in his own story. It means that he is dead to himself. Indeed, it is no accident that he names the cemetery as Gris's hiding place. His little practical joke plays out its comedy in the land of the dead. Soldiers run among the graves in order to kill a man. Ibbieta imagines the scene from the perspective of a dead man. Everyone is dead in this little farce. It is one hilarious practical joke on the dead.

But practical jokes invite others. After half an hour, one of the officers returns, the little fat one. Ibbieta expects to be executed, but the officer gives an order to put him in the courtyard with the others. There Ibbieta wanders about in a daze. He does not know who or where he is. Finally, that night, he recognizes his friend Garcia, and he tells Ibbieta that Ramon Gris has been killed. It appears that Gris had words with his cousin, and he left his hiding place. Many people would have been willing to hide him, Gris had explained to Garcia, but he did not want to owe anything to anyone. "I would have hidden myself at Ibbieta's," he had told Garcia, "but since they have caught him, I will hide in the cemetery" (233).

The soldiers discovered him there, on the advice of Ibbieta's lie. Garcia tells him that they found Gris in the gravedigger's shed and killed him on the spot.

The world begins to spin around, and Ibbieta's legs give way under him. Sartre ends the story with him lying there, on the ground, laughing so hard that tears come to his eyes.

Ibbieta fails to save his friend with his lie. He fails not because lying cannot save people, as Kant would argue, but because, as Sartre would say, existence is absurd. But Sartre's story strikes me as unavoidably Kantian nevertheless. The moral of the story may seem somewhat different from Kant's at first glance but the force of its poetic justice insists on a Kantian interpretation, in which one feels the immediate impact of one's own actions. When Ibbieta abandons practical reasoning for practical joking, he toys with his captors as they have toyed with him, and he therefore toys with himself. There on the ground, at the end of the story, he understands that he has become a toy of fate. Sartre loves irony. What a beautiful practical joke life has played on the practical joker! But the situation might have been different. If Ibbieta had spoken the truth, affirming himself as a person with the right to his own truthfulness, as Kant would put it, the joke would have been on the officials. The scene that Ibbieta imagines would have taken place at the house of Gris's cousin: soldiers turning over furniture, tearing up the floor to find secret hiding places, and exhausting themselves over their own evil intentions. They would have experienced as a result of their own toying with human beings the feeling of being toyed with, and only the unpredictability of life, not Ibbieta, would have been guilty of playing them as fools.

Understand that I am not responsible for the morality of this interpretation, although I agree more or less with its conclusions. It springs from the heavy-handed touch of Sartre. It is a story about poetic justice, and its conclusions are inescapable, although hopelessly negative in the example of Ibbieta. The story condemns Ibbieta as surely as the Spanish fascists have, and with as little fairness and sympathy concerning whatever his human situation may have been. This is where I find myself hesitating over the story. Ibbieta is to be preferred over the fascists, of course, but he is wrong in almost everything. He is reprehensible in many aspects. He falls as he has lived. But it may be too easy to pay heed to this poetic justice. Poetic justice often interferes with our ability to put ourselves in the place of another person. It tempts us not to retell the story. It puts an end to imagination, and it kills understanding, which is the ability to enter into the life of another person and to see it from his or her point of view. We say: "If I had been in that position, I would have acted differently." Or, we simply condemn the character for acting wrongly, having little understanding of the compulsion under which he or she may have lived. This is the problem as well with formal morals. If we accept them in isolation from their story, we excuse ourselves from retelling the story. The moral is no longer merely the end of the story. It spells the end of storytelling, and the end of storytelling brings an end to all hope of understanding.

Kant does not fall into this trap in my estimation, although he sometimes comes close. The categorical imperative is not a moral. It calls for the story of the moral. Kant may be as idealistic as Plato, but he never expels the poets. Kant understands that he needs storytelling, an aesthetic of morals, if his culture of moral feeling is to triumph. Nor does Kant embrace the easy solution to the problem of judgment. It is tempting to abandon judgment and to transform understanding into something utterly monstrous and useless. In this case, we refuse to render judgment for fear of doing an injustice and give ourselves over to a perverse view of understanding, in which *Tout comprendre, c'est tout pardonner* is the slogan that wins the day. No judgment, it seems, equals no injustice. But this simplistic equation does not work, and for at least two reasons. First, when we abandon judgment for fear of being unjust, we most often abandon our judgment either to people who are far less fearful than we are of injustice or to people who have no sense of justice at all. German history gives many examples. Second, to judge is part of retelling any story, its most important part, because it begins the work of telling the story from our own point of view, which means that it brings the story into our own life and puts our life into the story. Stories have no life in the absence of judgment. They are stupid without the aid of our intelligence. Kant, in fact, refers to the inability to judge as "stupidity," and when we abandon the right to judge, we are left with little more than the right to be stupid.

Judgment is not easy. It is necessary.

Hannah Arendt makes many of these points in her writings on German history in general and on the terror of living in the totalitarian state in particular. Her use of Kant is more sympathetic, more studied for political application, than Sartre's. She was perhaps the first person to understand that Kant's *Critique of Judgment* has far greater political implications than could be expected from a treatise on aesthetics, and she, in fact, works to expose the overtly political dimension of his theory of judgment. More importantly, she applies her reading of Kant directly to the problems of German history. One experiences in her writings on the origin of totalitarianism and on the trial of Eichmann a bold effort to see Kant's ideas in the light of these concrete and terrible events.

In *Lectures on Kant's Political Philosophy*, Arendt reveals that Kant's emphasis on the role of imagination in the work of judgment lays the groundwork for a political view of thinking, in which individuality, communicability, and sociability temper each other. The imagination is a political faculty because it alone devises the means by which human beings come to understand and to judge each other. It allows us to stand where someone else stands in order to understand another's actions and situation. But it also allows us to test the potential effects of actions on our future life, making it possible for us to tell whether we will be able to live with ourselves after performing a certain deed. Imagination in this sense is crucial to the judgments required by practical reason because it shows us the necessary limits of understanding.

It is the task of judgment, then, to find a middle ground between reason and understanding. It throws a bridge across the space separating them and makes their extremes less disconnected. On the one hand, its ability to emphasize an individual life story protects one from giving oneself over wholly to the understanding of another person too radically removed from oneself. In short, it permits us to reject unacceptable conduct on the basis of rational principles. Good and evil exist for judgment, and evil actions may be neither understandable nor pardonable. On the other hand, the ability to imagine someone else's situation tempers judgments tending toward bald condemnation by allowing us to put ourselves in another's place. Understanding prevents judgments of reason from growing hard and fanatical by softening them with sympathy and the desire to share our world with others.

Arendt's writings on totalitarianism place her squarely within the realm of the imagination, by which I mean that she returns again and again to the life stories of individuals in order to navigate between the extremes of understanding and reasoning by principle. For example, her book, *Eichmann in Jerusalem*, which is for all practical purposes a life story of Adolf Eichmann, was highly controversial, especially within the American Jewish community, because it tries hard to understand the reprehensible bureaucrat who engineered the Final Solution. In the same book, however, Arendt passes some negative judgments on Jewish collaborators, and for this she was accused of lacking understanding for their unbearable situation. I do not think that she deserved either of these criticisms. At a certain point, she stops trying to understand Eichmann and renders a harsh judgment against him, and her judgment of Jewish collaborators, especially of the Jewish Councils who performed too much of the work of identifying and selecting Jews from their numbers for transport to the camps, is always sympathetic and responsive to their impossible situation, without, however, relinquishing the right to reject their choices as the wrong ones.

Perhaps Arendt's most compact and intense articulation of these issues occurs in her little essay on "Personal Responsibility Under Dictatorship." It is also the place where her effort to apply Kant to political action is most evident. The essay reworks within the context of German history Kant's thoughts on the benevolent motives for telling lies. The reworking is most visible in Arendt's description of the moral excuses offered by collaborators and German officials. Both parties complained that they were either victims themselves or that they tried to choose the lesser of two evils. Some officials, including Eichmann, tried to excuse their behav-

ior by arguing that they were only following orders, and they made themselves out to be victims of Nazi Germany. It was all a terrible accident of
history, they said, and we were as much caught up in the terror as the
Jews whom we killed. We were cogs and wheels in the machinery of
history. Arendt rejects this defense straightaway because she believes in
taking personal responsibility for our actions. But then the question is:
What is our personal responsibility under dictatorship?

Arendt, following Kant, tries to answer this question by examining the
argument for the lesser of two evils. Both officials and collaborators offered a second moral justification for their conduct in the argument that
they tried to steer the evil system of the Nazis toward less immoral ends.
They had to serve the Nazi bureaucracy, they claimed, because they were
afraid to abandon their posts to less moral individuals, who would not
mitigate the crimes of the state. If you are faced with two evils, they
argued, it is your duty to opt for the lesser one, and it is irresponsible to
refuse to choose altogether. Their motives for lying sometimes, killing
occasionally, and keeping secrets almost always, they explained, were essentially benevolent, and they complained bitterly against those who
withdrew from political life completely during the years of terror, as if
their innocence had been bought by cowardice and an irresponsible attitude toward duty. The guilty held the innocent in disdain for not wanting
to dirty their hands in a dirty business. Notice that the argument for the
lesser evil sounds like Constant's objection to Kant's position. It scoffs at
lofty and inflexible principles for being impractical. But Arendt rightly
points out that only those people who placed personal responsibility
higher than political responsibility avoided becoming murderers.

Arendt rejects the argument of the lesser of two evils, just as Kant
does, because she identifies it as part of the machinery of terror and crime
imposed on people by totalitarian regimes. In such cases, there is no political solution, despite what Constant thought, because politics is the
problem. The choice of the lesser evil is a false choice because it leads the
individual to conform to a criminal state. Its great weakness is, according
to Arendt, that those who choose the lesser evil soon forget that they have
chosen evil. They also make their choices from those offered by the
enemy, and these choices remain enemy choices, even when they are internalized and taken as one's own. The Nazis consciously used the acceptance of the lesser evil to condition both government officials and large
populations. Arendt illustrates their technique with the example of anti-
Semitic measures. The extermination of Jews was preceded by a gradual

sequence of anti-Jewish ordinances, each of which was accepted because refusal to cooperate would have made things worse. But it soon happened that nothing worse could possibly take place, and by this time, cooperation was inbred and unquestioned. The officials of the Jewish Councils as well as some state bureaucrats tried valiantly to mitigate the evil, but they cooperated and supported evil in spite of themselves. Their motives were often benevolent and sympathetic. They are understandable. But they were still wrong.

The most important question, unless we are merely searching for negative examples, remains to be asked. How did it happen that some people did not cooperate? How were they different from the others? By what means did they reason their way out of an altogether impossible situation?

The answer is somewhat hypothetical, since it is difficult to recuperate reasons under such circumstances. But Arendt tries to trace out a response based on her experience with those who escaped becoming murderers. Their most singular quality, she points out, was that they dared to judge for themselves. Arendt is cautious to explain that these individuals were able to judge for themselves not because they necessarily possessed higher principles, a better system of values, or old standards of right and wrong. Rather, they were able to judge the situation because their conscience did not function in an automatic way, in which one applies oneself to duty or to preexisting rules. They were able to face choices as bearing directly on their most personal self. They asked themselves, Arendt reveals, whether they would be able to live in peace with themselves after having committed certain deeds, and they decided that it would be better to do nothing, to withdraw from the situation, not because the world would be a better place, but because only in this way could they live with themselves. They refused to participate, and they chose to die when they were forced to participate. "To put it crudely," Arendt writes, "they refused to murder, not so much because they held fast to the command 'Thou shalt not kill,' as because they were unwilling to live together with a murderer—themselves" (205).

There is something unsociable in the reasoning of those who resisted Nazi collaboration. It is the kind of reasoning found at certain points in Kant and which his critics sometimes call solipsistic or egotistical. It is a way of thinking about oneself in the world that invents the world on the basis of an individual life story. This life story is of first importance because Kant believes that everything necessary for moral life in general begins there. It is moral thinking as such. It is judgment. It combines understanding and reason, and it does not rely on either sophisticated or technical arguments. It relies only on the habit of living together with oneself and of being engaged in the story of one's own life. Moral thinking is, finally, the habit of telling a life story to oneself, and it refuses to tell no story, although it does refuse to live many, save the one that insists that there are such things as unstoried lives.

If more people had been able to think about themselves in this manner, Arendt implies, less crimes would have been committed, and fewer Jews would have died in the camps. For if other individuals had withdrawn from the Nazi bureaucracy of terror, the entire evil system would have collapsed. Those who shunned political responsibility were not irresponsible in the final analysis. They ended by contributing to the modern idea of nonviolent action and resistance, whose development, one imagines, was made necessary precisely because of the emergence of modern totalitarian regimes and methods of coercion. They embraced a form of resistance, a passive and nonviolent one, by avoiding those places—"places of responsibility" Arendt calls them—that required their blind obedience to the state.

I do not think it a perversion of Kant to place his ethics in this modern context, as in fact others have done by way of criticizing him. The categorical imperative recommends that we ask whether our maxim may be treated as a universal law. It asks us to tell ourselves a story to determine whether an action is acceptable. To describe its structure in a modern light, as Arendt does, it asks finally whether I can live with myself, if I act in a certain way. Despite his association with duty, Kant holds up individuality as the guide to moral conduct, and it is this emphasis that makes his ideas so valuable to Arendt's attempts to combat those regimes that exist to extinguish individuals and their moral faculties.

I am not arguing that Kant's ethics is flawless. Nor that he provides the final answer to living a moral life in the modern world. I am arguing that he exposes the limits of an ethics based wholly on experience, imitation, and political norms. In Nazi Germany, one could not depend on either political convention or the conduct of others to guide oneself in matters ethical. To be moral was a crime from the point of view of one's neighbors.

It is easy to make the claim in the abstract that Kantian ideas contributed to the creation of such a society. Kant can be blamed for a view of duty that takes no account of its consequences. But it is as easy to see that his way of thinking is the only way to survive as a moral person within the totalitarian state. When faced with evil, there can be no reason to choose it. If forced to choose evil, there can be no benevolent motive for the choice. The choice of evil is evil, and whenever it is possible, it is best to resist the evil choices that evil regimes would force upon us. Sartre's Ibbieta shows us why. German history insists. There can be no exception. Unbreakable principle. Distasteful to modern sense. But it is also nauseating to that modern form of evil represented most clearly by German history.

Such is Kant's unconditional response to modernity. It is an answer that leads not to the Final Solution but to a very different one.

CHAPTER 10

Jane Austen and Comic Virtue

One

THE MODERN AGE marks the end of philosophy, if only because our moral choices are now well rehearsed. The place of modern philosophy is one that we have seen before, with the difference that we have never before stood in a place where all the views are so familiar. We stand after Kant like Janus-figures, looking to the past and to the future. But the past and future are twins—Janus-figures themselves.

Perhaps a better way of describing the modern situation would be to apply the language of comic acting. Standing in this place, looking to the past and to the future, we are engaged in a perpetual "double-take." Doing a double-take at the past gives us the same effect as looking at the past and the future in rapid succession or the same effect as doing a double-take at the future.

It is a wonder that our heads do not detach.

Moral philosophy after Kant sees the future in the past. It returns to Aristotle because it wants to recapture an idea of moral judgment based not on principles but on experience. Post-Kantian philosophy values the principle of nonprinciple. It sees as a duty the refusal of duty. The distinc-

135

tion between an Aristotelian and Kantian world view, however, ends by possessing the dubious advantage of being itself a post-Kantian distinction. It is only after having been Kantians that we may decide to become Aristotelians once more. But in reality we can never go home again because the distrust of principles brought about by living in the post-Kantian world carries with it an equal distrust of character as a principle. Kant is just enough like Aristotle to make a radical rejection of Kant a difficulty for Aristotle's political view of ethics. For Aristotle's city could not have existed if its inhabitants were as distrustful of beliefs in duty, laws, principles, and virtues as some of our post-Kantian philosophers seem to be. In Aristotle's city, people study one another's character on principle, as it were, because they believe in each other, and the belief in character remains necessary, if anything like character building is to exist at all.

Characters are ethical because they manifest themselves as principles of self-reflection for people living in the world. Stories have morals because we make them our stories or at least try to make them our stories. These assertions apply to dispositions of social character, or virtues, as well as to dispositions of literary character. They apply to gossip, conversation, news stories, television, movies, history, and works of literature.

By referring to a real person or a literary character as a principle or moral of self-reflection, we risk falling into a Kantian and solipsistic view of the world, it may be objected, in which other people are not permitted to exist for themselves. It is a strange view of human character, some will say, that sees in other people the sources of personal maxims of action.

Is it not excessive to view others as mirrors of ourselves?

What of other people's reasons for acting and being as they are?

Other people and their motives are not transparent to us, and we should admit them as valuable in themselves apart from any private worth or usefulness that they might possess for us. In the jargon of the modern ethic of otherness, we say that we should respect the otherness of other people and not try to reduce it to the same. We have a moral duty to see other human beings as other human beings and not merely as versions of ourselves or as material for the work that we would like to do on ourselves.

Every person's life is worth a story. If we refuse to listen to someone's story and choose instead to use it to tell the moral of our own life story, we close ourselves off from the life of another human being.

A truly angelic description of experience would embrace this view of other people, and I would not want to live in a world where no such view existed, but I do not think that many people live according to so angelic a description of experience.

Nor do the modern philosophers most interested in the idea of experience usually believe in angels.

The tendency to characterize others and to see them in terms of ourselves is a method for living in the world. We may wish to live in a world where the other is the other, but we seem in reality to live in one in which the other is part of our vision of the self and in which the self plays the same role for the other, or so I, the self in this case, imagine.

If an increasing number of ethical thinkers have begun to turn to the writings of Jane Austen to face the historical conundrum posed by the end of philosophy, it is the case, I believe, because her irony and acknowledgement of people's tendency to look again at each other thematize the problem of the double-take.[1] This means, first of all, that we view Jane Austen as a student of character: we understand that her characters reflect on each other as a means of reflecting on themselves. Secondly, whether we like it or not, we understand that the relation between self-reflection and character study has an inescapably comic dimension, not a tragic one. Pre-Romantic philosophy is preponderantly tragic, but something happens to philosophy after Kant and Hegel. The romance of Romanticism—its ideas of love and of the relations between the sexes—drives us toward a comic finale, in which tragedy and comedy merge to describe life not as a tragic existence but as a human comedy.

The exact nature of Jane Austen's contribution to this change in philosophical reflection is nevertheless difficult to name. Philosophically, for example, it is hard to say whether her supposed Aristotelianism is an effect of not having been exposed to the Kantian revolution or of being a modern post-Kantian Aristotelian. Austen's vision of a human community in which individuals exist in close association with each other certainly gives her novels a political and ethical dimension that surpasses others, despite the fact that politics appears for all practical purposes not to be part of her world; and this vision is easily matched with a Greek view of the polis, especially with an Aristotelian one. But her novels possess another dimension that cannot be appreciated, if we deny them their modernity and view them as survivals of the classical tradition.[2] They describe a truly romantic view of morality, by which I mean that her ideas about ethics are all geared toward obtaining successful relationships between men and women. Hers is a world, then, in which the problem of learning for oneself from others is complicated by the fact that the others are usually of the other sex as well.

Jane Austen's world is the modern world of the novel. It is a world of novelty in which our vision of the novel relies on the novelty of being the same. In short, it is the world in which we increasingly find ourselves living.

To say that Jane Austen is Romantic is to understand that romantic attachments form the grounds of character building in her writings. Her people improve or worsen in character depending on their choice of partner. The selection of a partner is consequently of the utmost importance, and Austen's novels return again and again to the rituals of courtship by which people make acquaintances and fall in love. Indeed, it is tempting to coin the term "courtship novels" for her works because they are about the philosophical and conversational play in which men and women engage in order to test and to choose each other. Her interest in romantic attachments breaks with the classical view of ethics and demonstrates that she is preoccupied with the distinctly modern problem of sexual politics and morality. Her emphasis on the places—the grand houses, parks, and country villages—in which her English society develops may have the political and idyllic flavor of the Greek ethos, but it derives ultimately from a world in which the novel has replaced Greek forms of literature. The novel comes into its own during the same era as Kant's philosophy, and the novel is the literary form most concerned with courtship and marriage. If Jane Austen's society is somehow Aristotelian, then, it is Aristotelian with this difference. It is Aristotelian after Kant.

To situate Jane Austen's society, we need only contrast the ideas of friendship found in Aristotle and Kant, and recognize that she surpasses both points of view. Aristotle's *Ethics* includes a celebration of friendship, and although he mentions the "unequal friendship" found between husband and wife in his catalogue of friendships, it remains nevertheless clear that his ideal of living together is best captured by male society. When he explains that friends naturally wish to live together, for example, he lists drinking, dice-playing, athletic exercise, hunting, and the study of philosophy as the activities on which friendships may be built (1172a). These are not the usual activities shared by husbands and wives, except, perhaps, in the imagination of D. H. Lawrence.

Kant's view of friendship is more modern and romantic. *The Doctrine of Virtue* describes friendship in terms that recall the unions of men and women. Kant does not always speak favorably about these unions, it is true, but it is inescapably clear that he does mean to describe the romantic union of couples, which means that Jane Austen's view of attachments resembles Kant's more than Aristotle's. Kant explains, for example, that some "people cannot part with each other, and yet they cannot come to terms with each other since they need quarrels in order to savour the sweetness of being united in reconciliation" (143). This is not, I think, an Aristotelian description of friends playing dice.

Kant alludes to the squabbling found between couples having a romantic interest in one another. He is novelistic in his preoccupation with the frustrations and sweetness of marriage. But the story that Kant relates is not very important for the novels of Jane Austen. What is most distinctive about Jane Austen's novels is her ability to write about couples without succumbing to the melodramatic and sensational views of her contemporaries. If Jane Austen is credited with being the first "modern" English novelist, it is precisely because she leaves behind the cliché plots and characters of the sentimental novel and chooses to represent the emotional life of people who could live in the world and not merely in romances.

Jane Austen's refusal of tragedy also marks her distance from Greek philosophy and confirms the same conclusion. Her penchant for happy endings allows her to present the marriage of self and other as a fortunate one. This fact is in itself important to an understanding of modern ethics, which increasingly takes this theme as its main object, and we should not allow it to make us distrustful of Jane Austen's analyses of how people relate to other people, how they become like others, or how they represent to themselves the difference of others. Indeed, the many attempts by literary critics to ruin Jane Austen's happy endings bear witness only to their own inability to accept a notion of the couple that is not perfect and saintly. They reject Jane Austen's endings on principle as unreal, but it is their principled rejection of marriage that is unrealistic. Emma and Mr. Knightley, to take the usual example, do marry, and Jane Austen refers to the "perfect happiness of the union" (1002). If we cannot accept that this marriage will last, or if we demand that it be viewed as a compromise or a defeat on either one's part, we simply miss the main point. Emma and Mr. Knightley, in spite of their differences in character, love each other, which is to say that they successfully mark out where they shall become more alike, less alike, and stay neutral, and from this form of relating come both the happiness and the unhappiness of married life.[3] There is no other way of living together.

To express more fully the philosophical problem of joining Aristotle and Kant in a vocabulary conducive to Austen's writings, we might say that each represents in his turn the dispositions of character called pride and prejudice—only it is not at all certain that we are always talking about vices. For Aristotle, we recall, virtue is decidedly political. It would be more accurate to describe his ethics as civic because the city is the exclusive arena of character building. This means that dispositions of character associated with social harmony and hierarchy are bound to be most important. Oddly, however, the virtuous man in Aristotle is not, in fact, so different from the proud man. Pride (*megalopsychia*) is at the center of Aristotle's *Ethics:* he calls it the "crown of the virtues" (1124a). The proud man—for it is clear that pride is principally a masculine virtue in Aristotle—is "good in the highest degree" and possesses "greatness in every virtue" (1124a28–32). He is concerned most with honor, but he has a just understanding of his own merits. His ambitions are great, and he knows himself to be rightly superior to others. He is therefore justified, according to Aristotle, in despising those who imitate him without being equal to him in rank and ability. He is equally justified in honoring few things himself. His character is such that he is open in his hatred and love, free of speech because he is contemptuous, and given to telling the truth, except when "he speaks in irony to the vulgar." He refuses to permit his life to revolve around another person, unless it be a friend, for to do otherwise would be "slavish" (1124b25–1125a2).

Aristotle's view of pride is jarring from a modern perspective because he represents pride as the picture of virtue. We find his account baffling because we see as vices what Aristotle appears to be celebrating, and it is difficult to accept his point of view, even though we may understand it. His picture of the great-souled man reads rather like an excerpt from Nietzsche, and Nietzsche was, of course, thinking in part of Aristotle when he framed his idea of the "superman."

But pride also presents a difficulty for Aristotle's own idea of the virtues. The virtues in the Aristotelian conception supposedly express a mean between two extremes, but the virtue of pride does not easily fit the idea of the mean. It is true that vanity and humility may be considered the extremes between which pride finds itself, the former being self-esteem beyond merit and the latter being the tendency to underestimate one's own worth. But, in fact, Aristotle describes pride in such hyperbolic terms that it strikes one as an extreme in itself. In short, we again read it as a vice. Aristotle's idea of pride reminds us that his political views were not so very democratic after all, and that he was enamored of the aristocracy and too much inclined to be a king-maker.

Kant does not describe prejudice in the colorful terms that Aristotle gives to pride. But prejudice remains the Enlightenment vice. In *The Critique of Judgment,* Kant explains that the greatest of all prejudices is superstition and that emancipation from it is called "enlightenment" (§40). The principal goal of the Enlightenment is to do away with prejudiced thought, which Kant defines as a passivity of reason that leads people not to think for themselves. Kant in typical fashion gives a formula for attaining enlightenment. Enlightened thought demands that the thinker adhere to three maxims of human understanding: "They are these: (1) to think for oneself; (2) to think from the standpoint of everyone else; (3) always to think consistently" (§40). The first maxim encourages unprejudiced thought; the second leads to enlarged thought; and the third adheres to reason itself. Only by acquiring the mental habit of combining all three, does the thinker successfully achieve enlightenment. But it is obvious that this task cannot be simple. It asks one, in effect, to think for oneself from the standpoint of everyone else with consistency. A more difficult balancing act for the thinker could not be imagined.

Similar to pride in Aristotle's scheme, then, prejudice presents an obstacle for Kant's moral philosophy. Against it is set his Enlightenment project, but prejudice may be confronted only by a negative attitude, and for two reasons. First, a temptation exists to believe that we know what lies beyond our understanding, especially because other people, Kant notes, are always promising to satisfy our curiosity. We too easily accept the opinion of others about things and people, when often enough they know nothing about them. In this respect, it may be easier to think for oneself than to attain the standpoint of everyone else because the greatest temptation in Kantian thought is to believe that we have understood what may well lie beyond our understanding, in this case, the standpoint of everyone else. We have to remain skeptical of an easy understanding of other people, if we are to avoid prejudice. We have to question continually the possibility of our understanding of others, but this skepticism requires a negative attitude difficult to maintain because it contradicts the ultimate goal of enlightened thought, which is the enlarged point of view. How is one to be skeptical of one's understanding of others and strive to represent their standpoint at the same time? Moreover, how can one think these two thoughts simultaneously and continue to think with consistency? To put the dilemma simply, how can one be skeptical of the universal position and still remain a Kantian?[4]

Second, the attainment of enlightened thought requires that the thinker flirt with prejudice. The move from thinking for oneself (unprejudiced thought) to thinking from the standpoint of everyone else (enlarged thought or universal thought) risks plunging one into prejudice because enlarged thought resembles too closely the nature of prejudice itself. It escapes being prejudice, apparently, by virtue of the fact that the thinker is thinking for himself or herself at the same time. But thinking for oneself in this regard has once more a negative character. It appears merely as an antidote to prejudice and not as a significant grounds in itself for ethical thought. At this moment, Kant gives more weight to thinking from the standpoint of everyone else than he does to thinking for oneself, even though what is most distinctive about his ethics is his strong claim for the role played by the individual will in moral conduct. Kant opposes his ethics, we remember, to the classical models for the very reason that they seem to him to rest on prejudice of opinion. Enlightenment is freedom from tutelage (the inability to think without direction from another person), and tutelage is only another word for prejudice in Kant's vocabulary.[5]

In the case of Aristotle, to summarize, we have difficulty accepting his virtuous description of a vice. Pride is an "evil" in Aristotle because it encourages contempt for other human beings. In the case of Kant, we experience a similar problem. We have difficulty accepting his description of that quasi-virtuous state of prejudice called enlarged thought. It is precisely the strong sense that enlarged thought leads in the end to prejudice that tempts modern thinkers to reject Kantian "universalism" as proto-Nazi. We fail to distinguish, as Kant does, between enlarged thought and prejudice, and we end by viewing his ideal of duty not only as a failure but as a pernicious idea, and in spite of the fact that little in Kant actually leads to this view.

If Jane Austen were either an Aristotelian or an Enlightenment thinker exclusively, her view of character would not surpass these two positions. If she were Aristotelian, for example, the title of her novel would have been *Pride or Prejudice*, or merely *Pride*, and Darcy would not have married Elizabeth. Or if he had, she would have stabbed him to death in his bath in good tragic fashion. If Jane Austen were merely Kantian, she would have given her novel a different one word title. Prejudice is such an all-consuming vice in Kantian terms that one hardly needs to add *Pride* to the title and certainly not in the leading position. From the Kantian point of view, *Prejudice* suffices, as *Persuasion* seems to suffice. Indeed, it is difficult, unless care is taken, to see why pride has any real importance in the novel. Darcy does not dance with Elizabeth because his pride will not allow him to bend to one of her rank and connections, and his first proposal of marriage is an insult because it manifests his haughty confidence in his social superiority. But why not consider this pride as merely another prejudice, that of social class, for instance? When Frank Churchill, to take an example from *Emma*, recommends organizing a ball among the residents of Highbury, Emma quickly assesses it as proof of a flaw in his character. She faults him precisely for not having sufficient pride because he seems indifferent to the confusion of rank that such a ball would involve, and she fears that this indifference betrays an inelegance of mind. Here pride reveals itself to be merely a version of class prejudice.

Jane Austen's writings do not abandon the classical meanings of pride and prejudice, but their definitions are not nearly as sharp as we might expect because her perspective is not politically but romantically and ethically oriented.[6] She is not as concerned with creating an ideal republic, joining great houses, or preserving social distinctions as she is with bringing together couples who will improve each other morally and find happiness and goodness in their relationship as a result. Pride and prejudice are neither synonyms nor antonyms in Jane Austen's usage. Rather, their meaning relies on a certain historical development during which the language of character shifts its center from the world of politics to the couple.

In a sense, then, Jane Austen opens the age of the couple in which Freud's theory of the family romance will later find its impressive claim to authority. Her ideas of pride and prejudice are neither mutually exclusive nor redundant because they focus on the basic problems that men and women experience in relating to one another. Most fundamentally, they are dispositions that involve our perception of human difference and similarity, and whether we name them as a virtue or a vice is important because the shifting identity of the terms captures the fact that personal identity shifts as well when we try to place people in various moral settings. Human relationships are always complex, and within the practical sphere of daily life, the moral choice is not always to break down prejudices or to refuse pride any more than it is to allow them always to remain intact. To put it as simply as I can for the moment, if the other is to remain the other at times, it means that we have to acknowledge certain differences that exist among people, differences that may be essential to their well-being. But these very differences may appear in some cases as vices. At this point, we experience the moral dilemma of defending a vice to be virtuous, or of shedding our virtue to permit other people to keep their own vices. In short, we rediscover the double-take of what we have called the modern human comedy.

Two

The dilemma of our modern human comedy may be described for the sake of convenience as the problem of "comic virtue." Comic virtue shares certain elements with the modern ethic of otherness, but it differs ultimately in its attitude toward moral perfection. The ethic of otherness is essentially political, and so is the idea of comic virtue because it conceives of a relation between character and place. Moreover, both owe a debt to Aristotle, and they seem opposed to the Kantian view. But, in fact, the ethic of otherness flies to extremes, which is to say that it has little sense of humor, and this is the important difference. The ethic of otherness is often so anti-Kantian in principle that it ends by being Kantian in practice. Similarly, its Aristotelianism is so severe that it is not always recognizably Aristotelian.

The various applications of the ethic of otherness to the modern scene reveal these difficulties. The ethic of otherness is notably anti-Kantian because it describes human society not as a community of rational beings sharing the same cognitive abilities but as a group of heterogeneous individuals, whose individuality and uniqueness depend precisely on the fact that they cannot all be reduced to a common denominator (such as Reason, human nature, the male sex, etc.). We may therefore choose one of two moralities to deal with communal life. The first is a postmodern and radical form of Aristotelianism.[7] It argues that the extreme diversity of individuals in the community may be reconciled only through agonistic means. Conflict and conflict only establishes the architecture of society, and it bestows goods upon the winners and steals them from the losers. According to this view, theories of social harmony are an illusion, an illusion designed specifically by those in power, because they conceal the fact that all notions of community create victims. Beliefs in liberal notions of justice, for example, are described merely as the rationalizations used by the winners to justify their power over the losers. This is the morality of human being as wolf. In short, it believes in no morality at all.

The second morality based on the ethic of otherness does uphold the possibility of an ethical existence. It is largely traditional in effect, however, and to its chagrin, because it collapses back into Kantianism by virtue of its extreme anti-Kantianism. Here the moral relationship among persons does not spring from a notion of equality, since no such sameness can be said to exist, but from a respect for individual diversity and difference. But where does this respect come from, if heterogeneity and difference are the characteristic virtues of human society? It springs from nowhere. It merely surges forth, and we apparently experience it as an inner command or as a sublime imperative. The duty to acknowledge the otherness of the other remains a moral duty, then, and as surely as any duty found in Kant. In short, the principle requiring that we acknowledge the otherness of the other is a founding idea, and it cannot be demonstrated any more than we can demonstrate Kant's idea of "universal subjectivity," that is, the universal equality of cognitive ability shared by all reasonable beings. We might as well say after Kant that the otherness of the other is an idea given by reason.[8]

The ethic of otherness is serious business, and anyone commanding a view of the current scene in ethics will not doubt its gravity. It is linked to important political causes, and it allows us to give a voice to many marginal and underprivileged groups. Their suffering commands respect and high seriousness.

How, then, are we to recover a sense of comic virtue, if, indeed, we ought to? By what argument, by what expression of sympathy, by what confession, might we establish a rhetoric secure enough to communicate the importance of seeing the comic dimension of human difference?

Unfortunately, I do not believe that it can be done to everyone's satisfaction. First, no rhetoric will suffice because the power of rhetoric is precisely what is at stake. The instant that we have established an argument strong enough to defend ourselves against accusations of insensitivity, we will have succumbed in all probability to gravity, and the comic dimension of human life will elude us once more. Mistakes and double-takes fall out of favor. Storytelling is prohibited, and wit succumbs to high seriousness, since all comedy offends, and no joke exists that does not in some way marginalize the other. Confronted by Emma's joke at Miss Bates's expense, for example, we should, according to this ideal, recognize its cruelty and injustice. If we fail, Mr. Knightley is there to guide us to the truth. But the problem does not stop at Emma's insensitivity. Jane Austen is herself insensitive when she creates Miss Bates, for the character serves as a running joke throughout the novel. If we apply the ethic of otherness, *Emma* and the comic novel in general grow objectionable. Mrs. Bennet, Mr. Woodhouse, Miss Bates, and the many ridiculous characters in Jane Austen's novels become sins against the dignity and the diversity of the human race. In each case, we sacrifice an acceptance of the other as the other for a good laugh.

One alternative is to reject comedy for moral seriousness. But this choice leaves us with what can only be called a universal deadpan, where no one appreciates a joke. Irony is robbed of its ethical potential in favor of a one dimensional view. It is as if we suddenly find ourselves at the dinner table with Mr. Woodhouse and his basin of gruel. Mr. Woodhouse, we remember, can never recall a joke, and he comes to represent a parody of the view that all human beings are alike. His is a sympathetic perspective that believes that the well-being and harmony of all will come about if everyone adopts his diet and way of living. His life makes him comfortable, and since everyone is by his definition like he is, his life-style will serve everyone else as well. To respect Mr. Woodhouse's otherness means confronting this ethic. We must all by moral necessity share in his bowl of gruel, not to learn to like it, for that would mean becoming Mr. Woodhouse and relinquishing our own difference, but to suffer it as a distasteful and yet necessary communion with otherness.[9]

A more unappetizing solution could not be imagined, and if this is our only moral choice, we have reached a sorry state, indeed. It is a state, to pun on Plato, where storytelling is too dangerous to be approved. It is a state in which laughter is considered a risky business and the comic double-take has lost both its appeal and its value for ethical understanding.

Three

Jane Austen dearly loved a good joke, and she knew how to tell a story. Follies and nonsense, whims and inconsistencies did divert her, and she laughed at them, like Elizabeth Bennet, whenever she could. This fact irks some of her critics who cannot reconcile the morality of her novels with the stinging wit and the occasional cruel joke exposed in her letters.

"Dear Jane" falls from grace, and the critics then turn to her characters, who are submitted to the same kinds of moral censure. It is as if "Jane Austen" were made to act as the moral of her own stories, and when their ethical perspective cannot be supported by this persona, the critics grow disillusioned and take revenge on the novels.[10] But if "Jane Austen" is the moral, it is the case only because her stories do the work of composing the moral. "Jane Austen" has goodness because she writes good novels.

Pride and Prejudice ends with twin morals, and we will have to say something about them, but it is rather early to turn to them now. It is more useful to begin by examining how Austen's characters compose the morals of their life stories. It is a commonplace to discuss the ways in which *Pride and Prejudice* pivots on issues of identity and the mistakes caused by pride, egotism, and prejudice. Let us merely agree that the book cannot be easily read without understanding that its characters are enthusiastic about figuring out other people's emotions and motivations as well as their own, and that often enough they fail on both counts. The source of the novel's humor is its comedy of manners, but a comedy of manners is finally a story in which laughter and virtue merge. Since Elizabeth Bennet is the protagonist, we see her engaged in this study of character and this "comedy" most frequently, but I think it a mistake to pretend that only she has concerns about character. Everyone in the novel thinks to a great extent as Elizabeth does, although certainly with varying degrees of wit and foolishness. Some make grave errors that cannot be corrected, but they are errors in kind with those made by Lizzy.

On the first evening of her stay at Netherfield, Elizabeth confesses to being a "studier of character." The reader, of course, has already surmised it. Elizabeth has the sharp eye of a caricaturist and delights in putting other people's personalities in relief. But on the second evening we discover to what extent the other characters share Elizabeth's preoccupation with the issue of character. The three nights at Netherfield give us, in fact, as good a sense of how men and women get to know each other and how they compete with each other as any scenes in Austen's works. But they are also important for the emphasis that they place on a form of philosophical play having to do with virtue and character.

The conversation of the second night takes a philosophical turn with a joke made by Miss Bingley about her brother's penmanship. Her objective is clear. She has been trying to draw Darcy's attention away from his letter-writing to her own person, but she has not been having much suc-

cess. She finally succeeds in attracting Darcy's notice by making an un-
favorable comparison of her brother's writing with Darcy's. It is a comparison made at her brother's expense. She announces to all that he writes
carelessly, skipping words and blotting out the rest. Immediately, Austen
links Bingley's writing style to the style of his character. Bingley explains
that his ideas flow so rapidly that his hand cannot express them. Elizabeth
praises Bingley's humility, but Darcy recognizes an indirect boast. Darcy
complains that Bingley associates his carelessness with a power and rapid-
ity of mind. Darcy further explains that Bingley's pronouncement to Mrs.
Bennet earlier in the day that he would leave Netherfield in five minutes
if he ever resolved to quit was also a form of self-flattery. Bingley apparently cultivates rashness to compliment himself.

At this point the issue of character explodes forth as a general topic of
discussion. For Bingley counters that he did not "assume the character of
needless precipitance merely to shew off before the ladies" (251). He believes to have described himself accurately. But Darcy puts Bingley's character to the test with a case of storytelling: "if, as you were mounting your
horse, a friend were to say, 'Bingley, you had better stay till next week,'
you would probably do it, you would probably not go—and, at another
word, might stay a month" (251). Darcy has Bingley over a barrel, and
only Elizabeth, as a match for Darcy's intelligence, can save the man. She
enters the argument with some literary thinking of her own. She begins
to describe Darcy's part in the story of his own creation and holds him
responsible for remarks that she puts in his mouth. She accuses him of
being obstinate. Now Darcy needs help. He manages to escape only by
exposing the problem of creating character within ethical discussions:
"You expect me to account for opinions which you chuse to call mine, but
which I have never acknowledged" (252). The characters created by moral
philosophy are unacknowledged to say the least, and yet Darcy seems to
understand that ethical commentary cannot proceed without attribution
of character. For he does not call an end to the conversation but in fact
assumes the character created for him:

> "Allowing the case, however, to stand according to your representation,
> you must remember, Miss Bennet, that the friend who is supposed to
> desire his return to the house . . . has merely desired it, asked it without
> offering one argument in favour of its propriety." (252)

Darcy takes on the character of an autocrat, the domineering role that
he in fact plays in Lizzy's imagination throughout their early acquaint-

ance, but only to push the case to its limits. And, indeed, the more they argue, the farther they stray from the case at hand. They are playing with each other, and much of the enjoyment that readers take from the scene comes from our sense of the pleasure in witty conversations of this type. But the end of this play is as much to answer a question as to flirt. Finally, Elizabeth begins to see the futility of their argument. She puts a stop to the flirtation in order to answer the question, which is to say that at this point she is less interested in having Darcy's love than in deciding a philosophical point. (Philosophy is, after all, the love of knowledge, not the knowledge of love, and the comic novel is most philosophical, if it is philosophical, only in turning the heart of philosophy toward affairs of another knowing.) She suggests that one should discuss only real circumstances: "We may as well wait, perhaps, till the circumstance occurs, before we discuss the discretion of his behaviour thereupon" (252). Lizzy is suggesting that their argument is too abstract, and she is correct, but Lizzy likes to abstract character; that is her character, and she tries once more to catch Darcy off his guard:

> "But in general and ordinary cases between friend and friend, where one of them is desired by the other to change a resolution of no very great moment, should you think ill of that person for complying with the desire, without waiting to be argued into it?" (252)

Fortunately, Darcy knows how to answer a question with a question: "Will it not be advisable, before we proceed on this subject, to arrange with rather more precision the degree of importance which is to appertain to this request, as well as the degree of intimacy subsisting between the parties?" (252). Darcy drives the argument further toward particularity. His motivation comes from his characteristic love of precision, of course, but he also seems to know something about how moral discussions must work if they are to be moral themselves. We need to know about human motivations and emotions to make statements about people. Abstract stereotypes add nothing to ethical ideas because ethics delves into human character, and stereotypes are not human.

Darcy's question reveals his moral maturity, but it also invites a literary response. He wishes to trace the intimacy of the friends and to deepen our understanding of the story. Darcy is becoming an author figure. Bingley interrupts at this point to mock Darcy and Elizabeth, but his interruption is telling because its irony does not depart from the form of the argument; it merely twists it slightly as parody always does:

"By all means," cried Bingley; "let us hear all the particulars, not forget-ting their comparative height and size; for that will have more weight in the argument, Miss Bennet, than you may be aware of. I assure you that if Darcy were not such a great tall fellow, in comparison with my-self, I should not pay him half as much deference. I declare I do not know a more aweful object than Darcy, on particular occasions, and in particular places; at his own house especially, and of a Sunday evening when he has nothing to do." (252)

Bingley is teasing Darcy, but he completes his point. To hear all the particulars is to hear a story, the kind of story that Jane Austen is in the process of writing. Moreover, to hear all the particulars is exactly what Elizabeth and the others need, but what they consistently refuse to pur-sue. Rather, they allow their pride and prejudice to convince them that they already know everything that they need to know about someone.

The conversation breaks off at this moment, only to be resumed the next night, but it is important to stress how it comes to a conclusion because it introduces the theme of the third night's conversation and ex-poses an objection that is often posed against attempts to deal with moral issues by telling stories. Darcy smiles at Bingley's remark, and Elizabeth interprets him to be taking offense. Miss Bingley interprets the smile the same way, but she resents the indignity that Darcy has received and calls the whole conversation "nonsense." Darcy reacts by reading the hidden undercurrent of the conversation. He interprets Bingley's joke as an at-tempt to bring the conversation to a halt because of a dislike of argument, to which Bingley can only consent: "Arguments are too much like dis-putes. If you and Miss Bennet will defer yours till I am out of the room, I shall be very thankful; and then you may say whatever you like of me" (252–53).

Miss Bingley will never win the affection of Darcy for the very reason that she sees such conversations as nonsense, and Bingley will marry Jane because with her he need never worry about having an argument. Jane is, as it were, a Platonic idea. She is an angel, and a man who wants to live a life free from argument needs to marry an angel, or else to put his trust in a community based on something like Platonic idealism. But in such a community storytelling will be seen either as nonsense or as needlessly aggressive. Plato wants to expel conflict from his republic, and it is no accident that he identifies literature with conflict because storytelling is the principal means by which we confront disputes. It is a form of argument in which we try to hear the particulars about situations that trouble us.

It may never be clear how useful stories are for solving real problems. We may never believe that we can imagine a solution by telling a story and then make that solution work in reality. In some ways it is a matter of luck. But we do face problems by telling stories about them, and in the long run our solutions to problems or acceptance of them are tied to these stories. Stories, then, are not nonsensical; nor are they to be suppressed because they involve conflict.

Darcy and Elizabeth are not to be stopped in their conversation. It is even less likely that they will stop teasing each other. But the third and final night of Elizabeth's "captivity" at Netherfield sees the competition of the couple verge toward genuine argument and disagreement. The conversation again begins with Miss Bingley's attempts to win Darcy's attention. Darcy makes a joke at the expense of the two women as they take a turn around the room. Miss Bingley asks Elizabeth how they might retaliate, and, of course, Elizabeth knows, or thinks that she knows, Darcy's weakness: she proposes that they find a way to laugh at him. But Miss Bingley confesses that she knows no way of making him an object of ridicule. It would appear that Miss Bingley is forcing Elizabeth into a game that she cannot win; Miss Bingley would like it if Elizabeth ridiculed Darcy, for she believes that it will clear the field and leave her with a husband. In a sense, Miss Bingley and Elizabeth share the same misconception about Darcy: they both believe that he does not like to be laughed at. Apparently, Elizabeth believes this to her dying day. But Darcy does not object to laughter; he objects to ridicule—which is different. Darcy understands the distinction between derisive laughter and wit, and if he did not appreciate the latter, he would never have married Elizabeth.

When Elizabeth expresses her disappointment over the fact that her future husband is not to be laughed at, Darcy clarifies the difference between derision and wit for her. "The wisest and the best of men, nay, the wisest and the best of their actions," he says, "may be rendered ridiculous by a person whose first object in life is a joke" (256). Darcy is addressing the relation between virtue and comedy. Any action, he concludes, can be made to seem ridiculous by people who place laughter above everything and everyone. Mr. Bennet, for example, is such a man. Mrs. Bennet's personality is an easy target for ridicule, to be sure, but only a person whose first object in life is the ridiculous would risk turning his family life into a circus for a laugh. Mr. Woodhouse is as easy an object of ridicule as Mrs. Bennet, and Emma is as prone to snipe as anyone, but Highbury remains a place where Mr. Woodhouse has respect. Mrs. Bennet finds respect nowhere.

Elizabeth understands Darcy's meaning. It will soon dawn on her that she risks to be a person like her father. But she does not yet recognize the danger: "'Certainly,' replied Elizabeth—'there are such people, but I hope I am not one of *them*. I hope I never ridicule what is wise or good'" (256). Elizabeth believes that her love of virtue is never sacrificed to her love of a good laugh. When Mr. Collins proposes to her, however, she is so busy laughing at him that she cannot do what in all decency should be done. She has the chance to protect herself as well as Collins by stopping him early in the proposal, but she is stifling a laugh instead of him. Similarly, she does Darcy an injustice by holding up his pride to public ridicule. She justifies mocking him because she believes that pride is a vice, but her real motivations have more to do with her desire to appear uncommonly clever in public. Darcy tries to justify his pride by sketching a difference between pride and vanity. He claims in this same conversation that pride is under regulation where there is real superiority of mind, but Elizabeth (like Kant) cannot conceive of any form of pride as a virtue, and she turns from him to hide her laughter. Contrast her to the bookish Mary. Early in the novel, Mary tells Elizabeth that "vanity and pride are different things, though the words are often used synonimously [*sic*]. A person may be proud without being vain. Pride relates more to our opinion of ourselves, vanity to what we would have others think of us" (234).

Truly proud people cannot be vain because they are autonomous and vanity relies on others. But these truly proud people—people whose vision of themselves will not allow them to stoop to conquer the opinion of others—are rather hard to find in the real world. They are as rare as Aristotle's great-souled man. Elizabeth is right to laugh at Darcy's vain belief in his noble pride. And yet she will end by accepting Mary's Aristotelian view once she falls in love with Darcy, and his pride will prove in the end to be a genuine virtue because only his pride allows him to resist Lady Catherine's snobbish opposition to his marriage.

Darcy possesses great pride, but he still struggles with the temptations of egotism. He needs someone to tell him when his pride turns to vanity, and he knows it. He confesses as much to Elizabeth, when she accuses him of having no defects. "'I have made no such pretension. I have faults enough,'" he admits, "'but they are not, I hope, of understanding. My temper I dare not vouch for.—It is I believe too little yielding—certainly too little for the convenience of the world. I cannot forget the follies and vices of others so soon as I ought, nor their offences against myself. . . . My good opinion once lost is lost for ever'" (257). Darcy believes that some faults of character are natural and that the best education cannot overcome them. He confesses what he believes to be his defect: his inability to love people whose defects he cannot abide, even though he possess the intelligence to understand them. Elizabeth does not confess her defect, but she reveals it nevertheless. To Darcy's confession, she quips, "And *your* defect is a propensity to hate every body" (257). To which, Darcy replies, naming her defect: "And yours is wilfully to misunderstand them" (257).

Darcy's vice and virtue is pride.

Elizabeth's vice and virtue is prejudice.

Pride threatens Darcy's happiness, when it causes him to "hate" Elizabeth for her social rank, but it eventually secures his happiness because it permits him to "hate" Lady Catherine's snobbery and to claim his autonomy. Kant would say that Darcy's sense of pride is a vice, whereas Aristotle would find his aristocratic sense of himself justified.

Elizabeth's prejudice springs, declares Darcy, from willful misunderstanding, and Kant would surely have described Elizabeth's prejudice as a defect of the understanding. Prejudiced people render judgments that are nonjudgments, Kant argues, because they accept opinion and appearances rather than trying to think. They do not possess sufficient willpower to think for themselves. But Elizabeth *willfully* misunderstands, which is to say that she is as much of an anomaly in the Kantian universe as Darcy. Her act of falling in love with Darcy is made possible only by her willful misunderstanding of his vanity as noble pride. Elizabeth begins by being prejudiced against Darcy, but she ends by being prejudiced in favor of him.[11]

Elizabeth and Darcy share the comic fate of having vices that are virtues and virtues that are vices. This is why they are the only characters in the novel whom we do not ultimately wish to laugh at. In the modern world, we are as prone to laugh at virtue as we are at vice. Anytime we can isolate a trait, a difference, and ascribe it to a character, we can render him or her an object of ridicule. Despite the fact that Jane is the picture of virtue, for example, she is not immune to derision. Doubting her reality is a step in this direction. We may occasionally laugh at Darcy and Elizabeth, but we cannot make them into comic objects because their virtues and vices are not sufficiently different to allow us to mark them for ridicule—which is why we want to be them. Given the choice of identifications offered by the novel, most readers will select Elizabeth and Darcy as models. When we laugh at them, therefore, we laugh at ourselves. We attain through our identification with them the form of virtue, ironic self-reflection, most prized in the modern moral universe, and we come to believe in the high and romantic possibility of a happy marriage as a bonus.

What, finally, is Jane Austen's ethics of marriage? And why does it strike us as an ethics? She gives us several different views of couples in the novel. Mr. Collins's ethic of the couple seems to be the one espoused by many of Austen's critics. After Elizabeth refuses him and he weds Charlotte on the rebound, he offers this sanguine view of his marriage: "My dear Charlotte and I have but one mind and one way of thinking. There is in every thing a most remarkable resemblance of character and ideas between us. We seem to have been designed for each other" (347). Collins's inability to understand Charlotte is only exceeded by her dislike of him. His is a false vision of marriage because it is a false vision of his own marriage. But his general vision is one that seems attractive to many readers of Austen, especially those who quibble with the matches that her characters make. It does not seem possible that Austen's intelligent women characters would choose to marry men unlike themselves, and since they often do, the critics attempt to explain it by turning to external factors having little to do with human love.

Elizabeth marries Darcy not because she falls in love but because she is charmed by Pemberley and the spectacle of his wealth.

Emma has a father complex. She made a big mistake falling for Mr. Knightley.

Why cannot Fanny see that Edmund is a weakling?

Charlotte and Elizabeth debate at one point about how to choose a husband. They are discussing Jane and Bingley. Elizabeth believes that Jane has not had enough time to understand Bingley's character during the fortnight of their acquaintance. Charlotte disagrees, revealing the philosophy that will eventually lead her to make the disastrous match with Mr. Collins:

> "I wish Jane success with all my heart; and if she were married to him tomorrow, I should think she had as good a chance of happiness, as if she were to be studying his character for a twelve-month. Happiness in marriage is entirely a matter of chance. If the dispositions of the parties

are ever so well known to each other, or ever so similar before-hand, it does not advance their felicity in the least. They always continue to grow sufficiently unlike afterwards to have their share of vexation; and it is better to know as little as possible of the defects of the person with whom you are to pass your life." (236)

Elizabeth laughs at Charlotte's opinion as if it were a good piece of wit, but in this case no one has the last laugh because Charlotte ends by humiliating herself in marriage. But the fact remains that Elizabeth's ideal of marriage is closer to Charlotte's than to Collins's. Lizzy is not interested in Darcy's wealth. Nor does she believe that couples will inevitably grow further apart as time goes by. But she is not so naive to hope for someone of one mind and one way of thinking. She accepts that husbands and wives may bring different attitudes and personalities to a marriage. In this dream of what might have been, she reflects on Darcy's character, providing a description of marriage as one where partners see in one another liked unlikeness:

> She began now to comprehend that he was exactly the man, who, in disposition and talents, would most suit her. His understanding and temper, though unlike her own, would have answered all her wishes. It was an union that must have been to the advantage of both; by her ease and liveliness, his mind might have been softened, his manners improved, and from his judgment, information, and knowledge of the world, she must have received benefit of greater importance.
>
> But no such happy marriage could now teach the admiring multitude what connubial felicity really was. An union of a different tendency, and precluding the possibility of the other, was soon to be formed in their family. (400)

The marriage of Wickham and Lydia, a union of a different tendency, now makes Elizabeth's happiness impossible, or so she believes. Although she has just confessed her tolerance for Darcy's unlikeness to her, she does not yet comprehend that he is just as prepared to accept her differences. The marriage of Lydia and Wickham, of course, is the consummate example of this difference. Elizabeth's family is enough to scare off Darcy: it represents every type of vice abhorrent to him. Now foolishness is to be wed to dishonesty. How can Darcy, Elizabeth laments, tolerate such a connection to himself? But Darcy has already had the fear that he might have had to tolerate an even closer connection to Wickham, and far from being a reminder to him of an affront to his pride, as Elizabeth seems to think, the marriage between Lydia and Wickham makes Darcy think precisely of the similarity between Elizabeth and himself. He tolerates Wickham, difference incarnate, because he loves Elizabeth. He loves Elizabeth because his vision of her unlikeness duplicates her vision of his unlikeness.

The marriage of Elizabeth and Darcy, of course, will provide the space for further conversations about their likeness and unlikeness. In fact, their marriage is this very conversation, as all good marriages are. Not surprisingly, then, the twin morals of the novel spin off from one conversation in which we see them performing a typical negotiation about how to interpret their life story. It is an act of recollection. Elizabeth surmises that Darcy fell in love with her because she was unlike the other women in his life who were always seeking his approval. She fancies herself a bit of an outlaw in his experience. His virtue is willfully to misunderstand her vices as virtues, a virtue that she prays that he continue: "My good qualities are under your protection, and you are to exaggerate them as much as possible; and, in return, it belongs to me to find occasions for teazing and quarrelling with you as often as may be . . ." (440–41). Elizabeth's virtue and vice are to continue to tease Darcy, that is, willfully to misunderstand him and to remain unlike all the women who have sought to be liked by him.

This picture of vice and virtue leads Elizabeth and Darcy to formulate two opposing morals for their story. Elizabeth begins by expressing her concern that the moral of their story is immoral. She explains that they are together because she broke her promise never to reveal the story of Wickham's malicious attempts to entrap Miss Darcy. What "becomes of the moral," she worries, "if our comfort springs from a breach of promise, for I ought not to have mentioned the subject? This will never do" (441). "You need not distress yourself," Darcy replies to Elizabeth, adding a different kind of moral:

> "The moral will be perfectly fair. Lady Catherine's unjustifiable endeavours to separate us, were the means of removing all my doubts. I am not indebted for my present happiness to your eager desire of expressing your gratitude. I was not in a humour to wait for any opening of your's. My aunt's intelligence had given me hope, and I was determined at once to know every thing." (441)

Elizabeth's moral about broken promises jokes about the inadequacy of Kantian morality. But Darcy's moral is recognizably Kantian. It is a piece of poetic justice, a joke really, constructed at the expense of Lady Catherine. For Darcy describes a world in which Lady Catherine's unjust actions turn against her and bring about her own unhappiness. Darcy's poetic justice would replace Elizabeth's moral and restore Kant to his place. But, in fact, Darcy's moral does not actually displace Elizabeth's. The two morals are opposed, but they live together in the novel, like twins—identical and different—and just as well as Elizabeth and Darcy do. It does not matter that Lady Catherine's vice destroys itself. It only matters that Elizabeth and Darcy have their virtue. Darcy's moral justifies Lady Catherine's vices as easily as Elizabeth's justifies the vice in broken promises.

Perhaps there can be no benevolent motive for breaching a promise, but benevolence may come of broken promises all the same, and occasionally someone's injustice will end by justifying another's life. It all seems, however, to be a matter of chance. Is not one of the strongest impressions to be taken from the novel the sense that Elizabeth and Darcy are morally lucky? Elizabeth and Darcy listen while others do not. They learn while others do not. And they find each other in spite of the odds against them. They struggle with their own characters to put them in place, and in the end, they are fortunate to find that place in Pemberley. But in a world where vice can be virtue and virtue can be vice, it takes more than knowledge to find happiness. It takes luck and, perhaps, a good sense of humor.

Pride and Prejudice concludes happily, but it need not have. It describes a world imperiled, as do most of Austen's novels, a world in which the fabric of society is coming undone, in which the old guarantees of happiness are disappearing, and in which only the fortunate find another happiness by telling the story of their being together. Elizabeth and Darcy never tire of telling and retelling their story. They never tire of recollecting their life.[12] They have ears to hear the particulars about one another. But recounting a story does not necessarily bring an end to moral conflict. Nor does it guarantee a solution, since many moral arguments cannot be resolved. But hearing the particulars may at least give us a chance to find a place in the world.

CHAPTER 11
༄
Counting With Tolstoy

1. Moral philosophy purports to describe human life in the abstract, but abstraction cannot be maintained for long within any ethical discourse. Philosophy may begin by trying to create what Tolstoy would call "abstract human beings," but it ends by describing literary characters in a literary setting, if it succeeds in being moral philosophy. Moral philosophy grows out of literature, and to preserve its moral status, philosophy insistently returns to its origins.

2. It would be naive to assume that literature makes moral conflict impossible, or that it arms moral philosophy with a perfect ethical insight. Not all stories have happy endings; nor do all the problems of living have solutions, waiting somewhere, like a lost glove, to be pocketed by the moral philosopher. Literature does not by its existence alone resolve the moral conflicts of life. It is perhaps more interested in representing conflict than in resolving it.

3. Philosophy, too often, is fiction that refuses life as it is, and because it refuses life, it wants to change it. Literature is fiction that loves life as it is. The more fantastic literature becomes in its representation of life, the more

philosophical it becomes. Literature succeeds as literature when it is faithful to the necessities and particularities of human life.

4. Literature is more about the failures of moral philosophy than about its successes.

5. Plato is a philosopher who writes literature, or so it is said. But, in fact, Plato never comes so close to writing literature that we are tempted to refuse him the title of philosopher. All of Plato's stories remain utterly philosophical.

6. Tolstoy is, above all, a writer of literature. But he was taken as a philosopher in his own day, albeit as an esoteric one, because his stories easily translate into philosophical lessons. But what story does not conclude in a philosophical lesson? It is in the nature of philosophy that it be arrived at.

7. The Western classical tradition begins when Plato translates Homer into philosophy. Perhaps it ends when Tolstoy tries to translate himself into philosophy.

8. Tolstoy's fiction represents the poetic will trying to subject itself to philosophy. Fortunately, for Tolstoy, his philosophy usually fails to subject his poetry.

9. Dostoevsky, in contrast, remains always literary. This is why we call him a psychologist and not a philosopher. To be a psychologist is to remain within the province of literature, and only the epithet of philosopher really offers a threat to the storyteller.

10. "Tolstoy was the greatest storyteller of the modern age." But he was in his talent hopelessly out of date. We cannot, as moderns, read him, so grand is his talent. His stories are too large for our philosophic taste. We desire *contes philosophiques*, not epics. The epic is a prephilosophical form. My description has nothing to do with an innocent or theological view of the world. Only a philosopher could describe the epic as either innocent or theological, and only a philosophic culture, not a literary one, could accept such a description—which is why we all see the epic as a form of literature written before the fall of the gods, when gods have nothing to do with it.

11. Tolstoy writes epically to begin with and later molds his personality to the type demanded by a philosophic culture confronted by the epic. That is to say, he converts to religious zealotry. By this time, however, he has finished writing epic literature. His conversion is too much, too late, in short, superfluous to his talent as a writer. The best evidence against the modern equation between the epic and belief is the fact that Tolstoy, the modern writer with the greatest aptitude for the epic form, could not write an epic after his conversion to intense religiosity.

12. This is not merely one more way to call Tolstoy Homeric. To call Tolstoy Homeric is to give him a compliment that is not a compliment. In the end, Tolstoy is only Tolstoy.

13. We cannot read Tolstoy today because his works are full of more life than we can bear. This is the only trait that he shares with Homer.

14. There is no point in writing literary criticism of Tolstoy's epics. It cannot be read any more than Tolstoy can. Its enthusiasm always strikes the modern reader either as a form of nostalgia or as a form of fervor, if it is good and accurate criticism of the epic, which is to say that it takes on the sentiments of the epic as seen through the modern philosophic view. Epic criticism cannot escape the interpretation of a philosophic culture any more than the epic can. There are no terms in which it might be understood apart from innocence, zeal, or nostalgia. Better, then, for the critic to keep his most cherished thoughts and feelings to himself, to take the great fullness of life offered by Tolstoy into his own life, and to direct what words he has for the public sphere to the minor works, for these are the only works that can be digested by the public because they are minor in the way that modern life is minor.

15. Tolstoy's *The Death of Ivan Ilyich* is about a man who looks for an easy solution to his life but cannot find it. Ivan Ilyich is going to die. Most people interpret the novel as a spiritual statement on the nature of dying. Tolstoy, we insist, was morbidly preoccupied with death throughout his life, and *Ivan Ilyich* is his attempt to come to terms with his own mortality. But Tolstoy does not really describe death. The novel describes the life of Ivan Ilyich, and when Ivan dies, the book ends. Where is death? Ivan Ilyich's final confrontation with death leaves little understanding of dying, for his overwhelming sense of spiritual exultation in death is as personal as his own death. Ivan dies, but so does death in general: "'Death is over,' he said to himself. 'There is no more death'" (134). Tolstoy's novel appears to end in a paradox. It is a book about dying that does not allow death to be.

16. Philosophy, it has been said, teaches one how to die. But Ivan Ilyich does not want to learn. Apparently, Ivan Ilyich is not much of a philosopher because he does not know how to let go of life. He needs, it seems, to read some Plato. The problem, however, is not that simple. Ivan Ilyich cannot let go of life because he has no life to lose. His life has been meaningless. He has wasted it in pursuit of insignificance. He has neither loved nor been loved. He has touched no one. He has been an unreflective man. We say . . .

17. Ivan Ilyich must die, and yet how can a man die if he has already lost

his life? *The Death of Ivan Ilyich* was written to pose this question, and it asks us to see that the old maxim about learning how to die through philosophy is incomplete. Philosophy teaches one how to live, and if one knows how to live, one knows what it means to die. To die, then, Ivan Ilyich must learn how to live. But it is difficult to learn how to live on a deathbed.

18. Tolstoy describes an extremely complicated dilemma, in which a man struggles unwittingly but in the most effective manner to conceal himself from himself. Death compels Ivan Ilyich to hold more and more firmly to his life, even though that life is insignificant. He tries to think about his work as a judge; he thinks about his marriage; he decides to choose a doctor and stick to a method of treatment. But nothing eases the pain. The image of life that he opposes to death increasingly blinds him to life. But Ivan Ilyich has never behaved in any other way. His life has always blinded him to life. Only the suffering of death finally allows Ivan to penetrate the "screens" that he has raised between life and himself. The suffering of death is a precondition for Ivan's awakening to consciousness in his final moments of life. But, at first, death merely compels Ivan to block out the meaninglessness of his life, the loss of his life, with the greatest energy.

19. Philosophy colludes in Ivan Ilyich's need to block out his life. Midway through the novel, he turns to philosophy to grasp the meaning of death. But he ends by reciting Aristotelian syllogisms:

> In the depth of his heart he knew he was dying, but not only was he unaccustomed to such an idea, he simply could not grasp it, could not grasp it at all.
>
> The syllogism he had learned from Kiesewetter's logic—"Caius is a man, men are mortal, therefore Caius is mortal"—had always seemed to him correct as applied to Caius, but by no means to himself. That man Caius represented man in the abstract, and so the reasoning was perfectly sound; but he was not Caius, not an abstract man; he had always been a creature quite, quite distinct from all the others. He had been little Vanya with a mama and a papa, with Mitya and Volodya, with toys, a coachman, and a nurse, and later with Katenka—Vanya, with all the joys, sorrows, and enthusiasms of his childhood, boyhood, and youth. Had Caius ever known the smell of that little striped leather ball Vanya had loved so much? Had Caius ever kissed his mother's hand so dearly, and had the silk folds of her dress ever rustled so for him? Had Caius ever rioted at school when the pastries were bad? Had he ever been so much in love? Or presided so well over a court session?

Caius really was mortal, and it was only right that he should die, but for him, Vanya, Ivan Ilyich, with all his thoughts and feelings, it was something else again. And it simply was not possible that he should have to die. That would be too terrible. (93–94)

Caius begins as the "abstract man" of philosophy. Ivan believes that such abstractions may die. The reasoning of philosophy is perfectly sound. But, in fact, the Caius of the syllogism will never die, even though he represents in abstract form the universality of human death. Ivan instinctively opposes the reality of his life story to the general and abstract quality of Caius's existence. He disrupts the philosophical syllogism with his own particular autobiography. Philosophical discussion needs to hear all the particulars to be moral, Ivan seems to understand, but what he does not understand is that hearing all the particulars does not guarantee a solution. Ivan cannot solve his death by telling himself his life story.

20. "He saw his entire life pass before his eyes." Does this expression, this phenomenon, capture the desire to live in the face of death? As if telling one's own life story defeats death . . .

21. It may be argued that Ivan Ilyich cannot find a solution to death because he does not understand the problem. He wants to solve death, but his problem is life. Ivan tells his life story to oppose that of the mortal Caius. But he does not describe his life. It is true that he narrates a catalogue of emotions, sensations, and realistic events. They are all colored, however, by his own blind egotism. As the list moves from associations with family and friends to his profession, its falseness reaches satirical proportions. Tolstoy has narrated the life of Ivan Ilyich, and we know that he has not been that much in love. We know how he hands down decisions in court. Ivan Ilyich wants to kill off Caius but only to demonstrate his own uniqueness. Ivan believes that he has always been a creature "quite, quite distinct from all the others" (93): "If I were destined to die like Caius," he assumes, "I would have known it; an inner voice would have told me" (94). Death has not yet changed Ivan's mind about his own distinctiveness. Now he merely believes that he suffers more than others.

22. I have been talking like a skeptic and a Romantic, like someone who wants to change his life. I have been talking like Ivan Ilyich or Tolstoy. I am skeptical about Ivan's claims for his uniqueness, just as Ivan is and just as Tolstoy is skeptical about these same claims for himself. But in this skepticism toward their uniqueness lies their greatest claim for uniqueness.

23. A million conventions pervert our reality. A million screens stand as obstacles to the truth. An enormous distance separates me from everyone else. Tolstoy wants to strip away all conventions to reveal a stunning reality. He always fails because these fictions are the stuff of which life is made.

24. Fanya Kaplan, anarchist and failed assassin of Lenin, was removed from her strong room when it became clear that no information could be gotten out of her. Pavel Malkov, a Chekist, shot her in the head. Krupskaya, Lenin's wife, burst into tears at the news. She was deeply affected by the thought of revolutionaries condemned to death by a revolutionary power. This anecdote exposes the Romantic sentimentality inherent in movements. The solidarity of the movement, even of a revolutionary one, cannot escape the so-called injustice of institutionalization. Tolstoy felt the same way about society. Once society begins . . . *Alea jacta est.*

25. We must continue to believe in accidents. It is the greatest test of our faith.

26. "What you're all saying, you see, is that on his own a person can't distinguish the good from the bad, that it all depends on his environment, that a person's a prey to his environment. But the way I see it is that it's all up to chance. Listen, I'll tell you something that happened to me personally . . ." (*Kreutzer Sonata and Other Stories* 255). The narrator of *After the Ball*, a tale of love for a woman ruined by the violent behavior of her father, makes all discussions, abstract discussions about good and bad for example, the pretext for tales concerning episodes in his own life. The young Ivan Vasilyevich tells the story of how he fell in love with the daughter of a colonel, who personified all the grace and grandeur of military form, when in the ballroom, dancing with his daughter. But after the ball, he encounters him in the street in the act of brutally punishing a deserter. The horror of the spectacle revolts him, as he watches the deserter, crying out for mercy to the colonel, beaten within an inch of his life. But, rather than see the cruelty of the colonel as a vice, he believes himself to be inadequate. "Well," he tells his friends, "do you suppose I made up my mind then that what I had seen was something sickening? Not a bit of it. 'If it was done with such assurance and everyone thought it was necessary, then they must have known something I didn't,' was what I thought, and I tried to find out what it was. But I couldn't, no matter how hard I exerted myself. And since I couldn't, I couldn't join the army as I'd planned to, and not only did I not join the army, I couldn't find a

place for myself anywhere in society, and ended up being no good for anything, as you can see" (265).

27. In Tolstoy, as you can see, people are ruined by example, but it is no accident because "example" belongs to society, and society is corrupt. Therefore, virtue is no longer a matter of place. Ivan Vasilyevich's virtue depends on his not being able to find a place. He is displaced, being "good" in terms of an abstract virtue but being "no good for anything." Character in the modern world has become a matter, truly, of dispossession, of disposition.

28. The difference between deserving to be good and being good is a matter of luck.

29. The servant Gerasim, the only character in *The Death of Ivan Ilyich* shown without family and friends, is the one who knows how to live because, apparently, he accepts life and death. But Gerasim is a servant. What Gerasim knows is that the task of life is not to seek place after place but to see his task in his place. Gerasim is an Existentialist. It does not matter where he is; it only matters what he does. What we have not understood about Existentialism is that we can become an Existentialist only at the cost of being either dispossessed or so radically possessed as to feel dispossessed. That is why Existentialist heroes suffer from dizziness and dislocation. That is why Existentialist heroes are nihilists, clerks, slaves, prisoners, and servants. Why is the classic example of the Existentialist a waiter? Sartre thought of this example because he spent all of his time in cafés. But he was sitting at a table not waiting on one. The condition of Existentialist virtue is that the world remain in bad faith.

30. Levin on goodness and cause and effect: "If goodness has a cause, it is no longer goodness; if it has consequences—a reward—it is not goodness either. So goodness is outside the chain of cause and effect" (*Anna Karenina* 830).

31. The modern world is a train. Anna Karenina is a modern woman reading on a train. The only way to get off the train is to fall under it:

> At first she made no progress with her reading. For a while the bustle of people coming and going was disturbing. Then, when the train had started, she could not help listening to the noises. . . . Anna read attentively but there was no pleasure in reading, no pleasure in entering into other people's lives and adventures. She was too eager to live herself. If she read how the heroine of the novel nursed a sick man, she wanted to be moving about a sick-room with noiseless tread herself; if she read

of a member of Parliament making a speech, she wanted to be delivering that speech herself; if she read how Lady Mary rode to hounds and teased her sister-in-law and astonished everyone by her daring—she would have liked to do the same. But there was no possibility of doing anything, so she forced herself to read, while her little hands twisted the smooth paper-knife. (115)

The collection of characters presents no choice to Anna reading on the train. They are all equally tempting. They are all equally impossible. They are all moving, she thinks, more than she is. They are moving. She is sitting still on a moving train. She wants to be moving like the train. She wants to be the train. When she descends to the tracks, like the train, she dies. There is no living with this train.

32. There is no possibility of doing anything, so we force ourselves to read.

33. Tolstoy did not like to sit still. He taught himself to make shoes. Once Gorky came to visit him and found him soling shoes. Gorky could not believe that the greatest living writer was wasting his time on the task. Tolstoy assured him that it was very difficult, but Gorky did not believe it. Gorky tried, unsuccessfully, three times or two times, to pound a nail into the sole of the shoe.

34. Ivan Ilyich is a collector not a worker. He finds his self-worth in possessing objects of value. He fails in his work as a jurist, but he knows how to judge the *objet d'art*. He is a closet interior decorator. He dies because he has to mount a stepladder to show a perplexed upholsterer how to hang draperies. He misses a step and falls. He is assassinated by the knob of a window frame. His is a world of objects. He remembers the smell of his striped leather ball to banish the mortal Caius from his thoughts. In his dining room with the clock that he was so happy to have purchased at an antique shop, he feels at home. Ivan consults a friend about decorating his drawing room; Pyotr Ivanovich recommends pink cretonne with green leaves. None of this matters to Tolstoy. It is grotesque, and the grotesque in Tolstoy always serves morality, marking out those who have fallen. Value does not reside according to Tolstoy in possessions. He tries to dispossess himself, first of his material possessions and then of his talent. But he cannot give away his talent, no matter how hard he tries.

35. After reading Tolstoy on the Gospels, apparently, Wittgenstein divested himself of his wealth. He did not give it to the poor, whom it

could corrupt, but to his rich brothers and sisters who could not be further corrupted by possessions.

36. "An object in a museum case must suffer the de-natured existence of an animal in the zoo. In any museum the object dies—of suffocation and the public gaze—whereas private ownership confers on the owner the right and the need to touch. As a young child will reach out to handle the thing it names, so the passionate collector, his eye in harmony with his hand, restores to the object the life-giving touch of its maker. The collector's enemy is the museum curator. Ideally, museums should be looted every fifty years, and their collections returned to circulation" (Bruce Chatwin, *Utz: A Novel*).

37. What makes a collectible? Fate and the carefulness of its human guardians. Any object may become a collectible, if fate and carefulness will it so.

38. The museum rends the marriage of fate and carefulness in the life of the collectible. The curator's excessive carefulness dispossesses the object of its fate, sacrificing the objecthood of the object to its idea. The first museum is Plato's cave, in which prisoners look at the shadows of objects.

39. Walter Benjamin theorized that the mechanical reproduction of a work of art destroys its "aura." The aura is given to the object by its maker not by its owner. But it is the fact that the object is replicated in numbers to match the greatest potential of possible owners that destroys the aura. Benjamin was also a collector. Would not the aura of the object be protected by preserving the collector's right to private property? The reproduction of the work of art is the scheme of the museum curator and contrary to private ownership. Mechanical reproduction appears to be the democratization of ownership. But, in reality, it fakes private ownership for the masses.

40. "A real work of art," Tolstoy writes in *What is Art?*, "can only arise in the soul of an artist occasionally, as the fruit of the life he has lived, just as a child is conceived by its mother. But counterfeit art is produced by artisans and handicraftsmen continually, if only consumers can be found" (266).

41. Walter Benjamin packs and unpacks his library. But he does not give it away because each book is a memento of life:

> The most profound enchantment for the collector is the locking of individual items within a magic circle in which they are fixed as the final thrill, the thrill of acquisition, passes over them. Everything re-

membered and thought, everything conscious, becomes a pedestal, the frame, the base, the lock of his property. The period, the region, the craftsmanship, the former ownership—for a true collector the whole background of an item adds up to a magic encyclopedia whose quintessence is the fate of his object. In this circumscribed area, then, it may be surmised how the great physiognomists—and collectors are the physiognomists of the world of objects—turn into interpreters of fate. One has only to watch a collector handle the objects in his glass case. As he holds them in his hands, he seems to be seeing through them into their distant past as though inspired. So much for the magical side of the collector—his old-age image, I might call it.

("Unpacking My Library" 60–61)

For Benjamin to divest himself of these memories would be to dispossess himself of his own character. In his collection lies his virtue. Benjamin resembles Ivan Ilyich more than Tolstoy. Here are the limits of Walter Benjamin's so-called Marxism.

42. Family and friends are people whom we collect and recollect.

43. Virtues and vices are collectibles. The more they are collected, the more the taste for them grows. They are rearranged in our characters, like furniture brought into a new room. My mind is a vast chamber of collectibles, a memory theater, in which I stroll to remember myself.

44. Rye-bread we bake is as good as cake.

45. Levin at work:

He thought of nothing, wished for nothing, except not to be left behind and to do his work as well as possible. He heard nothing save the swish of the knives, saw the receding upright figure of Titus in front of him, the crescent curve of the cut grass, the grass and flowerheads slowly and rhythmically falling about the blade of his scythe, and ahead of him the end of the row, where would come rest. . . . Levin lost all count of time and had no idea whether it was late or early. A change began to come over his work which gave him intense satisfaction. There were moments when he forgot what he was doing, he mowed without effort and his line was almost as smooth and good as Titus's. But as soon as he began thinking what he was doing and trying to do better, he was at once conscious how hard the task was, and would mow badly.

(271–72)

Levin does not like to think about virtue. He does not like talking and hearing about the beauty of nature. Words for him detract from the beauty of what he sees. Levin is not a collector, but, like the collector, he wants to compose himself. Collectors compose themselves with the work of art. Workers compose themselves with work. In which lies the greater virtue? Levin prefers an aesthetics of action to that of the object. He is an aesthete of action.

46. Levin wants to make himself into a work of art. He believes, however, that the art is created by subtracting from himself rather than adding to himself. This is why he wishes to dispossess himself of everything he owns and go to work. But no feeling resides in the work for Levin. He feels satisfied only with himself. Levin is his own object.

47. The desire for action is the greatest egotism. It is amazing how much intellectuals admire men of action.

48. "Imagine you were walking along the street and saw some drunken men beating a woman or a child—I don't think you would stop to inquire whether war had been declared on the men: you would rush at them and defend the victim."

"Yes, but I should not kill them," said Levin.

"You might" (841).

49. In Tolstoy, people often fail to be good because they lose faith in their virtuousness. They do not believe that they are in possession of their virtue. They do not believe that their virtue is natural enough to count. Varenka in *Anna Karenina* is naturally good, or so Kitty believes. Ivan Ilyich thinks in the same way about Gerasim. Both Kitty and Ivan deserve to be good, but deserving is not possessing. Kitty tries hard to be good by imitating Varenka; she cares for the sick with enthusiasm. But, in short time, her actions seem a sham. She loses faith in her goodness and condemns herself:

> "What business had I to interfere with others? And now it's come about that I am the cause of a quarrel and that I've been doing what nobody asked me to do. Because it was all a sham, a sham, a sham! . . ."
>
> "To appear better to people, to myself, to God—to deceive everyone. No, I won't descend to that again! I'll be bad; but at any rate not a liar, a humbug! . . ."
>
> She did not give up everything she had learned, but she realized that she had deceived herself in supposing she could be what she wanted to be. (254–56)

50. Wittgenstein's Tolstoy:

> The greatest danger here is wanting to observe oneself.
>
> (*Last Writings* §459)

"Nothing is so certain as that I possess consciousness." In that case, why shouldn't I let the matter rest? This certainty is like a mighty force whose point of application does not move, and so no work is accomplished by it. (*Zettel* 402)

He did not move, but still he felt. (*Hadji Murád* 667)

51. Consciousness of your real self is the root of all evil. When you are conscious of the difference between yourself and the self of your actions, you are either acting better than you are and thus a hypocrite, or you are acting badly, worse than your true self, and thus a sinner. When there is no difference between yourself and the self of your actions, you are not conscious of yourself. This is either goodness or badness, the difference depending on luck. Therefore virtue has nothing to do with action.

52. Tolstoy's characters never live up to what one would expect of his religious fervor. Levin recognizes his moral ambitiousness as superfluous at the conclusion of *Anna Karenina*. Nekhlyudov has the same experience at the conclusion of *Resurrection*. Tolstoy never goes beyond this recognition: I must be good within the limits of who I am. "I" must be good.

53. The question of classical ethics is "How should one live?" The question of Romantic ethics is "How should I live?" Tolstoy's question: "What then must we do?"

54. Levin deliberates about how to care for his dying brother, Nikolai: "To talk of irrelevant things seemed to him shocking, impossible. To talk of death and depressing subjects was likewise impossible. To keep silent, equally so. 'I am afraid to look at him in case he thinks I am watching him. If I don't look, he will imagine my thoughts are elsewhere. If I walk on tiptoe, he won't like it: to tread firmly seems wrong.'" But Kitty cares for Nikolai: "But Kitty evidently did not think, and had no time to think, about herself. Occupied with the patient, she seemed to have a clear idea of something, and so all went well" (524).

55. "Is it possible," Levin was asking himself, "that one can be just only negatively?" (620).

56. One of the greatest paradoxes in Tolstoy lies in his relationship to Romanticism. The Romantics belonged to the first generation of thinkers who wished to live in the past not because they believed that their ancestors knew more than they (Classicism) but because they wanted to forget everything that history had taught them. Tolstoy knows this about Romanticism, but he wants to forget that he knows it.

57. Even though Tolstoy clearly sees that Anna is a Romantic and self-destructive creature, he treasures and "entitles" her. She becomes a parody of not knowing but an unconscious one. A morphine addict.

58. Tolstoy, known for his caustic treatment of his characters, is less ironic toward Anna than Flaubert is toward Emma Bovary. This is as unimaginable as having Levin fall in love with Anna. Nevertheless, it could happen. It happens all the time.

59. Anna says hysterically to Dolly in the famous scene in which she expresses her incompatible love for her son and Vronsky:

> "I love these two beings only, and the one excludes the other. I cannot have both; yet that is my one need. And since I can't have that, I don't care about the rest. Nothing matters; nothing, nothing! And it will end one way or another, and so I can't—I don't like to talk of it. So don't reproach me, don't judge me. With your pure heart you can't understand what I suffer."
>
> She came and sat down beside Dolly, and, peering into her face with a guilty look, took her hand.
>
> "What are you thinking? What do you think of me? Don't despise me! I don't deserve that. I'm simply unhappy. If there is an unhappy creature in this world, it is I." She turned away and began to weep.
>
> When Dolly was left alone, she said her prayers and got into bed. . . . Anna meantime returned to her boudoir, took a wine-glass and poured into it several drops of a mixture largely composed of morphine. After drinking it and sitting still for a little while, she went into her bedroom in a calm and more cheerful frame of mind.   (671–72)

Anna is unhappy. But what could she do to change her luck? Sometimes Tolstoy treats her as if she were merely a Romantic type responsible for her own problems. "Can you understand these desperate passions?" the Countess says. "All for the sake of being original" (812). At other times, Tolstoy behaves as if his interest in Anna springs from her originality, her beauty, and her uniqueness. He pities her misfortune and describes her in the words of a lover:

> She came out into the middle of the room and stood facing Dolly, pressing her hands to her breast. In her white dressing-gown she looked unusually tall and large. She bent her head and with eyes glistening with tears looked from under her brows at Dolly, a thin, pitiful little figure in her patched dressing-jacket and night-cap, trembling all over with emotion.   (671)

60. Anna begins in Tolstoy's mind as a homely woman, *une jolie laide*. Then he falls in love with her. He falls in love with a homely woman and makes her beautiful. But beautiful women in the novel are invariably unpredictable, and Anna does things of which Tolstoy cannot approve. One minute he loves her; the next minute he rails against her. When Tolstoy decides to transform Anna into a woman he can love, he surpasses in a single movement both the sentimentality of Karamazin and the irony of Flaubert.

61. Heidegger's Tolstoy: "Dying, which is essentially mine in a such a way that no one can be my representative, is perverted into an event of public occurrence which the 'they' encounters. . . . This evasive concealment in the face of death dominates everydayness so stubbornly that, in Being with one another, the 'neighbors' often still keep talking the 'dying person' into the belief that he will escape death and soon return to the tranquillized everydayness of the world of his concern. . . . At bottom, however, this is a tranquillization not only for him who is 'dying' but just as much for those who 'console' him. And even in the case of a demise, the public is still not to have its own tranquility upset by such an event, or be disturbed in the carefreeness with which it concerns itself. Indeed the dying of Others is seen often enough as a social inconvenience, if not even a downright tactlessness, against which the public is to be guarded" (*Being and Time* 51).

62. When Anna falls to her death, she asks herself three questions. The order is important for Tolstoy: "Where am I? What am I doing? Why?" (802). Where you are determines what you are doing. Doing in Tolstoy is naturally prior to asking, "Why?" "Why?" is what may never be known by the path of thought:

> And don't all the theories of philosophy do the same, trying by the path of thought, which is strange and not natural to man, to bring him to a knowledge of what he has known long ago, and knows so surely that without it he could not live? Is it not plainly evident in the development of every philosopher's theory that he knows beforehand, just as positively as the peasant Fiodr and not a whit more clearly than he, the real meaning of life, and is simply trying by a dubious intellectual process to come back to what everyone knows? (833)

63. Philosophy reverses the order of the dying Anna's questions. It asks "Why?" before it knows where it is and what it is doing. This is abstraction. This is the meaning of the mortal Caius.

64. When Ivan Ilyich dies, his body becomes a byword to all who view it. Ivan finally becomes a philosopher, achieving greater significance:

The body lay, as the dead invariably do, in a peculiarly heavy manner, with its rigid limbs sunk into the bedding of the coffin and its head eternally bowed on the pillow, exhibiting, as do all dead bodies, a yellow waxen forehead (with bald patches gleaming on the sunken temples), the protruding nose beneath seeming to press down against the upper lip. Ivan Ilyich had changed a great deal, grown thinner since Pyotr Ivanovich had last seen him, and yet, as with all dead men, his face had acquired an expression of greater beauty—above all, of greater significance—than it had in life. Its expression implied that what needed to be done had been done and done properly. Moreover, there was in this expression a reproach or a reminder to the living. This reminder seemed out of place to Pyotr Ivanovich, or at least inapplicable to him. (39–49)

65. Proverbs are words whose nature permits application to more than one case. They no longer stand in relation to the particular. They are universal. Ivan Ilyich's corpse is a proverb. All dead bodies are proverbs, since Ivan's body is like all dead bodies. Ivan's body is a proverb of dead bodies, which are, in turn, proverbs to be applied by their living witnesses.

66. The death mask and the *memento mori* are the natural extensions of the corpse. They obey the imperative to collect the memories of the remains. They obey the imperative to collect what cannot be collected. The corpse is the first collectible.

67. Heidegger's Tolstoy is Pyotr Ivanovich, who refuses to collect himself before Ivan's corpse. Pyotr does not see the beauty in Ivan's death mask, as he saw the beauty in the pink cretonne wallpaper with the green leaves. He is inconvenienced. But Tolstoy describes the beauty of Ivan's remains.

68. The beauty of the corpse is not the beauty of the work of art. It declares itself to be beyond beauty, of greater significance, of greater dignity. It possesses the beauty of the fragment, the aphorism, the ruin, which is in the realm of things, Benjamin says, what allegory is in the realm of thoughts. This is why Tolstoy calls Ivan Ilyich's body a "reminder" or a "warning" and not a "remains." When we look at a corpse, we do not see the remains of the person. We experience the corpse as a reminder. The corpse, like the collectible, works its magic, its inspiration, in memory. The corpse is a work of art, specifically as Tolstoy redefines

it, not because it is beautiful but because it unites human beings with God and with one another in memory.

69. "Seen from the point of view of death," Walter Benjamin writes in *The Origin of German Tragic Drama*, "the product of the corpse is life. It is not only in the loss of limbs, not only in the changes of the aging body, but in all the processes of elimination and purification that everything corpse-like falls away from the body piece by piece. It is no accident that precisely nails and hair, which are cut away as dead matter from the living body, continue to grow on the corpse. There is in the physis, in the memory itself, a *memento mori*; the obsession of the men of the middle ages and the baroque with death would be quite unthinkable if it were only a question of reflection about the end of their lives" (218).

70. Only shortly before dying does Ivan Ilyich begin to see the meaninglessness of his existence. "Yes," he realizes, "all of it was simply *not the real thing*" (132). The "real thing" refers to the object of life, and this instant of reflection leads Ivan to pose the most important question in the novel: "But what *is* the real thing?" (132).

71. It is entirely in character for Ivan Ilyich, the collector, to ask "What is the real thing?" If we think about it twice, we will realize that Marx allows himself to ask this question too, and with greater ease than Tolstoy.

72. "But what *is* the real thing?" Ivan waits for an answer. He hears only silence. No one says anything. He looks for the answer but cannot see it. His eyes are closed. Suddenly, he finds himself in his deathbed:

> Just then he felt someone kissing his hand. He opened his eyes and looked at his son. He grieved for him. His wife came in and went up to him. He looked at her. She gazed at him with an open mouth, with unwiped tears on her nose and cheeks, with a look of despair on her face. He grieved for her.
>
> "Yes, I'm torturing them," he thought. "They feel sorry for me, but it will be better for them when I die." He wanted to tell them this but lacked the strength to speak. "But why speak—I must do something," he thought. He looked at his wife and, indicating his son with a glance, said:
>
> "Take him away . . . sorry for him . . . and you." (132–33)

73. Ivan Ilyich has been lying in his deathbed, but he does not know where he is. He has struggled to think about what has been and what will be but not about what is. He has been literally out of place in the novel. Ivan is the object of Tolstoy's narrative, but the book is not about him

because Tolstoy does not allow him to share any of the moral values about life that sustain the story. Rather, he represents for Tolstoy only a negative example, or an object to criticize. Tolstoy's characteristic didacticism would seem to be responsible for this effect. The voice of moral intelligence is frequently Tolstoy's main protagonist, and he does not permit characters to find their place in a novel until they learn to understand the values that the storyteller already holds. Only when Ivan experiences his revelation, for example, does Tolstoy allow him to become the subject of the story. But the revelation itself is curiously lacking in didacticism and difficult to apply. It is true that the scene climaxes with a burst of light, but Tolstoy does not insist on a moral content: "He searched for his accustomed fear of death. . . . Instead of death there was light. 'So that's it!' he exclaimed. 'What bliss!'" (133). The light apparently has significance for Ivan, but Tolstoy does not provide an interpretation. Instead, he gives a brutal description of Ivan's death rattle.

74. Ivan Ilyich wishes to make over his life, and he seems to accomplish the feat in one moment of perception. He is able to give his life meaning through the sheer power of will. But this is the stuff of which Existentialism is made.

75. Ivan Ilyich does not make over his life at all. He falls into place. He falls off the stepladder into his life. He recollects himself—Ivan Ilyich, a father, a husband, a jurist, a dying man—on his deathbed, and he feels his son's kiss, sees his wife's tears, makes the just decision, and says what he thinks Ivan Ilyich should say on a deathbed.

76. Tolstoy is of two minds about Ivan Ilyich's death. The light is supposed to have significance for Ivan, but, in fact, it has meaning only for Tolstoy, and without Ivan's understanding, Tolstoy cannot express his own. The light is a symbol experienced by a man who dies before he can tell us its meaning: "He wanted to add: 'Forgive' but instead said 'Let it pass [Propusti],' and too feeble to correct himself, dismissed it, knowing that He who needed to understand would understand" (133).

Ivan "lets it pass." Tolstoy lights it up: "What bliss!"

77. "Instead of death there was light. 'So that's it!' he exclaimed. 'What bliss!'" (133). Tolstoy's special effects distract us from the experience of Ivan Ilyich's death. But he who needs to understand will understand.

78. Ivan Ilyich's "conversion" carries the burden of his misshapen life, for that life cannot be discarded at a moment's notice. To throw away his life now would be to repeat the error of which he has been most guilty. Nor does Tolstoy succeed in making over Ivan's epiphany as a miracle.

The revelation is finally quite minor, but, for Ivan, it is a revelation nevertheless. For a solitary instant, Ivan Ilyich takes his place among his fellow human beings, and in that place he has the fortune to step into character.

79. The conclusion of *The Death of Ivan Ilyich* reveals Tolstoy's desire to see the light in order to make up for what he saw as the lack of fullness of the novel. He displayed this same urge at the end of his own life in the train station at Astapovo. He fled from his life to change his life, when he had run out of time. But Tolstoy's death does not belong to the epic time of Ivan Ilyich's death. It is a media event: the movie cameras are running, the headlines are set—LEO TOLSTOY LEAVES YASNAYA POLYANA, the disciples crowd around the frail master, the journalists scramble for position, and Sofya's frantic and humiliating attempts to see her husband before he dies are recorded but not acknowledged. Tolstoy's death belongs to another time, the time of Eichmann's trial in Jerusalem or the time of another arrival at a train station, Lenin's arrival at Finland Station in Petrograd. This is the time of movements and photo opportunities.

80. Tolstoy to the very end: "I do not understand what it is I have to do."

81. "He drew in a breath, broke off in the middle of it, stretched himself out, and died." The last sentence of *The Death of Ivan Ilyich* reads like a proverb.

It stretches out like Ivan Ilyich.

It slouches toward death.

It concludes the story as if it were a moral.

It is meant to be remembered.

82. We may become moral philosophers, if we want, and tell the moral of the story. But we risk in telling the moral not to tell the story. The same may be said of any moral philosophy and any story. For the story comes first, and the moral, no matter how noble, can have no meaning in the story's absence.

CHAPTER 12

᠗

Chinua Achebe and Proverbial Wisdom

The impatient idealist says: "Give me a place to stand and I shall move the earth." But such a place does not exist. We all have to stand on the earth itself and go with her at her pace.   —Chinua Achebe, *No Longer at Ease*

An anthill rises from the savannah. Its name is *Truth Is Beauty, Isn't It?*

It is not so strange a thing for anthills to have such names on the savannah. After all, on the savannah, buses, lorries, and mammy wagons have such names that proverbs are made of: *Slow-and-Steady, God's Case No Appeal, Luxurious, Save Me O God, What A Man Commits.*

This raises some questions about anthills. Can anthills be like a proverb? Can anthills be like a collectible?[1]

So the songbirds left no void, no empty hour when they fled because the hour itself had died before them. Morning no longer existed.

The trees had become hydra-headed bronze statues so ancient that only blunt residual features remained on their faces, like anthills surviving to tell the new grass of the savannah about last year's brush fires.

(*Anthills of the Savannah* 28)

"Memory is necessary," Achebe insists, "if surviving is going to be more than just a technical thing." The anthills survive to tell stories to the new year about the last year. They wear their stories on their faces, like good storytellers. "The storyteller," Achebe also says, "creates the memory that the survivors must have—otherwise their surviving would have no meaning."[2] What has been collected on the faces of the anthills must be recollected for the new year. The story passes from face to face, from the old to the young, from the parent to the child, from the anthill to the grass. "The important thing then is to stay alive," Odili comments in *A Man of the People*. "The great thing, as the old people have told us, is reminiscence; and only those who survive can have it" (145).

Proverbs are stories that survive in the life of memory; and for Achebe, wisdom in life comes with the recollection of proverbs and their successful use in the places where people live. Knowledge stands up in its objects and its words to be collected and recollected, and this knowledge is affirmed in Achebe by the fact that sayings, phrases, adages, and proverbs crystallize into objects that circulate, like so many metaphors on the move, with the regularity and irregularity of public transports—buses, lorries, and wagons.

Christopher Oriko, in *Anthills of the Savannah*, rides one of these proverbs, *Luxurious*, to the place of the anthills and of another proverb, *The last green*, his dying words and a phrase in the private language of love between Beatrice and him. When his friend Emmanuel hears Chris murmur his dying words through a twilight smile, he misunderstands them as *The Last Grin*. Chris's words, for Emmanuel, name his last radiant smile, the comedy of which is not lost on Beatrice who knows the story of the last green bottle to be a bitter joke about the haughtiness of bottles that hang on the wall by a hair's breadth and yet look down pompously on the world. Chris's face swells with the bittersweet laughter of the last green bottle as he falls from the wall and mocks his own pomposity; and Beatrice apostrophizes this radiant smile as *Beautiful* and so as *True*—as a proverb worthy of being told to the new year. "Truth is Beauty, isn't it?" she asks (216).

Beatrice, if truth be told, knows something about apostrophe and also something about something. Her father, wanting a boy and being disappointed by her birth, named her Nwanyibuife—"A Female Is Also Something"—Buife, for short—or "Also Something" (79). But the name comes true in ways unexpected by her father. Agwu, the capricious god of diviners and artists, possesses Beatrice, and something happens to her. She becomes the figure of the storyteller in Achebe's novel. She tells tales of rebels, tyrants, lovers, taxi drivers, and villagers. She becomes wise by collecting and recollecting the stories and proverbs of her people.

And yet it is wise in a world where objects and words present themselves for gathering to keep in mind a proverb about the collecting of proverbs: "When a new saying gets to the land of empty men they lose their heads over it" (*Ease* 51).

Which brings me to my argument about Achebe. If knowledge stands up in objects (Is this why we call them objects of knowledge?) and if people may gather and use this knowledge, what is the relation between its possession and its use? Or, to rephrase the question, what types of stories make possible the fit between the possession and the use of knowledge? Or, what kind of story makes knowledge count? Immediately there arises at least one Scylla and Charybdis between which knowing is caught. If wisdom consists in the recollection and use of proverbs, how do we establish a difference between knowledge and phrasemongering, between wisdom and platitude, or between conversation and idle talk? Knowing lies between a rock and a hard place, the names of which are wisdom and cliché.

One further complication poses itself. Wisdom is the ecstasy of knowing, while cliché is its poverty. But how may we preserve the difference between proverb and cliché, if "Cliché is but pauperized Ecstasy" (*Anthills* 11)?

Does wisdom lose its knowing, if too many people know it?

In Achebe, at least, the relationship between the tyrant and the storyteller reproduces this rock and hard place. *Anthills of the Savannah* tells the story of the competition and betrayal among three boyhood friends, Chris Oriko, Sam, and Ikem Osodi, who rise to power when one becomes the head of state. Chris and Ikem are both journalists and storytellers. But Sam, who becomes His Excellency, is completely tone-deaf; he cannot hear that words turn sour when they are incessantly repeated. He collects favorite expressions and clichés. He hears another dictator use the phrase, "*Kabisa!*" ("Finished!" or "That's all!"), and he begins to use it himself as a handy way of shutting off all discussion of his authority. He reuses the phrase so often, for often must a tyrant shut off discussion of his authority, that it trickles down to the automobile mechanics of the capital. Soon the entire country is shouting "*Kabisa!*" with one rebellious voice.

The occasion of Sam's metamorphosis into a dictator hints at the relation between tyrant and phrasemonger. Sam returns from seeing the old emperor to tell Chris and Ikem with the excitement of a schoolboy about his hero. The old emperor, it seems, never smiles or changes his expression, no matter what happens. Ikem remarks that it is a strategy, "So he wears his mask-face only for the gathering-in of the tribes," to which Sam responds to Ikem's amazement, "I wish I could look like him" (48). At this moment, Ikem later realizes, Sam understood for the first time the potential of his role as a head of state, and he decided to "withdraw into seclusion to prepare his own face and perfect his act" (48). Such are the requirements of oppression, Ikem understands: "the nature of oppression—how flexible it must learn to be, how many faces it must learn to wear if it is to succeed again and again" (89). His Excellency is a collector who adds skill after skill to his repertoire. He amasses a collection of personality traits, tactics, phrases, jingles, and facial expressions, and he gathers to himself men, a cabinet, who thrill at the idea of adding to his collection. Indeed, as someone sarcastically remarks, the original meaning of a cabinet must refer to people "put away in a wooden locker," making inescapably clear that His Excellency's cabinet is merely a product of his collecting mania (52).

At the other extreme, the telling of proverbs takes a liberty with words that frees them to rise to a register that the tyrant either cannot hear or does not want to hear. Consider three brief examples. Professor Okong, hardly a storyteller and in fact a phrasemonger himself, nevertheless raises His Excellency's ire, when he recites proverbs in meetings. "Please cut out the proverbs," His Excellency interrupts (18). But wisdom flies from a fool's mouth. Okong is trying to tell the tyrant that the cabinet shares responsibility in a bad political situation, that "one finger gets soiled with grease and spreads it to the other four" (18). But his recital, so much like the traditional use of proverbs at tribal gatherings, where decisions are taken on the basis of such speeches, has no place in a regime where collective responsibility does not exist. And the wisest proverb may turn to naught in the mouth of the phrasemonger.

At the conclusion of *Things Fall Apart*, to take a second example, Achebe again illustrates the idea that people in authority do not love the proverbial use of words and stories. Okonkwo, the novel's protagonist, murders the District Commissioner's messenger and then kills himself. The Commissioner arrives at Okonkwo's compound to place him under arrest, not realizing that he has committed suicide. To the Commissioner's orders that the murderer be produced, the men in the compound can only respond, with deep metaphysical knowledge of Okonkwo's fate, "He is not here!" (189). The Commissioner does not understand the words, turns red, and demands to know where Okonkwo is, but the villagers cannot respond because he is departed to the nowhere land of suicides.

Finally, they offer some information: "We can take you where he is, and perhaps your men will help us" (189). The Commissioner finds infuriating and superfluous this use of everyday courtesy. To his mind, there is no question of a "perhaps" or of his men helping the villagers. He exercises authority there, and his authority excludes the possibility of placing his power at the service of inferiors. When they discover Okonkwo's body dangling from a tree, and the villagers again repeat their request, "Perhaps your men can help us bring him down and bury him" (190), the Commissioner finally understands from them that it is against custom to touch the body of a suicide. But this revelation does not in the slightest change his attitude toward the villagers' love of superfluous words. Achebe's novel concludes with the Commissioner's intention to write a book about his adventures in Africa, as "the story of this man who killed a messenger and hanged himself would make interesting reading" (191). This story, which is Achebe's novel, becomes in the Commissioner's handling, first, a fit subject only for one chapter and, eventually, fit only for one "reasonable paragraph," because Okonkwo's life story must be sacrificed a second time to authority. One "must be firm," the Commissioner moralizes, "in cutting out details" (191).

Third, consider an example in which Achebe emphasizes how storytellers may take liberties with proverbs, and here I stress that taking liberty with proverbs may in fact be a form of taking liberty from them. One of Beatrice's girlfriends, nicknamed Comfort, suffers the misfortune of being twenty-six and still unmarried. When her fiancé takes her to meet his family, an aunt makes a proverb at her expense. Beatrice narrates the story:

> an aunt or something of his made a proverb fully and deliberately to her hearing that if *ogili* was such a valuable condiment no one would leave it lying around for rats to stumble upon and dig into! Well, you can trust Comfort! The insult didn't bother her half as much as her young man's silence. So she too kept silent until they got back to the city and inside her flat. Then she told him she had always suspected he was something of a rat. I can hear Comfort saying that and throwing him out of her flat! Now she is happily married to a northerner and has two kids.   (*Anthills* 81)

Comfort turns the proverb to her advantage by redirecting it. A story told for the purpose of expelling her is sufficiently thick to permit her to expel someone else. What the Commissioner in *Things Fall Apart* calls the love of superfluous words is really an understanding of the delicacy of the fit between phrases and the world. This understanding does not equate brevity with wisdom. Brevity is the soul of wit, not of wisdom. Rather, wisdom is a matter of counting, and the love of superfluous words expresses a generosity toward a superfluous world, a world in which many things and ways work. It discovers pleasure and comfort in extending the conversation among things, numbers, and words, and recognizes that words may make easier the uttering of other words. We have to say "one" and "two" to get to "three." To cite another Ibo proverb about proverbs, "proverbs are the palm oil with which words are eaten" (*Things* 10).

And yet proverbs may at times take on the appearance of idle talk and jinglism. At the tragic moment of Ezeulu's undoing in *Arrow of God*, when his god deserts him, the priest's mind cracks, and from his mind flows a procession of empty proverbs:

> Why, he asked himself again and again, why had Ulu chosen to deal thus with him, to strike him down and cover him with mud? What was his offense? Had he not divined the god's will and obeyed it? When was it ever heard that a child was scalded by the piece of yam its own mother put in its palm? What man would send his son with a potsherd to bring fire from a neighbour's hut and then unleash rain on him? Who ever sent his son up the palm to gather nuts and then took an axe and felled the tree? But today such a thing had happened before the eyes of all. What could it point to but the collapse and ruin of all things? Then a god, finding himself powerless, might take to his heels and in one final, backward glance at his abandoned worshippers cry:
> If the rat cannot flee fast enough
> Let him make way for the tortoise! (260–61)

When proverbs cease to work, the world is shaken and turned upside down. The inadequacy of proverbs to tell of that world exposes either that they have become clichés, with no power to tell the truth, or that the possibility of wisdom itself has vanished, if it ever existed. In earlier scenes, Ezeulu had used many of these same proverbs to guide his life and to persuade others to follow his advice. Now a powerful wind, the wind of the ruin of the world, blows over him, and it scatters before it all knowledge, leaving potent words in its wake, tossed about and aimless, like so many pieces of straw exploded from the rooftops.

If this wind surprises the gods themselves, what can human beings do about it?

In the modern world of skepticism we are most concerned with things fallen apart because we do not believe that they have ever been together. For the skeptic, who arrives after things have come undone, the world is a pile-up, a heap of wreckage, in which we try in vain to put things together. Nostalgic is the belief that things once fit with other things, that words had meaning, and that we could count them as being somewhere; and the skeptic hates, above all, nostalgia. We skeptics like to contest nostalgia rather nostalgically by hovering in our thoughts above places of origin, denying that we have lost something or that we see anything at all. Our places of origin are therefore desolate places. They are stages that have been unset by our skepticism, although no amount of skepticism can rid us of the empty stage. Wordsworth called it the unfitting of the mind for thought. But such is the nostalgia of skepticism that it loves to dwell upon its lack of fitness and that it must keep returning to the same places to find nothing.

But to find something, you have to have lost it, and in this case nothing counts for something. "A man whose horse is missing will look everywhere even in the roof," says the kindly captain in *Anthills of the Savannah* (163). Let us look everywhere for what we have lost, until what we find begins to look like a horse.

But, first, I add a word of caution about looking for horses, which I take to be an activity, like most activities, that risks to end well or not. I do not know that I will be able to square the extremes of wisdom and phrasemongering between which knowing finds itself, perhaps for the simple reason that these may not be extremes at all. It may not be the case that wisdom and phrasemongering involve usages that exclude one another. I advance, nevertheless, one fragile idea to consider. There are good and bad proverbs, and the bad proverbs are more important to the good ones than the good ones are to the bad. By this I do not mean that proverbs are good or bad in themselves, since "what is good in one place is bad in another place" (*Things* 71), but that their goodness and badness are determined by the degree to which they fit with other proverbs. Things go with other things, until they fall apart.

"When we hear a house has fallen do we ask if the ceiling fell with it?" (*Arrow* 20).

"Wherever something stands, another thing stands beside it" (*Ease* 149).

"But in all great compounds there must be people of all minds—some good, some bad, some fearless and some cowardly; those who bring in wealth and those who scatter it, those who give good advice and those who only speak the words of palm wine. That is why we say that whatever tune you play in the compound of a great man there is always someone to dance to it" (*Arrow* 113).

Looking for something, a horse or anything else, involves learning how to be successful in finding things. It is, in part, the art of looking for meaning. We learn this art by imitating other people's searching. When people do not know what they are looking for, they cannot expect to find anything, unless they follow the example of those who do know what they are looking for, or at least believe that they do. Then a person looks for something inside the bag of a person looking for something (*Anthills* 174).

Among the characters of Achebe's novels, people look for wisdom in conversation and proverbs, and if we look where they look, we may find out something about what it means to be wise. Each novel contains scenes of public debate, in which argumentation by proverb determines the political direction of a people. These scenes do not tell us a great deal about the origin of wisdom, it is true, but they may give us an idea of how proverbs work in certain settings. The scenes are often protracted, as political debates necessarily are, and difficult to cite, but the use of sayings, jokes, and parables differentiates them from the kinds of rhetoric that we have come to associate with political argument in the West. Whereas political leaders in the West are likely to give prepared speeches, to cite statistics, and to underplay the rhetorical nature of debate, the characters in Achebe's novels take great pleasure in argument, confrontation, and rhetorical display.[3]

The meeting of the Abazonian delegation, described in *Anthills of the Savannah*, provides the flavor of argumentation by proverb. The background is that the Abazon do not vote to give His Excellency the title of President-for-Life, and he takes revenge on them by refusing to develop a system of wells for the region. As a result, drought ravages the countryside, and a delegation goes to the capital to plead for mercy. It even offers to reverse its vote. But the delegation is portrayed as a mob of agitators, and when Ikem, who comes from the area, goes to a meeting, his attendance is used by His Excellency as an excuse to have him shot for treason. Here is a truncated version of the meeting, which takes off when an old man stands up to defend Ikem for having missed various social gatherings:

"I have heard what you said about this young man, Osodi, whose doings are known everywhere and fill our hearts with pride. Going to meetings and weddings and naming ceremonies of one's people is good. But don't forget that our wise men have said also that a man who answers every summons by the town-crier will not plant corn in his fields. So my advice to you is this. Go on with your meetings. . . . But leave this young man alone to do what he is doing for Abazon and for the whole of Kangan; the cock that crows in the morning belongs to one household but his voice is the property of the neighborhood. . . .

"If your brother needs to journey far across the Great River to find what sustains his stomach, do not ask him to sit at home with the layabouts scratching his bottom and smelling his finger. . . . I have heard of all the fight he has fought for people in this land. I would not like to hear that he has given up that fight because he wants to attend the naming ceremony of Okeke's son and Mgbafo's daughter.

"Let me ask a question. How do we salute our fellows when we come in and see them massed in assembly so huge that we cannot hope to greet them one by one, to call each man by his title? Do we not say: To everyone his due? Have you thought what a wise practice our fathers fashioned out of those simple words? To every man his own! To each his chosen title! We can all see how that handful of words can save us from the ache of four hundred handshakes and the headache of remembering a like multitude of praise-names. But it does not end there. It is saying to us: Every man has what is his; do not bypass him to enter his compound. . . ." (112–13)

By the end of the speech, which goes on to great lengths, the old orator has mesmerized the audience. It greets his words with great silence and even greater applause. His main topic, to which I will return, becomes the place of storytelling in political struggle, called the place of tortoises and leopards. What I take to be the old orator's wisdom is his ability to recollect what everyone knows—the proverbial—in a situation about which everyone is nevertheless in doubt. It is not the case that he dominates his audience or tells it what to think, as His Excellency would like to dominate those around him. Rather, he thinks with his audience and accepts the idea that his telling is owned by the story, that his wisdom is embedded in stories familiar to his friends and family, and that their understanding and agreement contribute to any power that he might be said to gain in his oratory. No person, however powerful, can accomplish anything good or bad without the help of other people to see the task to its end.

Part of the power of proverb is the summoning of this help. It calls on a power that is already there. For when does power ever spring from nowhere? Proverbs align what a people knows of itself with what it hopes to know of itself, knowing that hope is also part of what a people hopes to know. Their power of conviction lies solely in these terms.

The sense of "the proverbial," like so many terms popular to theories of meaning today, embraces the extreme positions of knowledge and its opposite. Proverbial wisdom appears to be caught between contradictory uses. But I do not want to suggest in any manner that this fact threatens its status as knowledge. Rather, it exposes what knowledge is all about, which is a certain movement between what may be proverbial, commonplace, even cliché, and what may strike one as beyond knowing, as knowing's ecstasy. The proverbial defines a case in which the everyday world and the need for an intelligence beyond worlds collide. Sometimes, proverbs capture a wisdom beyond words and worlds. At other times, our wisdom is not up to the task of facing what seems beyond knowing. Sometimes, it may seem as if we force the unknown into the proverbial in order to tame it. At other times, our inability to understand something unknown convinces us that we do not know what we have always thought that we knew. But none of these cases is in itself extraordinary, beyond the world, and proverb tells us as much about them as anything else. "It is like a bird that flies off the earth and lands on an anthill. It is still on the ground" (*Ease* 150). What escapes the proverbial, we might say, does not belong to the story. It means the end of storytelling.

To find oneself in the proverbial is part of learning how to look for oneself. Proverbs are the manner of looking that those who find keep to. We are not so lucky in Achebe to see the conditions of this finding traced out or to bear witness to the birth of knowledge. (Perhaps, to bear witness to the birth of such knowledge is more than can be expected of a writer who knows enough to understand that the birth of knowledge is worth witnessing.) But Achebe does give us many examples of a thing becoming something else, which is perhaps the best that can be hoped for in the case of beings who do much of their knowing in function of language. When something becomes something else, we have entered into the form of knowing usually called naming, but we may also consider that knowing in general shares with naming a result in which something comes to mean something else.

Most often, something becomes something else in Achebe in that form of address called apostrophe. Public transports are vehicles of apostrophe; people become proverbs and phrases, horses bearing wisdom from place to place. Now a problem arises about the conditions of this wisdom. It is one thing to describe the proverbial as a form of storytelling concerned with what a people knows and hopes to know about itself. It is another thing to view naming as concerned with what a person knows or hopes to know about himself or herself. This assumes, first of all, that names tell stories. The obvious question asks whether the names and stories that people acquire contain an understanding of them or of anyone else? If a woman, for example, acquires a derogatory nickname does it count as a form of knowledge about her?

I pose this question and others of its kind not because they are questions that I can answer but because they are questions that I would like to think about in public.

A Man of the People devotes a chapter to such questions, but it does not, I warn in advance, provide many answers. Chapter 2 opens by citing a proverb and concludes by cursing the jingles that stick in our mind. Odili, the narrator, insists that the common saying, "It doesn't matter *what* you know but *who* you know," is not idle talk in his country (17). But it is not clear whether other common sayings and forms of address escape this fate. Odili's girlfriend, Elsie, has the habit in lovemaking of summoning the name of her last lover until she makes the transition to a new one. During her first time with Odili, she calls out "Ralph darling," and a next-door-neighbor, who hears the commotion, takes to calling Odili "Ralph" from that day (25). The neighbor, in turn, is nicknamed Irre, short for Irresponsible. He is himself a celebrated womanizer, whose fame in the area is achieved when he manages to seduce a beautiful and inaccessible young woman, whom the other boys have apostrophized as Unbreakable. When Odili finally discovers the origin of Elsie's apostrophe, he confides the story to Irre, who promptly takes to calling him Assistant Ralph or, in Elsie's presence, simply A. R.

Minister M. A. Nanga, the populist of the novel's title, nicknames himself. In the early days, his friends referred to him simply as M. A., to which he always called out in a joke, "Minus Opportunity." But when Odili remakes his acquaintance years later, the man is horribly offended when someone uses the old nickname. Odili cannot shake the episode from his thoughts, and the chapter concludes with a meditation on jinglism and an interpretation of why Nanga should wish to refuse his old name:

For days after the Minister's visit I was still trying to puzzle out why he had seemed so offended by his old nickname—"M. A. Minus Opportunity." I don't know why I should have been so preoccupied by such unimportant trash. But it often happens to me like that: I get hold of some pretty inane thought or a cheap tune I would ordinarily be ashamed to be caught whistling, like that radio jingle advertising an intestinal worm expeller, and I get stuck with it. (26)

The riddle is as much a jingle as Nanga's nickname. They are both things that stick in the mind. Jingles are perhaps one of the best cases in the modern world of superfluous language. They advertise products and people. We invent them to get attention for things and persons that are important to us and that we want to be important to others. Their status as knowledge is at best questionable and at worst contemptible, but jingles are one way that we come to know something, as least in the modern world. Nicknames seem equally superfluous. A person given a nickname already has one given name and does not require another. But naming is such and people who name are such that they do not want to stop the process of naming any more than we would wish to stop the process of getting to know other people. Jingles and nicknames express the love of superfluous language for which the Commissioner has contempt. They are forms of counting and collecting. They appear to serve no other purpose than to make dear to us things and people unknown to us.

Odili goes on to solve the riddle. He surmises that Nanga could admit his yearning for higher education in 1948, but now in 1964, in the anti-intellectual climate of the country, he prefers to represent himself otherwise. Odili is right. Nanga adjusts his public face in the same way that His Excellency does in *Anthills of the Savannah*. In the early years, the nickname, "Minus Opportunity," serves to make Nanga memorable to those around him. Now the Minister represents himself as a populist, seeking a new nickname or title, "Man of the People." His character is like a weathervane; it points in whichever direction the political wind blows.

Before returning to the question of whether apostrophe is at all instructive about the conditions of knowledge, I want to focus on a final example of the process. It is a fine example because it involves both phrasemongering and an account of the origin of a common saying. Minister Nanga arrives at the school where Odili is teaching to receive an honorary degree. The degree is bestowed by the principal of the school, one Mr.

Nwege. Nwege is an infamous phrasemonger, who regularly reads such literature as "Toasts—How to Propose Them" (7). And his introduction of Nanga practices what he has acquired from such tracts in abundance. After going on for over twenty minutes, largely about himself, Nwege begins to stir grumbles from his audience. But Nwege, ever insensitive to anyone who would wish to shut his mouth, continues droning on, until, suddenly, a young tough stands up and shouts, "It is enough or I shall push you down and take three pence" (13). The audience bursts into laughter, and Nwege is driven from the podium.

Such phrases make no sense without an understanding of their story. The point is precisely that they permit an economical access to a body of shared knowledge and narratives, and if one does not belong to the group to which the stories belong, the phrase has no meaning. Among the Anata, the phrase, "Push me down and my three pence is yours," has the currency of a proverb. I am not sure myself what it means. Indeed, one difficulty in reading Achebe for any Westerner is the interpretation of the many parables, proverbs, and common sayings used in his novels. I can retell the story of the proverb's origin because Achebe tells it, but I do not have access to the story of its application, its fitness as a proverb among the Anata, because I have not learned it by being exposed to many applications. I imagine that this is true of all or most proverbs. Even the most accessible of proverbs, "A stitch in time saves nine," for example, may prove enigmatic, if I have no experience with the sphere of its application. Besides understanding what a stitch is and what the nature of holes in material is all about, I have to know about sewing, and I have to know that this proverb, which is ostensibly about sewing, has broader applications to situations in which sewing is not at issue. And to use this proverb well, presumably, I must be able to apply it creatively to new situations, while preserving the knowledge that there are some situations in which it will not work.

The laughter of the audience tells us that the young tough understands the proverb, and the story of the proverb confirms its appropriateness to the situation. First, the phrase originates in association with Nwege, although this is not necessary for the proverb to work. The story has it that when Nwege was a poor elementary school teacher, he owned an old rickety bicycle of the kind to which the villagers gave the onomatopoetic name of *anikilija*. The brakes did not work, and one day as Nwege was cascading down a steep slope on a narrow path, he saw a truck coming in the opposite direction. Faced with a head-on collision, Nwege began to call out to passing pedestrians, "In the name of God push me down" (13). But nobody helped him, and so he added an inducement, "Push me down and my three pence is yours" (13). From that day forward, the phrase became a popular Anata joke.

Notice that the two usages provided by Achebe concern Nwege's inability to stop. But it is worth stressing that the kinds of stopping involved are sufficiently different as to make the transfer between them a minor miracle of adequation; and yet such miracles happen everyday. They are part of the everydayness of language. They are the proverbial as such.

I suppose that some such miracle is necessary as well if we are to accept these examples as ways of talking about the conditions of knowledge. The miraculous involves the luck of finding out how things work. But this is no easy task, as implied by the idea of miracles. For instance, to the question whether nicknames, derogatory or otherwise, count as knowledge of a person, one can respond only that the question requires more conversation and, specifically, conversation about particular individuals and their nicknames. Some of these conversations will come to satisfactory ends, while others will not. I expect that a major obstacle in such conversation would be ethical. For example, to accept the name Unbreakable as a form of knowledge about a woman means characterizing the knowledge of women in a certain way. Elsewhere, in *Anthills of the Savannah*, Achebe cites a case of a woman apostrophized as *Black is Beautiful* (70). These examples run the risk of finding evil in knowledge. For, in the extreme case, the argument is not that people may acquire a nickname that victimizes them but that such cases exemplify an irresponsibility inherent to naming and knowledge as such. We call signification inadequate when we object to the fact that it represents something as something else instead of representing the thing as itself. Words compromise the purity of their objects, the argument goes, when they take their place. The thing itself has a dignity that the naming and knowing of it breaches.

The problem with this argument, of course, is that it has lost touch with the story of knowledge. Knowledge, at least as one story has it, is the knowledge of good and evil. To reduce knowledge to an understanding of the good alone produces a form of wisdom in which evil has no importance. Knowledge is cruel because we need to know cruel things. It is saintly because saints are worthy of our acquaintance. The temptation is great to make language the guarantor of virtue, but only this temptation is finally worth anything, not the theory. Or, rather, the temptation is the best that the theory can provide.

One of Chris's historical analyses exposes the fact that values shift in ethical argument and, perhaps, that a desire for knowledge beyond the shift, beyond good and evil, has only a little to do with knowledge as such. Ikem and Chris are having an argument about His Excellency's plan to refurbish the Presidential Retreat. Ikem thinks that the money should be spent on the poor. Chris is certainly not opposed to the idea, but he punctures Ikem's idealism by rubbing his aestheticism in his face. Chris seizes on the bloody history behind our most prized monuments:

> "Nations," he said "were fostered as much by structures as by laws and revolutions. These structures where they exist now are the pride of their nations. But everyone forgets that they were not erected by dem-ocratically-elected Prime Ministers but very frequently by rather unat-tractive, bloodthirsty medieval tyrants. The cathedrals of Europe, the Taj Mahal of India, the pyramids of Egypt and the stone towers of Zimbabwe were all raised on the backs of serfs, starving peasants and slaves." (67–68)

The Taj Mahal does not risk to vanish into thin air because human beings attach contrary values to it. The wisdom of the proverb is such a structure. An origin in evil does not necessarily compromise its present goodness, importance, or applicability. Good and evil are not extremes that exclude each other, and searching for a knowledge beyond good and evil will not provide a happy escape from the clash of the world. The point is to use what is there and what works, when it does not harm anyone. "A man who lives on the banks of the Niger should not wash his hands with spittle" (*Ease* 17).

Politics and ethics are not so different that they do not sometimes find themselves being debated in the same place. It is difficult to decide whether I have been talking here about politics or ethics. I sense a shift in my argument, and I experience the temptation to write "political" in those places where I have customarily written "ethical." (Perhaps it is because I am trying to find out how proverbs first began to work, and this brings me to a moment when politics and ethics are not yet distinguishable.) There is an urge in most of us to keep ethics and politics apart. We would like for purity's sake to imagine them as existing in separate houses, but, like good neighbors, they are not beyond keeping an eye on each other's property, especially when one has gone on holiday. We may wish to treat ethics and politics as polar opposites, but we rarely succeed.

Proverbs carry the wisdom of a people. That this wisdom belongs to a

political body is inescapable, and yet the constraints on the use of proverbs are not always political. Proverbs often express a knowledge similar
to that of the moral of a story. They claim to work beyond their particular
circumstances, aspiring to a form of general wisdom. Perhaps wisdom is
itself ethical for this reason; we call those people wise who appear to
possess a knowledge beyond their own limited purview. We call them the
worldly wise, as if they inhabited the entire planet and not merely one
corner of it.

Achebe is, of course, a good choice to aid thought about politics because his novels aspire to large political claims. But I do not want
to address the politics of colonialism or of African dictatorships here.
Achebe is without question a master in these large political concerns. He
has, however, achieved an equal mastery in a smaller sphere of influence,
in which ethics and politics merge, and this mastery is especially apparent
in those places in his novels in which the proverbial turns political or,
rather, reveals that its impulse is already political. In *Things Fall Apart*,
for example, the enormous political struggle between the colonial church
and native belief takes place on the diminutive site of the proverbial. The
children who feel the most nostalgia for the stories told to them in their
mother's hut are most susceptible to conversion to Christianity because
they find the parables of the Bible irresistible. Colonialism works in part
here because it inspires nostalgia for one's own life story.

When this struggle continues in *No Longer At Ease*, it takes the same
forms. The opening chapter concludes by telling the story of Obi's departure from Umuofia for England in order to be educated for the "European
post" in the civil service that will eventually prove his ruin. The ceremony
attending his departure explodes in an enthusiastic combination of village
oratory and proverbs with Christian hymns and recitations. It would seem
that the village of Obi's grandfather has now been entirely absorbed by
Christianity. But it is not clear who has swallowed whom. The fervor of
the villagers' belief also absorbs Christianity because its community demonstrates a greater capacity to embrace Christianity than the Christian
community does it. The village stands as an example of the perfect past
of Christian utopic future; the vision promised by Christianity appears
retrospectively to be intelligible only within a prehistory not its own.[4]
Converts are drawn to Christianity because its stories remind them of
something they have once had more perfectly, and this perfection is expressed as the proverbial.

I want now to turn to two overtly political uses of the proverbial in the hope that I can clarify some of the ways in which the wisdom of the story relates to the everydayness of politics. Achebe recounts both episodes in *Anthills of the Savannah*. Ikem calls the first one an impeccable scenario, and he tells it in the context of a meditation on the military vocation and authoritarian politics. In fact, it is important to keep in mind that he concludes this story of a confrontation between a soldier and a clothing vendor by reflecting on His Excellency's tone-deafness because the explicit theme of the story, its parabolic function, is that violent people are often stupified by proverbial language. Ikem is waiting in his car at the Gelegele Market while a girlfriend, named Joy, is having her hair plaited. The street is littered with stands, and unlicensed second-hand traders rush into hiding whenever the police pass by and just as quickly stampede back into business when they depart. But one trader does not manage to clear out quickly enough when an army car arrives, and the driver almost runs him over, causing general alarm. Ikem is the narrator:

> A cry went up all round. The driver climbed out, pressed down the lock button and slammed the door. The young trader found his voice then and asked timidly:
> "Oga, you want kill me?"
> "If I kill you I kill dog," said the soldier with a vehemence I found totally astounding. . . . I watched the ass walk away with the exaggerated swagger of the coward. . . . But then the one who had had the brush with the car suddenly laughed and asked:
> "Does he mean that after killing me he will go and kill a dog?"
> And the others joined in the laughter.
> "No, he means that to kill you is like to kill a dog."
> "So therefore you na dog . . . Na dog born you."
> But the victim stuck to his far more imaginative interpretation. "No," he said again. "If I kill you I kill dog means that after he kill me he will go home and kill his dog."
> Within ten minutes the life of the group was so well restored by this new make-believe that when the offensive soldier returned to his car to drive away his victim of half an hour ago said to him:
> "Go well, Oga." To which he said nothing though it diminished him further still, if such a thing could be conceived. (44)

This is indeed an impeccable scenario. The trader takes a liberty with the soldier's words that is central to the way that proverbs work. Proverbs allow individuals to tell the types of stories necessary to see situations differently. Proverbs tinker with situations, permitting us to see what a situation is and what it might be. The trader and the soldier are locked in a struggle to tell a story about this situation. But their stories serve different ends. The soldier desires to silence the trader. His story is a curse in which the trader metamorphoses into a dog and a son of a bitch. It ends in the present moment with the affirmation of his power and the trader's obedience. But the trader's story points toward the future. In this scenario, the soldier kills the vendor and then goes home to continue venting his rage by killing his own dog. It is a crazy story, not unlike the crazy fable that Kant tells about the consequences of lying; but in its madness lies a form of wisdom about the adverse situation in which the storyteller finds himself. The trader characterizes the soldier's rage and his own helplessness by telling a story suitable to their excess. Whereas the first story exists to preempt struggle and to control opposition, the second one describes the soldier's injustice by playing out his disgraceful and arbitrary rage to its logical conclusion. It memorializes the struggle between the soldier and his victim as the first event in a series of outrageous and violent actions that are worth recollecting and opposing. It is, to recall Achebe's political view of storytelling, a reminiscence to be recounted to survivors.

I have been looking for something called a horse, but I seem to have found a dog. I beg forgiveness and excuse myself by recalling that we already know, from proverb, that a horse is so valuable that we look in the wrong places when we have lost one. We may also find horses everywhere to compensate for our loss. A few years ago a human interest item appeared in newspapers across the United States that captures this tendency. It arrived from Africa, like Achebe, but neither its transit nor the reasons for it seem as innocent. A revenge-minded Masai tribesman whose brother had been killed by a lion attacked a stuffed lion in a glass cage at the Tourist Ministry in Nairobi. Friends had told him that the ministry kept a live lion. He ran into the downtown office on a Saturday, broke the glass with his bare hands, and began strangling the lion. When asked why he did it, he said that his brother had been killed by a lion and he had sworn that one day he would kill a lion with his bare hands.[5]

That the wire service chose to recount this local story to the global community already shows the mark of discrimination; and it is easy to reject this poor man's actions as a form of peculiar madness, excessive grief, or exotic mania. But I am not sure that any one of us behaves any differently when everyday we use words to call things other things in order to stave off the immensity of our losses.

What does the difference between stuffed and unstuffed matter to the stories that we tell ourselves in order to live where other people live? What matters, finally, are the promises that we make to ourselves and to others and whether we can find ways to fulfill them without going crazy or hurting someone.

After Sam kills Ikem, to turn to my last example of political proverb, Chris goes into hiding. His Excellency alerts his forces, and they look for Chris everywhere, in right and wrong places. The search makes of Chris a horse whose value lies in his death, not in his life. It is a search that proposes to end in not finding the horse ever again. But the man whom His Excellency chooses not to find the horse ever again loves horses too much to look for one in this manner. The captain and his troops storm into Beatrice's apartment to look for Chris, and, not finding him, they look with great energy where he is not. The captain explains the frantic search with the proverb that we have been using here to look for the proverbial: "My people have a saying which my father used often. A man whose horse is missing will look everywhere even in the roof" (163). But Beatrice does not understand at the moment that this is the captain's way of telling her that he is presently looking where he knows the horse is not, and that, consequently, he is her friend.

The next day as Beatrice rises from bed, the telephone startles her. The voice on the line alludes to the proverb of the night before and begins the work of telling her the real story: "I know where the horse is. But I don't want to find him. Get him moved. Before tonight" (164). Beatrice is alarmed. She does not know whether to try to contact Chris to tell him of the danger or whether the real danger to him is in trying to find him. Will a message to him, she puzzles, expose his hiding place or help him to leave a hiding place that has already been exposed? She risks contacting him, and Chris moves to another location. The next day she again hears the voice on the telephone. He congratulates her on having moved the horse but impresses upon her that it would be better to think about a "cross-country gallop," if the horse is still in the city. "It's not me," he concludes, "you should worry about; I can promise never to find a horse. It's the others who are more efficient than myself in the matter of finding horses" (170). Caught off guard, Beatrice asks whether the captain is "genuine," as he cuts off the conversation, and then reminds herself that she "should not look a gift-horse in the mouth" (170). But the gift-horse calls that evening to offer his mouth: "You asked was I genuine? If by that you mean do I ride horses or do I play polo the answer is an emphatic no. But if you mean do I like horses, yes. I am a horse-fancier" (170).

The proverb is the medium for a struggle, a conversation, in which enemies become friends. They converse in what seems to be the cryptic words of a secret language. But this language is not really strange to the normal way that friends and lovers talk. The proverb opens the possibility of a joking relationship, not unlike that between Chris and Beatrice, "a couple of tired swimmers," Achebe calls them, who tread water and rest at the railing together and who share each other's sweet breath (57). Beatrice learns to trust the captain in spite of who he has been because his ability to take liberty with proverbs teaches her that he respects freedom. A person who speaks in such words may be trusted not to speak the language of tyranny. A person who answers questions that do not have to be answered for his own peace of mind but for that of others understands peace of mind. He is a horse-fancier, one who respects the nervousness of horses and has a calming effect upon them. He understands that horses need to be talked to even when we have nothing to say to them.

In the proverbial are found the enormous resources of the extraordinary and of the ordinary, of moments when a person becomes a horse and of moments when someone knows not to look a gift-horse in the mouth. It is easy to be charmed by the proverbial when it is ecstatic, especially in its literary guises. Literature is the proverbial taken to the limits of ecstasy. For when the proverbial works, we experience the visitation of wisdom in a phrase or story that we have heard before. But let us not underestimate the virtue of having something to say, when there is nothing to say. "Proverbs are the palm-oil with which words are eaten," which means that they help to ensure that we continue to talk (*Things* 10). At these moments, proverbs may seem small, as do those who use small proverbs. But, as proverb says, to succeed as a small person is no small thing (*Anthills* 179).

Having nothing to say is the state that tyrants wish their subjects to live in, but storytellers know how to tell a story about nothing, as if it were something, thereby making memories and meaning possible. This is why tyrants hate storytellers. As long as people share memories freely they will have something to say to a tyrant. Proverbs, sayings, adages, and stories involve such recollections. Storytellers tell a story that owns them and their kind, and this story strikes its hearers as the wording of their own thoughts and dearest recollections. Storytellers care nothing for the desire to take things apart or to succumb to silence, whether it be motivated by the skeptic's valuable doubt or by the tyrant's worthless treachery. Storytellers are most interested in meaning and, above all, relation: "Whatever happens in the world has meaning. As our people say: 'Wherever something stands, something else stands beside it'" (*Ease* 149). Storytellers hold this proverb dear. For it is the ethic of storytelling. Each world has a world within it, Beatrice realizes as she discovers within her-·self the moral vision of the storyteller. "*Uwa-t'uwa! Uwa-t'uwa! Uwa-t'uwa!*" she sings: "World inside a world inside a world, without end" (77).

Agwu, the god of the story, gives this song to Beatrice, and she tells a story, the story of Achebe's novel, in order that those who survive her will not be convinced by tyrants that nothing happened in their past. Beatrice is not present when Chris dies. Emmanuel and the others witness his murder and recount his dying words, but it is Beatrice who remembers Chris for them because she has the words to describe his beauty and his truth. Like the old orator at the assembly of the Abazonian delegation, the maker of fables about leopards and tortoises, Beatrice tells the story of politics in order that politics might continue to exist. To call out the name of politics, whether it be present or not, to apostrophize it for those who are not attending to it—this is Achebe's ideal of storytelling. I conclude by citing the old orator's belief that storytelling is superior to warfare and by recalling his fable about the role of storytelling in political struggle. Recalling is greatest, he remembers:

> "Why? Because it is only the story can continue beyond the war and the warrior. It is the story that outlives the sound of war-drums and the exploits of brave fighters. It is the story, not the others, that saves our progeny from blundering like blind beggars into the spikes of the cactus fence. The story is our escort; without it, we are blind. Does the blind man own his escort? No, neither do we the story; rather it is the story that owns us and directs us. It is the thing that makes us different from cattle; it is the mark on the face that sets one people apart from their neighbors. . . .
>
> "Whether our coming to the Big Chief's compound will do any good or not we cannot say. We did not see him face to face because he was talking to another Big Chief like himself who is visiting from another country. But we can go back to our people and tell them that we have struggled for them with what remaining strength we have. . . .Once

upon a time the leopard who had been trying for a long time to catch the tortoise finally chanced upon him on a solitary road. *'Aha,'* he said; *'at long last! Prepare to die.'* And the tortoise said: *'Can I ask one favour before you kill me?'* The leopard saw no harm in that and agreed. *'Give me a few moments to prepare my mind,'* the tortoise said. Again the leopard saw no harm in that and granted it. But instead of standing still as the leopard had expected the tortoise went into strange action on the road, scratching with hands and feet and throwing sand furiously in all directions. *'Why are you doing that?'* asked the puzzled leopard. The tortoise replied: *'Because even after I am dead I would want anyone passing by this spot to say, yes, a fellow and his match struggled here.'*

"My people, that is all we are doing now. Struggling. Perhaps to no purpose except that those who come after us will be able to say: *True, our fathers were defeated but they tried.*"   (114–17)

All of which suggests a moral for this story.

If we cannot rise to a political or ethical solution to our problems on this earth, the wise thing is to keep rolling around on the ground.

CONCLUSIONS

CHAPTER 13

∾

Between a Rock
and a Hard Place

IN BOOK 16 of the *Iliad*, Patroklos pleads with Achilleus to beat down his anger and to reenter the battle in order to save his friends and compatriots from the violent grasp of the Trojans. But Achilleus will not let his anger go. Patroklos describes the genealogy of his friend's hardheartedness with what looks like a famous proverb:

> Pitiless: the rider Peleus was never your father nor Thetis was your mother, but it was the grey sea that bore you
> and the towering rocks, so sheer is the heart in you turned from us.
> (16.33–35)

Achilleus was born "between a rock and a hard place," and this phrase remains an apt expression of the difficulties in which he finds himself throughout the epic. Whether the rock and hard place be his divinity and his humanity or his wrath and his grief, the point is that Achilleus is torn, even though being torn is not a trait that we tend to associate with the godlike. But, as Homer makes clear, Achilleus is not so godlike that he cannot be torn. He may not be quite human, but neither is he divine. In fact, in being torn, he shows that he may be more human than divine.

The human characters in the *Iliad* are for the most part torn in one way or another, which is to say that they are torn by the nature of their judgments. Achilleus is torn between his own honor and the honor of the Greeks. Agamemnon is similarly torn. He must decide between being the king and giving kingly due to Achilleus, but he cannot decide, because if he chooses to be the king, he loses the support of Achilleus who is necessary to defend the community without which he would have no reason to be king. Patroklos is caught between his loyalties to Achilleus and to the Greeks. One is larger than life, and the other is life itself. Priam struggles between grief and hatred, having to play the father to his son's murderer to have again his son.

It would be possible to show in any one of these cases or, rather, choices that the characters are on both sides of an argument. Agamemnon, for example, wants both his kingship and to save his kingdom. But how could we show that these characters *must* be on both sides? It might also be possible to show that, as readers, we are on both sides of the argument. But, again, how could we show that we *must* be on both sides? I am not necessarily referring to the judgments of tragedy. Tragedy is sometimes defined as an action in which a person in search of goodness encounters a choice that cannot be made without sacrificing his or her goodness. The problem is that this definition implies that tragedy haunts only certain choices and situations, certain houses, as Aristotle would say, and not the action of choosing to live well in the places where people live. But what would it mean to claim that living for the good necessarily places us on many different sides? To phrase the question differently, to what extent do the terms by which we make a decision remain as a residue of the decision? After we have made the choice, do we leave the odd term behind or does it slouch with us toward death? When we try to make decisions, do we always find ourselves between a rock and a hard place?

Ethics tells the story of this want, which is to be on the side of both lacking and desiring. We fill holes, Achebe says, by digging other holes. If a choice could be made, there would be no need for a decision, a *decidere*, a cutting. Decision involves the impossible and necessary task of cutting one thing that we want into one thing that we can want and another thing that we cannot want. We end by choosing between one thing, as if it were two things. It appears, for example, as if Anna Karenina and

Achilleus are trying to decide between two sides of an argument. In fact, they are torn because they are trying to decide between one thing, as if it were two things. Anna understands the dilemma intuitively, when she tries to decide between her son and Vronsky: "I love these two beings only, and the one excludes the other. I cannot have both; yet that is my one need" (671). Achilleus, similarly, cannot separate his honor from that of the Greeks. For, as Homer amply demonstrates, Achilleus cannot be himself in isolation from the Greeks, so his decision to cut himself off in order to honor himself is doomed from the start. Achilleus is nobody outside of Greek society.[1] Ethics tells such stories. It asks us to relate what we cannot want and what we cannot not want. It asks us to give an account of a configuration of meaning that strikes us as profoundly alien to our wants.

The demand of ethics bears most heavily when we are trying to decide something in everyday life. But it casts its weight as well when we contemplate life and try to decide how to decide, and our theories strain under the burden of deciding well. It may look as if we cannot make up our minds between theory and practice, for example, or between character and action, or universal and particular, objectivism and relativism, fact and fiction, skepticism and belief, can and ought, doing and knowing, having and knowing, ethics and politics, flesh and spirit, moral and story, philosophy and literature, and on and on and on. But it is not merely that we cannot make up our minds. That would mean that it is possible to decide between such terms, when thinking about it shows and situation after situation shows that we tend to leap from position to position, even as we condemn one or another position as untenable.[2] We ought to be able to decide, we think, but we cannot, and yet we do. Nor can we decide whether the "ought" is better than the "can," and yet we do. We are like Peter Freuchen, leaping from ice pan to ice pan and telling the story of our leaping. The higher Kant climbs, the more he comes to solid ground. The deeper we dig into Aristotelian bedrock, the less substance we find. Wittgenstein said that it is only in language that we can mean something by something. But in order to have language you have to mean something. "To have language," "to possess language," is already a metaphor that makes language into an object.

The idealism of theory is attractive to ethics because it allows us to conceive of things as they ought to be. But there is also idealism in conceiving of things as they are. Kant's old saw, "That might be right in theory, but it won't work in practice," captures the tension. It is good to be right in theory, if theory is the only place in which one has the chance to be right. Our idealism is crushed as we pass to practice and know that it will not work. But when anything works it also entails a rightness and an idealism. It is good to have something work in practice, if practice is the only place in which one has the chance to have it work. The mind and the hand thrill at the experience of a fit. Something counts. It works. An adequation results that bespeaks the coming together of two impossibilities, or three, or four. Within being right is working and within working is being right. Being right and working are a rock and a hard place.

The political world is a hard place where we look desperately at times for a rock to cling to. It is difficult, however, to judge whether the rocks are to be theories and moralities or whether the rocks are the hard places where we come to stand. Ethics and politics are a rock and a hard place, but which is which and how do we tell them apart? Today we like to divorce politics and ethics in the hope that each will be purer as a result. But when we separate off politics to purify ethics do we also produce a purer politics? The mind rebels at the idea of purifying politics by distancing it from ethics. What would a pure politics be anyway?

Let us turn the question over to language for a moment. On the one hand, politics has to do with a *polis*, a community, whose end is being served. Politics is interested in the realm of practice, although its notion of practice might be better described as an essentially hypothetical operation geared toward obtaining an ideal state of human cohesiveness. The political aspires to a wholly inclusive community, but it practices on a community already in existence and therefore tends to restrict itself to the temporal and geographical limitations of that community. It struggles to discover how it may affect a specific group, but it strives at every turn to preserve this group against other political bodies. It is possible, therefore, to create "political alliances," whereas it does not make any sense to speak of "ethical alliances," for politics concerns the relation between essential and distinct groups, and ethics believes ultimately that there ought to be only one group. Whence the necessity, for example, that Kant take as given the existence of a community of rational beings before turning to a description of the categorical imperative.

That may be right in theory, but it won't work in practice.

Our language exposes a limit: that "political alliances" are possible and that "ethical alliances" are impossible. But the practice of politics is willing to go a long way toward conceiving of its constituencies as an ethical alliance. Countries and the world swarm with political bodies coming together to preserve what is "right" and "good."

On the other hand, our language tells us something about the relationship among politics, ethics, and action. The phrase, "political activist," is current coin for the most theoretical and idealistic of political practitioners. We suspect that the political activist is more ethical than the politician. But if this is the case, why can we not conceive of an "ethical activist"? Let us try to define one. This ethical activist is a man, and he belongs to those who . . . "do"? . . . "think"? . . . "have"? . . . "speak"? . . . "write"? . . . I suppose part of this description would end up claiming that in whatever the ethical activist does, he produces ethics as an activity or he makes ethics active. Does this also imply that he would give ethics a place? A hard place, perhaps? Would something ideal take on a more rocky substance? We talk of ideas that rock the world. Is ethical activism that process by which ethical ideas rock the world? In short, to come full circle, would the ethical activist be the most "political" of ethical thinkers?

You will say that I am merely bending language. But language bends this way and that because it means something.

Nor do I think that it is ultimately an issue of language. Consider a current idiom of literary theory: "There is no outside the text." This idea presumably refers to the claim that human beings exist exclusively in the world of language. What would it mean to reverse the proposition? "There is no inside the text." I suppose this idea would claim that human beings cannot enter into a world of language. What we have here is a metaphor in which it is hard to know whether metaphoricity consists of the determination of objects by language or that of language by objects. Current fashions side with the former. But they continue to speak about language as if it were a thing. Ideas of depth, density, thickness, loftiness, and baseness are strange (and wonderful) ways to speak about language. In the idiom of poststructuralism, for instance, we celebrate "gaps," "fissures," "breaches," and the like. Describing language in such terms is a bit like using human virtues to extol wine. It tells us more about what is supposed to be good in human beings than what is good in wine. Thus we drink of the wine of human kindness. When we express a preference about the nature of things in our descriptions of language, are we talking about language or are we still talking about things?

Current idiom permits things to be linguistic, but it cannot accept that language might be thinguistic.

In Achebe's *Things Fall Apart*, there is a scene in which Okonkwo tries to fathom how it can be that his virility has not been passed on to his son, Nwoye. Okonkwo becomes fixated on one of his nicknames, "Roaring Flame," as he stares into the log fire in his hut:

> Okonkwo was popularly called the "Roaring Flame." As he looked into the log fire he recalled the name. He was a flaming fire. How then could he have begotten a son like Nwoye, degenerate and effeminate? Perhaps he was not his son. . . . He pushed the thought out of his mind. He, Okonkwo, was called a flaming fire. . . .
>
> He sighed heavily, and as if in sympathy the smoldering log also sighed. And immediately Okonkwo's eyes were opened and he saw the whole matter clearly. Living fire begets cold, impotent ash. He sighed again, deeply. (143)

Things Fall Apart is an apt title for a story in which people are confronted by their thingness and its falling apart. Is it unnatural for a man who "pushes" thoughts from his mind and whose "eyes are opened" to look to a smoldering log for guidance? Okonkwo sees in the smoldering log his life story. Does the smoldering log see in Okonkwo its life story? Each is a parable for the other. How far and in how many senses does the metaphor extend? Can a metaphor extend to the point where it is no longer a metaphor but a thing? Does a metaphor become a thing when we "extend" it? "Roaring Flame" is no mere metaphor in this sense. It is *something* else.

To confront the knowledge of things is to come to a knowledge of what it means to belong. Language is one thing by which we understand belonging and belongings. Philosophers have written one history of thought in terms of "being" and "becoming," and knowledge has fallen away from being as a possibility. Perhaps we might write another history in terms of "beings" and "belongings," in which knowledge reveals itself in its belonging-to. Knowing cannot necessarily be cut off from having. The question is to decide, if we can, which has first importance or whether knowing and having can be conceived as two things.

There is a story about a toad and a leopard. The toad owned a magnificent stallion. One day the leopard saw the toad riding toward him. The toad was riding sidesaddle, bouncing about the horse most comically, and the horse's path was erratic and ugly. The leopard stopped the toad.

"Let me show you how to ride a horse," he said.

The leopard mounted the magnificent stallion swiftly and surely. He brought it to a canter and directed it in tight, elegant patterns over the field. Finally, he brought the horse to a halt in front of the toad and dismounted with a bow.

The toad remounted the horse in the same way, sidesaddle, and, looking down at the leopard, said, "Knowing is not the same as having." Then the toad rode off as before, bouncing comically along the path.

Two tramps stand beside a tree not sufficiently large to stand beneath. They are waiting for someone or something, and to pass the time, they tell stories, play games, move objects, and perform parts. Other people pass through, bringing objects and ideas along with them. They all tell stories and want to hear stories. Occasionally, people have the idea that some object or idea is not part of the story, and they try to throw it away. Other people have the idea that this idea is not part of the story, and they try to throw away the idea of throwing ideas away.

Limits are not easily thrown away. They are not merely the old binary oppositions (whose polarity is, in the end, merely imagined by freeze-framing language in motion), but rocks and hard places. What appear as contrasts and opposites are extremes in our experience, complementary poles in the field of human activity, in which neither pole is completely reducible to its counterpart and through which understandings and mis-understandings happen. These are always in flux to some degree but not completely so. Kantianism changes over the years. A Kantian today is something different from a Kantian before World War II. An Aristotelian is different from a post-Kantian Aristotelian. A label such as "post-Kantian Aristotelian" makes sense, if it makes sense, because the same things have changed in terms of other same things. But such labels cannot be applied to anyone. If I were to say that Richard Rorty is a "Kantian," many people would disagree. The same could be said about Bernard Williams, Alasdair MacIntyre, or Jacques Derrida. But if I then asked what is Kantian about these thinkers, we would begin to think about the problem in a different way. We would begin to ask what counts as Kantianism. The question then becomes: how many things have to be Kantian about a thinker before we call that thinker a Kantian?

We like to assume that interpretation is open-ended. We capture our freedom through the allegory of interpretation, as Kant knew so well. But interpretation has rocks and hard places. In the case of the moral of a story, for example, we may say at one extreme that every story has a different moral, or at another extreme that any moral can be made to fit any story. There is a great deal of flexibility in the relation between morals and stories precisely because it involves relation. But this flexibility does not exclude the possibility of a "fit." We may find two stories that have the same moral, or find it impossible that a particular story and moral fit together.

There is freedom in the fit as well. There is freedom in belonging.

Terms such as "adequation" or "fit," "counting," "collecting," and "recollecting" describe ways of marking the rocks and hard places of interpretation. Some interpretations are more adequate to particular stories. We experience a fit, and if this fit survives, it will influence other forms of adequation. Validity in interpretation will never be more than this. Interpretation proceeds not by spontaneously inventing its applications but by collecting and recollecting applications that are already in place. (This is not to say that there is no invention; it is to say that all is not invention, and that invention may be applied with justice to the creative remembering, collecting, and arranging of things and ideas whose applications have a history.) What we choose to collect or what we collect inadvertently contributes to our make-up. But all is not accident. Collection relies on fate, but it also relies on carefulness, neither of which ever defeats the other completely. They are, rather, another rock and hard place between which we find ourselves.

What would a dictionary of these limit terms look like?

Collecting looks for things that count and it looks for fits. Things are in a collection or outside of it. Some things fit better in an existing collection than other things, but every collection includes things that do not fit as well as others. What counts as something to be collected may depend on the collection, but it may just as well depend on the thing. It may just as well count on who has counted the thing as worth collecting before, or who wants to have it now, or in the future. In 1988 at Sotheby's a manuscript by Beethoven, including passages from his Ninth Symphony, sold for $158,000. In the same year, Andy Warhol's cookie jar collection sold for about the same price. What counts is subjective, an effect of want rather than intrinsic worth. ("Intrinsic worth" is also decided on the basis of whether something counts for somebody.) Modern taste often exposes this aspect of value precisely because the emergence of greater individual desire has heightened the eccentricity of what counts in objects. For possession by someone now holds more worth than the object. Some cookie jars once belonging to Andy Warhol have equal value to an original Beethoven manuscript because people care as much about Warhol's desire as they do about Beethoven's art.

Counting judges things, people, and stories. It adds, subtracts, multiplies, and divides. But it also confronts reality, which is what will not go away, even though it may not fit with preconceived notions of what is. Different things count in different places because counting is one way of taking account of what different places are. To count on someone or something expresses a fundamental optimism about the future of where we are. We also count in order to begin. 1 ... 2 ... 3 ... Go! We start at three, not at zero. Zero had to be invented, as did imaginary numbers, because counting judges what is. Those who want us to start at zero in anything, especially in ethics, are asking the impossible, or we might say that they are asking too little of us. Alasdair MacIntyre, for example, criticizes Kant's doctrine of the categorical imperative in *A Short History of Ethics* because he argues that it is "parasitic upon some already existing morality" (197). The categorical imperative provides a test for rejecting proposed maxims, according to MacIntyre, but it fails because it does not tell us from where we are to derive maxims to test. MacIntyre wants Kant to be able to say "Go!" without counting. But only God in the history of the world said, "Let there be light!" without first counting to three.

Fit. To fit is when things go together, whether we want them to or not. We cannot make things fit, if they do not. If something fits, we cannot get rid of it. When we collect something, we may, because of a fit, get something that we do not count on.

Recollecting is a way to reaffirm the activities of collecting, counting, and finding fits. We remember things past in a recollection of a collection, and when we recollect, we count and count on anew; the act of recollection reaffirms what we have counted on as something worth counting on again. Things sometimes lose their objecthood in the process of recollection as they are fit together with our memories of people, other things, situations, and places. Sometimes the opposite happens: things become things in the act of recollection. As we recollect the thing in our hand, we remember the thingness of the thing as it had been held before in our hand or in another's hand. Recollection is temporal, and it tells a story steeped in time. Recollection is, then, intimately related to the retelling of a story. It is a story about recovery and judgment, in which we decide whether to collect anew or to discard. The active recollection of a person is therefore a special type of storytelling. We recognize a person in the act of recollection as someone who belongs to us by virtue of having been in the places where we have been, and when we recollect someone, we choose again to collect him or her. To recollect is to affirm past acts of counting people and to decide anew whether they belong to us. We can collect ourselves by recollecting people and things that do and do not belong with us.

Work. To work takes account of adequations and countings. Collecting, recollecting, counting, and looking for fits are all forms of work. But, most important, work counts on surprises. We say, in the jubilation of being completely surprised by our luck, "It works!"[3] Work is surprising because it recollects the fit between what is and what is not, between what we cannot want and cannot not want, between what is and what ought to be, and between being and belonging. To provide an example, we are disposed today against the idea of the autonomous self à la Kant. Bernard Williams offers a coherent critique of this form of subjectivity, when he argues that it expects us to leap to a midair position when we are faced with a decision in the here and now. Since we cannot leap to a midair position to make a decision—basically because we need to make the decision where the decision is—the disinterested self may be said not to exist. It is an elaborate fiction. But the next question is, "Does it work?" Or, to put the question differently, "Can it come into being?" If I am led by the history of idealist philosophy to accept myself as an autonomous self, might I not persuade others of it in certain situations? Might I not summon extra strength because of the belief in my autonomy? Consider the case of those who refused to collaborate with the Nazis. Where did they summon the strength to exercise their character? It did not always work. It did not have to work. But sometimes it did work.

Sometimes it works, and we are surprised by virtue.

When work stops being surprising, it stops working. To be surprised at work is to be overtaken by belief, or undertaken, to reverse a direction that is unimportant, as if the rug were pulled out from under us and we remained intact, upright, like a fine set of china does when the master illusionist tugs away the table cloth.

Literature is a form of work because it makes us think about what is work to think about. It stirs astonishment, thoughtfulness, and memory. The work of literature is proverb, saying, parable. A proverb is a star of light. A saying is a clay pot or a wooden toy in our path. A parable is a story that we tell to picture an idea too difficult to understand.

But if life is an idea too difficult to understand, all stories are parables.

There is no story that is not true.

CHAPTER 14

∾

A Parting Shot

ONCE RABBI ELIJAH, the Gaon of Vilna, said to his friend, the Preacher of Dubno, "Tell me, Jacob, how in the world do you happen to find the right parable for every subject?"

The Preacher of Dubno answered, "I will explain to you my parabolic method by means of a parable."

"Once there was a nobleman who entered his son in a military academy to learn the art of musketry. After five years the son learned all there was to be learned about shooting and, in proof of his excellence, was awarded a diploma and a gold medal.

Upon his way home after graduation he stopped at a village to rest his horses. In the courtyard he noticed on the wall of a stable a number of chalk circles and right in the center of each was a bullet hole.

The young nobleman regarded the circles with astonishment. Who in the world could have been the wonderful marksman whose aim was so unerringly true? In what military academy could he have studied and what kind of medals had he received for his marksmanship?

CONCLUSIONS

After considerable inquiry he found the sharpshooter. To his amazement it was a small Jewish boy, barefoot and in tatters.

'Who taught you to shoot so well?' the young nobleman asked him.

The boy explained, 'First I shoot at the wall. Then I take a piece of chalk and draw circles around the holes.'

"I do the same thing," concluded the Preacher of Dubno with a smile. "I don't look for an appropriate parable to fit any particular subject but, on the contrary, whenever I hear a good parable or a witty story I store it in my mind. Sooner or later, I find for it the right subject for pointing a moral" (Ausubel 4).

NOTES

1. A Childhood Memory

1. Murray Krieger, "In the Wake of Morality: The Thematic Underside of Recent Theory," *New Literary History* 15.1 (1983): 119–36, esp. 135.

2. Life Stories

1. See Bernard Williams's discussion of this question and its impersonal form, "How should one live?" in *Ethics and the Limits of Philosophy*, pp. 1–21, 66–70.

2. The literature on conventions and norms in the social sciences is exploding at the present moment. For recent theories about how norms and conventions are formed and internalized, see the References, especially Axelrod (1984, 1986), Hamilton (1964), Lewis (1969), and Scott (1971). Robert Axelrod takes a neo-Darwinian perspective on norms drawn from William Hamilton's path-breaking work on kin selection and inclusive fitness, in which he argues that cooperation is evolutionarily motivated because it contributes to the success or fitness of individuals who share genes. I am indebted to some of his descriptions of cooperative behavior.

3. The ultimate unreliability of action is revealed by the concept of acting. Acting

(dramatic or other) presents a threat to social relationships because it is all acting and no character. It follows, in other words, the demands of aesthetics as Aristotle established them, where character exists only for the sake of acting. A person may, for example, play the part of the virtuous man and perform those actions characteristic of it. But this playing does not make him a virtuous man (although Aristotle does argue that playing a role for a long time may in fact bring about a change in character to the good). He may be either an actor or a hypocrite, which explains to some degree the body of literature dealing with the so-called paradox of the actor.

But other cases present themselves. Consider the acting involved in courtship. The desire for the beloved may lead someone to behave, consistently over a period of time, in ways different from his or her character. The practice is not hypocritical because the change is not necessarily a masquerade. It is rather a change brought on by trying to make oneself desirable to another person, so that one begins to mirror that person's preferences.

Whether courtship can bring about true character change or modification is here at issue, for the agent may lapse into old habits after the romance cools, or he or she may indeed be changed by the relationship. Jane Austen's notion of romantic relationships characteristically depends on this process. There is always the possibility of one person being changed for the better or the worse by a romantic attachment. Moreover, part of courtship involves trying to fathom whether certain character traits are real or contrived. Austen's tendency is usually to distrust the actions of people over the short run in favor of descriptions of their character provided by those whose character is already known to be reliable. See chapter 10 for further discussion of Austen's sketch of courtship.

4. Plato approaches the idea of cooperation and its relation to ethics at one point in the *Republic*, when Socrates challenges Thrasymachus's claim that injustice is a source of strength (351c–352). Socrates argues against Thrasymachus that no group of men, whether a state, army, or set of gangsters or thieves, can undertake any wrongdoing if they wrong each other. Injustice renders joint undertakings impossible, according to Socrates, and any group that wishes to embrace a common action must accept the idea of justice to be successful.

3. The Case Against Linguistic Ethics

1. The shift to the analysis of practices from that of language is pervasive on the contemporary scene, and often startling in its resources. In *Pursuits of Happiness*, for example, Cavell discovers in Hollywood comedies of the 1930s and 1940s a language for discussing the relation among love, self-transformation, and the habits of living together. MacIntyre has devoted his efforts in recent years to redescribing vices and virtues on the basis of a strong sense of the traditions by which the conflicts of ethics are worked out. Nussbaum stresses the fragility of goodness through a reading of Aristotle and Greek tragedy, steeping the good in the problem of luck and disabusing one of the idea that it could ever be associated with a single idea or a single word. Finally, Williams is at the heart of the resurgence of the idea of moral luck in philosophy today. He replaces linguistic trends in recent analytic philosophy with a view of practical life described in terms of "thick concepts."

2. Beauty is the symbol of morality in Kant because in beauty the will discovers the analogy for its own autonomy: thought unbound by concepts. Therefore, to put constraints on interpretation, as Miller does, by arguing that the language of the text coerces the reader, is to destroy the analogy, the symbolism, by which literature represents morality. Moreover, the replacement of the categorical imperative by a linguistic imperative misunderstands the role played by the categorical imperative in Kant's ethics. The categorical imperative is not a law that coerces the will. It is the formula by which the will discovers its freedom in self-legislation. A true categorical imperative for texts, a "linguistic imperative," could only have the autonomous self-legislation of a text for its object, not any reader, and this is an absurdity.

3. This development in deconstruction is somewhat regressive when we consider that Roland Barthes proposed the analogy between sentence units and narrative structure with the advent of structuralism. Deconstruction withdraws from this already dubious analogy to one that parallels narrative and single words. See Roland Barthes, "Introduction to the Structural Analysis of Narratives": "If a working hypothesis is needed for an analysis whose task is immense and whose materials infinite, then the most reasonable thing is to posit a homological relation between sentence and discourse insofar as it is likely that a similar formal organization orders all semiotic systems, whatever their substance and dimensions. A discourse is a long 'sentence' (the units of which are not necessarily sentences), just as a sentence, allowing for certain specifications, is a short 'discourse'" (83).

To a certain extent, of course, the emphasis on a small group of words has also plagued moral philosophy. Ethical theorists tend to focus on "good," "right," or "ought," assuming that an understanding of them will give a general comprehension of ethics. When they find the words to be ambiguous, they lose faith in the possibility of describing ethical representation. Cf. Bernard Williams, *Ethics and the Limits of Philosophy*, pp. 127–28, 131.

4. The Moral of the Story

1. Hedayat's story was given to me by Gernot L. Windfuhr, upon whose translation the following is based. Professor Windfuhr also related to me that the names of the characters have the following meanings: Mashdi, "one who has made the pilgrimage to the shrine of the Eighth Imam in Mashad"; Zolfaqar, "master of backbone, name of the sword of Ali, the champion of the Shiites"; Gowhar Soltan, "jewel/essence of the king"; Setare Khanom, "star/fate lady"; and Ostad Mashallah, "master wonderful." I thank Professor Windfuhr for his translation and for bringing the story to my attention.

2. In addition to the work of MacIntyre and Williams, which I discuss below, I recommend the writings, listed in the References, of Cavell (1981), Diamond (1983), Medina (1979), Nussbaum (1983, 1986), Phillips (1982), and Raphael (1983).

3. This is not to say that there are no problems with MacIntyre's account. For example, it is clear that MacIntyre arms himself against liberal individualism at every turn, and when he tries to trace the rise of current attitudes, he uses the vivid case of different translations of Homer. He focuses on Achilleus's struggle with whether to kill Agamemnon in Book I of the *Iliad* and performs a pointed analysis of the trans-

4. The Moral of the Story

lations of Chapman, Pope, and Fitzgerald, assigning each to a different theory of rationality (*Whose Justice? Which Rationality?* 16–19). Chapman (1598) represents Renaissance ideals of rationality; Pope (1715), the eighteenth-century opposition between reason and passion; and Fitzgerald (1974), the psychological style of the present and its emphasis on alternating impulses of passion. Fitzgerald composes an Achilleus who holds within his breast an army of competing individuals, making him a metaphor for the body politic of liberal individualism. But when MacIntyre goes to define "tradition," he produces an account of it that resembles all too sharply Fitzgerald's portrait of Achilleus (12). Does MacIntyre thereby fall back into liberal individualism?

In fact, Bernard Williams, in "Modernity," *The London Reviews of Books* 11.1 (January 5, 1989): 5–6, has criticized MacIntyre for failing to stress the traditional nature of liberal individualism, arguing that it may be better equipped than MacIntyre believes to deal with modern ethical situations. If MacIntyre does unwittingly embrace it in his description of tradition, Williams may be right. Williams also disputes MacIntyre's apparent belief that only a great catastrophe could clear away our present difficulties in ethics. Here, however, Williams goes too far. While MacIntyre obviously stresses the past and often excessively, I do not see that he believes that a catastrophe is required to provide modernity with a clean slate. He seems, rather, to use the catastrophe as a metaphor for the historical rise of liberal individualism, and if he believes in some future disaster, it is not that he desires it but that he thinks its occurrence likely.

4. It is worth noting here the extent to which both Williams and MacIntyre share the same philosophical models. Both are post-Kantian Aristotelians, and both have embraced a certain Hegelianism. Williams refers specifically to Hegel's idea of *Sittlichkeit* to ground his notion of "custom" or "folkways" (104), and Hegel's idea seems to be behind MacIntyre's definitions of practices and traditions. *Sittlichkeit* in Hegel contains the norms of a society's public life. Notice, however, that neither MacIntyre nor Williams is wholly faithful to Hegel: their embedding of ethics in "folkways" and practical life cuts Hegel's idea loose from the path of *Geist*. For a discussion of *Sittlichkeit*, see Charles Taylor, *Hegel*, pp. 376–78, 382–88.

5. Perrault's version is more complex. Jupiter, not a fairy, appears to the woodcutter. The woodcutter drinks too much before wishing for the sausage; and his curse against his wife renders her speechless. He also considers making himself King with his last wish, but he abandons the idea because he does not wish to make his wife Queen with such a nose. Perrault's moral, taken from Charles Perrault, "Les Souhaits ridicules," *Contes en vers et en prose*, pp. 85–93, follows:

> Bien est donc vrai qu'aux hommes misérables,
> Aveugles, imprudents, inquiets, variables,
> Pas n'appartient de faire des souhaits,
> Et que peu d'entre eux sont capables
> De bien user des dons que le Ciel leur a faits. (93)

We may ask whether the power given to the woodcutter is not enough power. He cannot do what he ought to do with the three wishes. He is simply not capable of it. Am I wrong to suppose that his only recourse would have been to ask for his first wish to possess the knowledge necessary to make such wishes? But, perhaps, in this case, he would have had no further need to use the remaining wishes because possessing this knowledge could be the most to be expected from such wishes. If, for instance, this knowledge made him happy, he would be left with the false choice of not using the wishes or of using them to affirm his present life. Ironically, in fact, the woodcutter stumbles upon this conclusion by using his wishes as he does. But who am I to guess about knowledge of which I am not capable?

If it amuses the reader, I add my daughter's application. She advises the woodcutter to save his last wish by eating the sausage off his wife's nose. For my three-year old daughter, a sausage is a sausage, and a nose, a nose, while the story tends to confuse the sausage and the nose. My own reaction at first was that it would be too painful to bite or to cut into this sausage-nose.

5. The Place of Ethics in Homer

1. A large debate has centered on the question of the moral rationality of Homer's Zeus. On the one hand, E. R. Dodds, *The Greeks and the Irrational* and A. W. H. Adkins, *Merit and Responsibility: A Study in Greek Values* have taken the position that Zeus does not behave in a consistent and rational manner. On the other hand, Hugh Lloyd-Jones, in *The Justice of Zeus*, places Zeus at the center of the Greek idea of justice. He claims against Dodds and Adkins that Zeus is rational and that he acts specifically to punish the aggressor in human violence. The fall of Troy is therefore the Trojans' punishment for stealing Helen, and Patroklos is killed only when he turns from defending the Greek ships to advancing on Troy. Achilleus and Agamemnon are punished for their injustice to each other. While I find Lloyd-Jones's idea ethically appealing, it has several flaws. First, it places this ethical ideal in the figure of a god, when it is obvious that the Greeks and Trojans have an equally clear understanding of justice. Both Menelaos and Paris, for example, feel pangs of guilt for involving their people in their affairs, and Helen regularly curses herself. Moreover, the constant speech about the injustice of the gods reveals a sense of human fairness not connected to the gods. Second, Zeus's prolongation of the fighting to buttress Achilleus's honor does not serve this ethical ideal. Finally, as Lloyd-Jones admits, his theory ends in paradox, since we can only wonder at the justice of a god who causes people to commit injustice and then punishes them for it.

2. I am indebted throughout to the philology of Charles Chamberlain, "From 'Haunts' to 'Character': The Meaning of *Ēthos* and its Relation to Ethics," *Helios* 11.2 (1984): 97–108. On the Homeric ethic, I also recommend Redfield (1975).

3. In fact, Homer uses variations of *ēthos* twice in the *Odyssey*. When Odysseus and Eumaeus, the sow-herd, are talking in Book 14, the sows are brought home by their keepers and enclosed in their *ēthea* (14.411). Earlier, Eumaeus has spoken of Odysseus as *ētheios*, even though far away (14.147).

4. Aias, in fact, argues that the dispute with Agamemnon is over a trifling matter:

> "Pitiless. And yet a man takes from his brother's slayer
> the blood price, or the price for a child who was killed, and the guilty
> one, when he has largely repaid, stays still in the country,
> and the injured man's heart is curbed, and his pride, and his anger
> when he has taken the price; but the gods put in your breast a spirit

not to be placated, bad, for the sake of one single
girl. . . ." (9.632–38)

Indeed, the prize is insignificant when we consider that it is not the real issue between Achilleus and Agamemnon. They would fight over a grain of sand, if they saw it as a token of the highest kingship.

5. For the best commentary on Achilleus's relation to Thetis, see W. Thomas MacCary, *Childlike Achilles: Ontogeny and Phylogeny in the Iliad*. MacCary also notes on pp. 29–30 the role played by Homer's epics in the myth of the integrated society. He remarks that James Redfield and others look to Homer to represent a perfect integration of nature and culture, from which the modern world has inevitably fallen. Alasdair MacIntyre represents Homer in a similar way in *Whose Justice? Which Rationality?* (chapter 2). This same myth could be traced as well from Schiller through Georg Lukács, where it comes to symbolize the difference between epic forms and the novel.

Finally, permit me to add a disclaimer of my own. I do not begin with Homer because I believe in this myth of perfect integration. Homer demonstrates the integrity between story and moral as well as between literature and ethics, but this integration exists in spite of an absence of perfect social integration (because, I claim, the first integration is a social fact apparent whenever we find the smallest residue of social organization). The *Iliad* is, after all, a story about war. Let us not pretend that it represents the ideal existence for human beings.

8. Kant's Character

1. I am most indebted to Hannah Arendt, *Lectures on Kant's Political Philosophy*; Ernst Cassirer, *Kant's Life and Thought*; H. J. Paton, *The Categorical Imperative*; Rex P. Stevens, *Kant on Moral Practice*; and H. Vaihinger, *The Philosophy of 'As If'*.

10. Jane Austen and Comic Virtue

1. Among the many ethically minded critics writing on Jane Austen are Wayne Booth, *The Company We Keep: An Ethics of Fiction*; Alasdair MacIntyre, *After Virtue*; and James Boyd White, *When Words Lose Their Meaning*.

2. Jane Austen's earliest commentators began the tradition of placing her in a Greek context, and the tradition continues today. Writing in 1821, Richard Whatley traced Jane Austen's power back to Homer, comparing their talents for writing conversation and claiming that her novels fulfill Aristotle's idea that fictive biographies effectively convey moral experience. Gilbert Ryle, in "Jane Austen and the Moralists," argues that Austen's moral system is secular and Aristotelian and that she took her Aristotelianism from Shaftesbury. More recently, in *After Virtue*, Alasdair MacIntyre describes Jane Austen as the last great voice in the classical tradition of the virtues, implying that her Aristotelianism flows directly and untainted from the source. On the other hand, there have been attempts to view Austen in terms of Kantian ideas. See, for example, Claudia Brodsky's *The Imposition of Form*.

3. *Mansfield Park* provides another example. Edmund is not a bad sort, although he is far from perfect and Fanny's inferior in understanding. But his early acts of

kindness distinguish him in the novel and in Fanny's eyes. These acts are sufficient to make him worthy of love. Marriage does not require the doubling of minds. It requires but the faith that one's partner desires to do good and the proof that he or she sometimes succeeds.

4. Chapters 8 and 9 are an attempt to answer this question.

5. It is worthwhile looking at Kant's idea of pride in contrast to Aristotle's. For by the time that Kant writes about pride, it has become a vice, and for the same reasons that Aristotle's account gives us pause. It is the vice, Kant explains in *The Doctrine of Virtue*, most "opposed to the respect which every man can rightfully claim" (135). In the desire to be always on top, the prideful person abuses other people, for no amount of inferiority may convince Kant that one is justified in such abuse. When Kant tries to single out pride proper as a virtue, therefore, he fails, explaining that it, too, tends toward vice. Pride proper à la Aristotle, sometimes called "noble pride," has the virtue of representing one's dignity as a person, but it may also become the "anxiety" to yield nothing of one's dignity to others. It easily becomes an affront because it demands that others be most concerned with our importance. Proud people believe themselves deserving of followers, whom they think that they are entitled to treat contemptuously. But pride is, in the final analysis, nothing but stupidity, for Kant stresses that it desires respect but it goes about obtaining it in a way guaranteed to bring about disrespect. It fails to understand other people because it is too concerned with itself. Pride is egotism exalted, Kant concludes, and the proud person is always an abject human being.

6. Both pride and prejudice are dispositions expressing the relations between people having to do with social standing and rank. They are extremes in the relationship between self and other. They define, respectively, the esteem attributed to oneself and the value placed on the general opinion of others. If we give each term its classic interpretation, we can see that they apply to different social realms, since pride has to do more with the individual than prejudice does. A list of prejudices given by most modern readers would probably include racism, sexism, nationalism, and biases of religion and class. Each entails the idea of a community of opinion to which one bends one's own thought.

7. The main proponent of this view on the current scene is Jean-François Lyotard, whose notion of the *différend* describes disputes that cannot be reconciled justly because any such reconciliation creates by definition a victim. Lyotard argues that it is the purpose of those in power to hide the fact that agreements conceal conflicts. See *The Differend: Phrases in Dispute* and the issue of *Diacritics* (Fall 1984) devoted to Lyotard's work.

8. This ethic is widespread today. The majority of Anglo-American feminists embrace it. It also lies at the heart of the so-called critical pluralism. For a recent example, elaborated entirely in the language of ethics, see Wayne C. Booth, *The Company We Keep: An Ethics of Fiction*.

Richard Rorty's position on social democracy is important to mention here as well. Rorty, of course, does not believe in the necessity of founding ideas, and so he does not need to justify our respect for others according to ideas of general humanity, Reason, or God. He argues, in effect, that these are ladders that have helped some cultures reach their current positions and that we are now in a position to throw away the ladders. Like Bernard Williams, then, Rorty views the ability to have "thick concepts" and to defend them as the most that can be expected in matters of practical reasoning. I find this view attractive, although I like the idea of keeping the old ladders around a bit longer. But, then, I have already confessed to being a collector of "old tools." The thing about old tools is that you can never tell when a job might come along that suits them better than the new-fangled ones that the kids have been giving to you on birthdays and holidays. Our difference is that Rorty sees human history as a vertical ascent, and I see it as mountain climbing. Since climbing down is as important in mountain climbing as climbing up, I think it is a good idea to hold on to our ropes and ladders for awhile. Cf. Rorty, *Contingency, Irony, and Solidarity*, part 1.

9. Austen does not consider this choice viable, of course, since no one excepting Isabella ever shares a bowl of gruel with Mr. Woodhouse. Mr. John Knightley, however, comes perilously close, and Austen describes his inclination precisely in terms of his desire to express regret over a previous act of rudeness toward his father-in-law: "Mr John Knightley, ashamed of his ill-humour, was now all kindness and attention; and so particularly solicitous for the comfort of her father [Mr. Woodhouse], as to seem—if not quite ready to join him in a basin of gruel—perfectly sensible of its being exceedingly wholesome . . ." (798).

10. In *The Company We Keep: An Ethics of Fiction*, Wayne Booth applies the idea of that "great woman, the implied Jane Austen, the dauntingly mature human being who underwrites every act of imagination she takes us through," to defend *Emma* against feminist attacks (433). But, more typically, critics begin with the idea of a great moral thinker working behind the scenes and end by attacking the novels because biographical information does not confirm Jane Austen's moral perfection.

11. The conversation in which Elizabeth attempts to win her father's acceptance of Darcy is critical in this respect:

> "He is rich, to be sure, and you may have more fine clothes and fine carriages than Jane. But will they make you happy? . . . We all know him to be a proud, unpleasant sort of man; but this would be nothing if you really liked him."
>
> "I do, I do like him," she replied, with tears in her eyes, "I love him. Indeed he has no improper pride. He is perfectly amiable. You do not know what he really is; then pray do not pain me by speaking of him in such terms." (438)

Mr. Bennet first voices the doubts about Elizabeth's character that critics have always used against her, but she convinces him that she is not marrying a prideful man merely for money. She cannot consider Darcy as improperly prideful, despite the fact that she has never been able to conceive of any form of pride as a virtue until this moment. Her love consists of a leap of faith in the possibility that Darcy's pride is noble.

The word, "amiable," is also crucial to the description of Darcy. Besides carrying the sense of "love and friendship" necessary to Jane Austen's ethics of the couple, it is a word that falls squarely within the problematic of likeness and unlikeness as described in *Emma*. When Emma believes that she loves Frank Churchill, she describes him as "amiable" to Mr. Knightley. But Mr. Knightley rightly understands that Emma is falsely impressed with Churchill because of her own vanity, and he makes this point with a pun. "He may be very 'aimable,' have very good manners," Knightley says of Churchill, "and be very agreeable; but he can have no English delicacy towards the feelings of other people: nothing really amiable about him" (807). To say that Churchill is "aimable" is to say that he is "Emmable." Knightley reveals that Emma likes Churchill for herself and as herself, as if they were of one mind and one thinking, but this condition does not make him truly "amiable."

Of course, the pun does not work when Elizabeth uses the word, nor should it, because Darcy is neither "Emmable" nor "aimable." He is in Elizabeth's mind "amiable" in the sense required by English delicacy.

12. An emblem of this love of their own story, which is also a love of the conversation that is marriage, appears in the last sentence of the book in the form of the Gardiners. They unite the couple, of course, and the friendship that Darcy and Elizabeth feel for them cannot be separated from the origins of their own marriage. To befriend them is to embrace their own story again and again.

12. Chinua Achebe and Proverbial Wisdom

1. Can anthills, for example, be like a Grecian urn? One reading of *Anthills of the Savannah* might compare it to Keats's "Ode on a Grecian Urn" because the novel ends with an allusion to its concluding moral. I will not pursue this reading, although I will intimate it from time to time in the notion that storytellers and poets find words that appear to the people who hear them as their own memories. My interest here is not to reduce Achebe's work to its resonances with Western classics, even though he might be said to encourage such readings when he chooses to allude with such titles as *Things Fall Apart* and *No Longer At Ease* to Eliot's "The Journey of the Magi" and Yeats's "The Second Coming." Rather, I think it more important to recognize that Achebe is collecting such phrases for a particular use (see note 4).

This may also be the place to chart my motivations for reading Achebe, even though I am not prepared for it. I cannot make up for my lack of experience with the places about which he writes, but I have chosen to include him here because I owe many of my ideas to my reading and rereading of him, and it would now be an act of intellectual dishonesty not to try to interpret him in public.

2. Achebe makes these remarks and others about memory in an interview with Bill Moyers in *A World of Ideas*, p. 337.

3. The pleasure in the political process, however, creates certain ironies once Western civilization comes to Nigeria. *No Longer At Ease* opens, for example, with the trial of Obi Okonkwo, the grandson of the warrior in *Things Fall Apart*; but now Western justice has entirely engulfed the family. Obi is a civil servant who is being tried for taking bribes. He is a criminal within the system, not outside of it, as his grandfather was. The trial mirrors disjointedly those debates in the marketplace that decided the fates of individuals and peoples during Okonkwo's time. Indeed, Achebe is careful to provide many contemporary examples of such debates at the meetings of the Umuofia Progressive Union, the village council of Obi's home town. But attendance at the trial, while it is based on curiosity and pleasure in the proceedings, signifies not an integral part but an obstruction of social life. The trial creates a sensation, and other civil servants bribe doctors to obtain certificates of illness so that they may

skip work to hear the judgment. One does not need such excuses to attend the political debates at the Umuofia Progressive Union.

4. This is also the effect of Achebe's use of Western allusions in the titles of his novels. He chooses phrases that make sense only if we see them as naming Africa as the retrospective origin of their own poetic power.

5. "Wrath vented on stuffed lion," *Detroit Free Press*, Monday, February 14, 1983, 4 A, column 4.

13. Between a Rock and a Hard Place

1. Since nobody can be identified without reference to those who surround one, Odysseus's experience with Polyphemos ends by being a gloss on the problem. Homer describes the Cyclopes as alien to society as such:

> These people have no institution, no meetings for counsels;
> rather they make their habitations in caverns hollowed
> among the peaks of the high mountains, and each one is the law
> for his own wives and children, and cares nothing about the
> others.   (9.108–15)

Predictably, given the Cyclopes' customs, Polyphemos treats Odysseus and his men as if they were nobodies, a sense of identity that Odysseus justly and poetically returns to him when the Cyclops wants to know the name of his vanquisher. Homer, of course, plays upon the name, "Nobody," but notice as well that he emphasizes that this naming creates a mock society that is identical to the one inhabited by the Cyclopes, in which "each cares nothing about the others," and that Polyphemos's treatment of the Greeks reproduces. Odysseus claims that his parents and his companions care nothing for him, as if he were a Cyclops himself:

> Nobody is my name. My father and mother call me
> Nobody, as do all the others who are my companions.
>   (9.366–67)

2. For example, consider the work of Barbara Herrnstein Smith on relativism and objectivism in *Contingencies of Value: Alternative Perspectives for Critical Theory*. Smith argues for a strong relativism in which all statements and beliefs are contingent. Now, as is always the case with relativism, Smith opens herself to self-refutation by making the claim that everything is relative, except for her own relativism. But she takes an audacious step in order to meet the dilemma of self-refutation. She claims that objectivists who describe relativists as self-refuting are trapped within an objectivist idea of relativism and that they expose the fact by reading other, nonobjectivist forms of thought as always already objectivist. In short, according to Smith, the objectivist simply cannot understand the relativist.

The problem with this view is that Smith cuts off relativism from objectivism in an absolute manner—so absolute, in fact, that her claim for the difference between the two kinds of thinking appears as pseudoracist. It reminds one of Lévy-Bruhl's argument that Western anthropologists will never come to understand so-called primitive societies because "primitive" and "modern" thinking are radically different. Indeed, Lévi-Strauss's entire analysis of the "savage mind" strives to dislodge this prejudice. Smith's fear of sharing any position with the objectivist reproduces this problem, concealing from her the relation between the two positions. Just as objectivists find themselves inside and outside of their position when they claim that one can attain an objective, disinterested view of things (what Bernard Williams calls the "midair position" and Thomas Nagel calls the "view from nowhere"), relativists find themselves both inside and outside of relativism when they claim that everything is relative except relativism. Both relativism and objectivism entail leaping from position to position, and eventually they leap to the same one. This means neither that their positions are incoherent (or more incoherent than they already are) nor that they collapse into the same position. Rather, they are rocks and hard places in a single field of analysis.

3. I confess that this phrase summons for me the ghoulish joy expressed by Henry Frankenstein when (in the 1931 film *Frankenstein*, directed by James Whale) he sees the hand of his creation move and exclaims until he faints, "It's alive! It's alive! It's alive!" Frankenstein stiffens and rises toward unconsciousness, turning rigid and inanimate, like his creation. The monster is Frankenstein's work of art, but this piece of work is really a collection. Indeed, the opening scenes of the film show Frankenstein in the midst of his collecting mania. The creator becomes his creation because his collecting and recollecting fuse in his investment in the "object."

REFERENCES

Unless there are page references in the text, no editions have been specified for philosophical classics.

Achebe, Chinua. *Anthills of the Savannah*. New York: Anchor Books, 1987.
———. *A Man of the People*. 1966; reprint, New York: Anchor Books, 1967.
———. *The Arrow of God*. 1964; reprint, New York: Anchor Books, 1969.
———. *Chike and the River*. Cambridge: Cambridge University Press, 1966.
———. *No Longer at Ease*. New York: Fawcett Premier, 1960.
———. *Things Fall Apart*. New York: Fawcett Crest, 1959.
Adkins, A. W. H. *Merit and Responsibility: A Study in Greek Values*. Oxford: Oxford University Press, 1962.
Aesop. *Fables*. Drawings by Fritz Kredel. New York: Grosset & Dunlap, 1947.
Arendt, Hannah. *Eichmann in Jerusalem: A Report on the Banality of Evil*. 1963; revised, New York: Penguin, 1977.
———. "Isak Dinesen, 1885–1963." *Men in Dark Times*. New York: Harcourt, Brace & World, 1968.

References

———. *Lectures on Kant's Political Philosophy*. Chicago: University of Chicago Press, 1982.

———. *The Origins of Totalitarianism*. 1951; revised, New York: Harcourt Brace Jovanovich, 1973.

———. "Personal Responsibility Under Dictatorship." *The Listener* (August 6, 1964): 185–87, 205.

Austen, Jane. *Complete Novels*. New York: Penguin, 1983.

Ausubel, Nathan, ed. *A Treasury of Jewish Folklore*. New York: Crown, 1948.

Ayer, A. J. "Editorial Foreword." P. H. Nowell-Smith. *Ethics*. London: Penguin, 1954.

Axelrod, Robert. "An Evolutionary Approach to Norms," *American Political Science Review* 80.4 (1986): 1095–1112.

———. *The Evolution of Cooperation*. New York: Basic Books, 1984.

Barthes, Roland. "Introduction to the Structural Analysis of Narratives." *Image, Music, Text*. London: Fontana, 1977.

Benjamin, Walter. *Illuminations*. Ed. Hannah Arendt. New York: Schocken Books, 1969.

———. *The Origin of German Tragic Drama*. Trans. John Osborne. London: NLB, 1977.

Brodsky, Claudia. *The Imposition of Form*. Princeton: Princeton University Press, 1987.

Carr, David. "Life and the Narrator's Art." *Hermeneutics and Deconstruction*. Ed. Hugh J. Silverman and Don Ihde. Albany: State University of New York Press, 1985.

Cassirer, Ernst. *Kant's Life and Thought*. New Haven: Yale University Press, 1981.

Cavell, Stanley. *Pursuits of Happiness: The Hollywood Comedy of Remarriage*. Cambridge: Harvard University Press, 1981.

Chamberlain, Charles. "From 'Haunts' to 'Character': The Meaning of *Ēthos* and its Relation to Ethics." *Helios* 11.2 (1984): 97–108.

Chambers, Ross. *Story and Situation: Narrative Seduction and the Power of Fiction*. Minneapolis: University of Minnesota Press, 1984.

Chatwin, Bruce. *Utz: A Novel*. New York: Viking Press, 1989.

Culler, Jonathan. "Issues in Contemporary American Critical Debate." *American Criticism in the Poststructuralist Age*. Ed. Ira Konigsberg. Ann Arbor: University of Michigan Press, 1981.

Diamond, Cora. "Having a Rough Story about What Moral Philosophy Is." *New Literary History* 15.1 (1983): 155–170.

Dodds, E. R. *The Greeks and the Irrational*. Berkeley: University of California Press, 1951.

Freuchen, Peter. *Arctic Adventure: My Life in the Frozen North*. New York: Farrar & Rinehard, 1935.

Gans, Eric. *The End of Culture: Toward a Generative Anthropology*. Berkeley: University of California Press, 1985.

Goodman, Nelson. *Of Mind and Other Matters*. Cambridge: Harvard University Press, 1984.

Heidegger, Martin. *Being and Time*. Trans. John Macquarrie and Edward Robinson. New York: Harper and Row, 1962.

References

Hamilton, William. "The Genetical Theory of Social Behavior." *Journal of Theoretical Biology* 7 (1964): 1–52.

Herodotus. *The Histories*. Trans. Aubrey de Sélincourt. New York: Penguin Books, 1972.

Homer. *The Iliad*. Trans. Richmond Lattimore. Chicago: University of Chicago Press, 1951.

———. *The Odyssey*. Trans. Richmond Lattimore. Chicago: University of Chicago Press, 1965.

Jakobson, Roman and Claude Lévi-Strauss. "*Les Chats* de Charles Baudelaire." *L'Homme* 2 (1962): 5–21.

Jameson, Fredric. *The Political Unconscious: Narrative as a Socially Symbolic Act*. Ithaca, NY: Cornell University Press, 1981.

Kant, Immanuel. *The Critique of Judgement*. Trans. James Creed Meredith. Oxford: Oxford University Press, 1957.

———. *The Doctrine of Virtue*. Trans. Mary J. Gregor. Philadelphia: University of Pennsylvania Press, 1964.

———. *Foundations of the Metaphysics of Morals*. Trans. Lewis White Beck. Indianapolis: Bobbs-Merril, 1969.

———. "On a Supposed Right to Tell Lies from Benevolent Motives." *The Critique of Practical Reason and Other Works on the Theory of Ethics*. Trans. Thomas Kingsmill Abbott. 1873; 6th ed., New York: Longmans, Green, 1923.

———. "What is Enlightenment?" *Philosophical Writings*. Ed. Ernst Behler. New York: Continuum, 1986.

———. "Perpetual Peace." *Philosophical Writings*. Ed. Ernst Behler. New York: Continuum, 1986.

Kirk, G. S. *The Iliad: A Commentary*. Vol. 1. Cambridge: University of Cambridge Press, 1985.

Konigsberg, Ira, ed. *American Criticism in the Poststructuralist Age*. Ann Arbor: University of Michigan Press, 1981.

Krieger, Murray. "In the Wake of Morality: The Thematic Underside of Recent Theory." *New Literary History* 15.1 (1983): 119–36.

Kristeva, Julia. "The Ethics of Linguistics." *Desire in Language*. Trans. Thomas Gora, Alice Jardine, and Leon S. Roudiez. New York: Columbia University Press, 1980.

———. *Polylogue*. Paris: Seuil, 1977.

———. *The Revolution in Poetic Language: A Semiotic Approach to Literature and Art*. Ed. Leon Roudiez. Trans. Alice Jardine and Thomas Gora. New York: Columbia University Press, 1980.

Lewis, David. *Convention: A Philosophical Study*. Cambridge: Harvard University Press, 1969.

Lloyd-Jones, Hugh. *The Justice of Zeus*. Berkeley: University of California Press, 1971.

Lyotard, Jean-François. *The Differend: Phrases in Dispute*. Trans. Georges Van Den Abbeele. Minneapolis: University of Minnesota Press, 1988.

MacCary, Thomas M. *Childlike Achilles: Ontogeny and Phylogeny in the Iliad*. Berkeley: University of California Press, 1982.

MacIntyre, Alasdair. *After Virtue*. 1981; second edition, Notre Dame, In.: University of Notre Dame Press, 1984.

References

————. *A Short History of Ethics*. New York: Collier, 1966.

————. *Whose Justice? Which Rationality?* Notre Dame, In.: University of Notre Dame Press, 1988.

Medina, Angel. *Reflection, Time, and the Novel*. London: Routlege & Kegan Paul, 1979.

Miller, J. Hillis. "The Critic as Host." *Critical Inquiry* 3.3 (1977): 439–47.

————. *The Ethics of Reading*. New York: Columbia University Press, 1986.

Moore, G. E. *Principia Ethica*. Cambridge: Cambridge University Press, 1923.

Moyers, Bill. *A World of Ideas*. Ed. Betty Sue Flower. New York: Doubleday, 1989.

Mudimbe, V. Y. "Reading Waving Margins." Colloquium on Reading Literature and Culture: Comparative Literature and the Methods of the Disciplines. The University of Michigan, April 14, 1988.

Nagel, Thomas. *The View from Nowhere*. New York: Oxford University Press, 1986.

Nussbaum, Martha Craven. "Flawed Crystals: James's *The Golden Bowl* and Literature as Moral Philosophy." *New Literary History* 15.1 (198): 25–50.

————. *The Fragility of Goodness*. Cambridge: Cambridge University Press, 1986.

Paton, H. J. *The Categorical Imperative*. Chicago: University of Chicago Press, 1948.

Perrault, Charles. "Les Souhaits ridicules." *Contes en vers et en prose*. Geneva: Albert Skira, 1944.

Phillips, D. Z. "Philosophizing and Reading a Story." *Through a Darkening Glass*. Notre Dame, In.: University of Notre Dame Press, 1982.

Plato. *Republic*. Trans. Desmond Lee. New York: Penguin, 1974.

————. *Republic*. Trans. Paul Shorey. 2 vols. Cambridge: Harvard University Press, 1935.

Raphael, D. D. "Can Literature be Moral Philosophy?" *New Literary History* 15.1 (1983): 1–12.

Redfield, James M. *Nature and Culture in the Iliad: The Tragedy of Hector*. Chicago: University of Chicago Press, 1975.

Riffaterre, Michael. "Describing Poetic Structures: Two Approaches to Baudelaire's *les Chats*." *Yale French Studies* 36/37 (1966): 200–42.

Rorty, Richard. *Contingency, Irony, and Solidarity*. Cambridge: Cambridge University Press, 1989.

Ryle, Gilbert. "Jane Austen and the Moralists." *Critical Essays on Jane Austen*. Ed. B. C. Southam. London: Routledge & Kegan Paul, 1968.

Sartre, Jean-Paul. "Le Mur." *Oeuvres romanesques*. Paris: Gallimard, 1981.

Schank, Roger C., and Robert P. Abelson. *Scripts, Plans, Goals and Understanding: An Inquiry into Human Knowledge Structures*. Hillsdale, NJ: Lawrence Erlbaum Associates, 1977.

Schein, Seth L. *The Mortal Hero: An Introduction to Homer's Iliad*. Berkeley: University of California Press, 1984.

Scott, John. *Internalization of Norms*. Englewood Cliffs, NJ: Prentice Hall, 1971.

Sedgwick, Sally S. "On the Relation of Pure Reason to Content: A Reply to Hegel's Critique of Formalism in Kant's Ethics." *Philosophy and Phenomenological Research* 49.1 (1988): 59–80.

Shklar, Judith. *Ordinary Vices*. Cambridge: Harvard University Press, 1984.

References

Smith, Barbara Herrnstein. *Contingencies of Value: Alternative Perspectives for Critical Theory*. Cambridge: Harvard University Press, 1988.

Stevenson, C. L. *Ethics and Language*. New Haven: Yale University Press, 1944.

Stevens, Rex P. *Kant on Moral Practice*. Macon, Ga.: Mercer University Press, 1981.

Taylor, Charles. *Hegel*. Cambridge: Cambridge University Press, 1975.

Tolstoy, Leo. *Anna Karenin*. Trans. Rosemary Edmonds. New York: Penguin, 1954.

———. *The Death of Ivan Ilyich*. Trans. Lynn Solotaroff. New York: Bantam, 1981.

———. *Hadji Murád*. Trans. Louise and Aylmer Maude. *Great Short Works*. New York: Perennial Library, 1967.

———. *The Kreutzer Sonata and Other Stories*. Trans. David McDuff. New York: Penguin, 1985.

———. *Resurrection*. Trans. Rosemary Edmonds. New York: Penguin, 1966.

———. *War and Peace*. Trans. Ann Dunnigan. New York: Signet, 1968.

———. *What is Art?* Trans. Aylmer Maude. Oxford: Oxford University Press, 1930.

Vaihinger, H. *The Philosophy of 'As If'*. New York: Harcourt Brace, 1924.

Watkins, C. "A propos de MĒNIS." *Bulletin de la société de linguistique de Paris* 72 (1977): 87–209.

Williams, Bernard. *Ethics and the Limits of Philosophy*. Cambridge: Harvard University Press, 1985.

———. "Modernity." *The London Reviews of Books* 11.1 (January 5, 1989): 5–6.

———. *Morality: An Introduction to Ethics*. New York: Harper, 1972.

Wittgenstein, Ludwig. *Last Writings on the Philosophy of Psychology*. Ed. G. H. von Wright and Heikki Nyman. Trans. C. G. Luckhardt and Maximilian A. E. Aue. Chicago: University of Chicago Press, 1982.

———. "Lecture on Ethics." *The Philosophical Review* 74 (1965): 3–26.

———. *On Certainty*. Ed. G. E. M. Anscombe and G. H. von Wright. New York: Harper and Row, 1972.

———. *Zettel*. Ed. G. E. M. Anscombe and G. H. von Wright. Trans. G. E. M. Anscombe. Berkeley: University of California Press, 1970.

White, James Boyd. *When Words Lose Their Meaning: Constitution and Reconstitution of Language, Character, and Community*. Chicago: University of Chicago Press, 1984.

Wilson, A. N. *Tolstoy*. London: Hamish Hamilton, 1988.

INDEX

Index

Index

Literature, 34, 56, 80, 82, 196, 210; defined, 34, 159–60; and desire, 81; and philosophy, 159–60; and society, 81; *see also* Fiction; Story; Storytelling

Love, 137–38

Luck, 54, 157, 164–65, 170–71, 214n1; *see also* Fate

Lying, 31, 118–20, 194

MacIntyre, Alasdair, 22, 46, 54, 67, 71, 109, 207, 214n1, 215n2, 215–16n3, 216n3, 218n5; *After Virtue*, 38, 49–51, 67, 72, 108, 218nn1, 2; on Kant, 111–12, 115; *A Short History of Ethics*, 107, 114, 209; *Which Justice? Whose Rationality?*, 46, 51–52

Marriage, 22, 139, 154–56, 221n12; *see also* Ethic of the couple

Marxism, 25–26, 168

Memory, 173–74, 177–78, 196, 221n1,2; *see also* Recollection

Metaphysics, 14–15

Midair position, 54–55; *see also* Ethic of nowhere

Miller, J. Hillis, 26, 29, 30–31, 52; "The Critics as Host," 28–30; *The Ethics of Reading*, 28–29

Mimesis, 78

Modernity, 24, 54, 113, 133, 135, 138, 153–54, 161, 165–66, 208

Moral and story, 55, 136, 207–8; *see also* Ethics of storytelling

Moral education, 37, 62

Morality, 55; defined, 54; and society, 114

Moral of the story, 57, 156, 176, 192, 198

Moral philosophy, 38; defined, 98; in Kant, 159

Morals, 136, 212; outmoralizing of, 44; rejection of, 41

Nazism, 115–16, 118, 120, 122–23, 128, 130, 132, 142, 210; and resistance, 132; *see also* Final Solution

Nicknames, 186–88, 190

Nonsense, 17, 150–51

Nostalgia, 161, 183

Nussbaum, Martha, 22, 214n1

Objectivism, 203, 222n2

Objects, 4, 166–67, 169, 203, 205, 207–8, 223n3; and words, 190; *see also* Things

Otherness, 25, 139, 145; *see also* Difference

Parables, 210–12

Particularity, 149–50, 157, 163, 173, 192, 203

Perrault, Charles, 56–57, 216–17n5

Personhood, 104; in Kant, 109–10

Philosopher king, 81, 83, 87

Philosophic culture, 160–61

Philosophy, 56, 94–95, 149, 159–61

Phrasemongering, 179–80, 183; *see also* Cliché

Place, 37, 52, 81, 94; in Austen, 138, 157; beloved, 66; and character, 72; defined, 63; in Homer, 62, 75–76; and law, 66; of philosophy, 94–95; and stories, 61

Plato, 18, 66, 77–87, 89–96, 127, 146, 150, 160–61, 167, 214n4; "The Allegory of the Cave," 82–83, 89, 90–94; expulsion of poets, 82, 86–87, 93; "The Myth of Er," 89, 97; myth of imperfect societies, 83–86

Platonic ideas, 78, 90, 94, 97, 150

Poetic justice, 43, 126–27, 157

Political movements, 164, 176

Politics, 24, 66, 82, 132; and activism, 205; and alliances, 204; defined, 204–5

Politics of storytelling, 25–26, 194, 197

Post-Kantian Aristotelianism, 137, 207, 216n4

Power, 17, 124–25, 185–86

Practical joking, 125–26

Practical reasoning, 125–26; defined, 102

Practice, 3, 18, 39, 46, 53–54, 214n1; defined, 50–51

Prejudice, 16, 140, 142, 153; in Austen, 143; defined, 219n6; in Kant, 142–42

Pride, 140, 153, 220n11; in Aristotle, 140–42, 219n5; in Austen, 142–43; defined, 152, 219n6; in Kant, 219n5

Principles: *see* Theory

234

Index